# Origami Symphony No. 5

*Woodwinds, Horns, and a Moose*

Books by John Montroll
www.johnmontroll.com
Instagram: @montrollorigami

## Origami Symphonies

*Origami Symphony No. 1: The Elephant's Trumpet Call*
  First movement: Allegro: Theme and Variation on the Classic Crane
  Second Movement: Andante: Crawling Simple Bugs
  Third Movement: Minuet of Platonic Solids with a Trio of Sunken Solids
  Fourth Movement: March of the Large African Animals

*Origami Symphony No. 2: Trio of Sharks & Playful Prehistoric Mammals*
  First Movement: Allegro Agitato: Sharks in the Sea
  Second Movement: Andante: Dulce, Peaceful Creatures
  Third Movement: Minuet of Dimpled Polyhedra with a Trio of Archimedean Solids
  Fourth Movement: March of the Prehistoric Mammals

*Origami Symphony No. 3: Duet of Majestic Dragons & Dinosaurs*
  First Movement: Allegro: Quacking Chorus of Dinosaurs
  Second Movement: Andante: Colorful Australian Birds
  Third Movement: Minuet of Diamonds with a Trio of Dimpled Diamonds
  Fourth Movement: Presto: Flight of the Dragons

*Origami Symphony No. 4: Capturing Vibrant Coral Reef Fish*
  First Movement: Allegro: Songs of the Tropical Birds
  Second Movement: Andante: Colorful Coral Reef Fish Swimming in Harmony
  Third Movement: Minuet of Deltahedra with a Trio of Duo-Colored Octahedra
  Fourth Movement: Allegro: Deep Melodies of the Sea Invertebrates

*Origami Symphony No. 5: Woodwinds, Horns, and a Moose*
  First Movement: Allegro: Triplets for Birds with Toes
  Second Movement: Andante: Woodwinds in the Woods
  Third Movement: Minuet of Catalan Solids with a Trio of Sunken Quadruplet Solids
  Fourth Movement: March of the Horns & Antlers

## General Origami

*Origami Fold-by-Fold*
*DC Super Heroes Origami*
*Origami Worldwide*
*Teach Yourself Origami: Second Revised Edition*
*Christmas Origami: Second Edition*
*Storytime Origami*
*Origami Inside-Out: Third Edition*

## Animal Origami

*Dogs in Origami*
*Perfect Pets Origami*
*Dragons and Other Fantastic Creatures in Origami*
*Bugs in Origami*
*Horses in Origami*
*Origami Birds*
*Origami Gone Wild*
*Dinosaur Origami*
*Origami Dinosaurs for Beginners*
*Prehistoric Origami: Dinosaurs and other Creatures: Third Edition*
*Mythological Creatures and the Chinese Zodiac Origami*
*Origami Under the Sea*
*Sea Creatures in Origami*
*Origami Sea Life: Third Edition*
*Bringing Origami to Life: Second Edition*
*Bugs and Birds in Origami*
*Origami Sculptures: Fourth Edition*
*African Animals in Origami: Third Edition*
*North American Animals in Origami: Third Edition*

## Geometric Origami

*Origami Stars*
*Galaxy of Origami Stars: Second Edition*
*Origami and Math: Simple to Complex*
*Origami & Geometry*
*3D Origami Platonic Solids & More: Second Edition*
*3D Origami Diamonds*
*3D Origami Antidiamonds*
*3D Origami Pyramids*
*A Plethora of Polyhedra in Origami: Third Edition*
*Classic Polyhedra Origami*
*A Constellation of Origami Polyhedra*
*Origami Polyhedra Design*

## Dollar Bill Origami

*Dollar Origami Treasures: Second Edition*
*Dollar Bill Animals in Origami: Second Revised Edition*
*Dollar Bill Origami*
*Easy Dollar Bill Origami*

## Simple Origami

*Fun and Simple Origami: 101 Easy-to-Fold Projects: Second Edition*
*Super Simple Origami*
*Easy Dollar Bill Origami*
*Easy Origami Animals*
*Easy Origami Polar Animals*
*Easy Origami Ocean Animals*
*Easy Origami Woodland Animals*
*Easy Origami Jungle Animals*
*Meditative Origami*

# Origami Symphony No. 5

## Woodwinds, Horns, and a Moose

Antroll Publishing Company

John Montroll

*To Marky and Leslie*

**Origami Symphony No. 5:** *Woodwinds, Horns, and a Moose*

Copyright © 2020 by John Montroll. All rights reserved.
No part of this publication may be copied or reproduced by any means without the express written permission of the author.

ISBN-10: 1-877656-54-2
ISBN-13: 978-1-877656-54-5

Antroll Publishing Company

# Introduction

Welcome to the world premier of the Fifth Origami Symphony! By combining origami with music and storytelling, an elaborate presentation in four movements brings origami to a higher level. With a Woodwinds and Horns section, the four movements highlight the richness, beauty and challenges of origami.

Each of the four movements presents a wide range of subjects and styles. The symphony is unified with a woodwinds and horns section. From the first movement, birds with toes add complexity to the folding and detailed expression to the birds. The peaceful second movement of the woodwinds presents familiar smaller animals of the woods. The minuet and trio of the third movement takes us out of the world to the least familiar of origami subjects, with the mind-boggling structures of the Catalan Solids. The fourth movement concludes triumphantly with mammals with horns and antlers found around the world

Great care has been taken to keep the designs as simple as possible, given their inherent complexities. Almost all of the animals of the woods are folded in under 30 steps. This includes a Banded Snake with four white stripes and an open mouth in only 21 steps and a cute Squirrel in 24 steps. Most of the Catalan Solids are folded in under 30 steps, yet the shapes are complex. Even the complex mammals with horns are accomplished in fewer steps. This includes the Musk Ox in 32 steps and the Arabian Oryx in 28 steps. The fewer steps for these complex subjects show a higher level of origami design, and a richer folding experience. The 31 models from this symphony can be folded from standard origami paper, and will hold together.

The diagrams are drawn in the internationally approved Randlett-Yoshizawa style. You can use any kind of square paper for these models, but the best results will be achieved with standard origami paper, which is colored on one side and white on the other (in the diagrams in this book, the shading represents the colored side). Large sheets, such as nine inches squared, are easier to use than small ones.

Origami supplies can be found in arts and craft shops, or at Dover Publications online: www.doverpublications.com. You can also visit OrigamiUSA at www.origamiusa.org for origami supplies and other related information including an extensive list of local, national, and international origami groups.

Please follow me on Instagram @montrollorigami to see posts of my origami.

I thank my editor, Charley Montroll. I also thank the many folders who continued to encourage me to develop the presentation of origami through an origami symphony.

I hope you enjoy the richness and complexities of Origami Symphony No. 5.

John Montroll
www.johnmontroll.com

# Contents

| | |
|---:|:---|
| Symbols | 9 |
| Origami Bird Designs | 9 |
| Origami Symphony No. 5 | 10 |
| First Movement | 11 |
| Second Movement | 38 |
| Third Movement | 69 |
| Fourth Movement | 99 |

★ Simple
★★ Intermediate
★★★ Complex
★★★★ Very Complex

**First Movement**
**Allegro: Triplets for Birds with Toes**

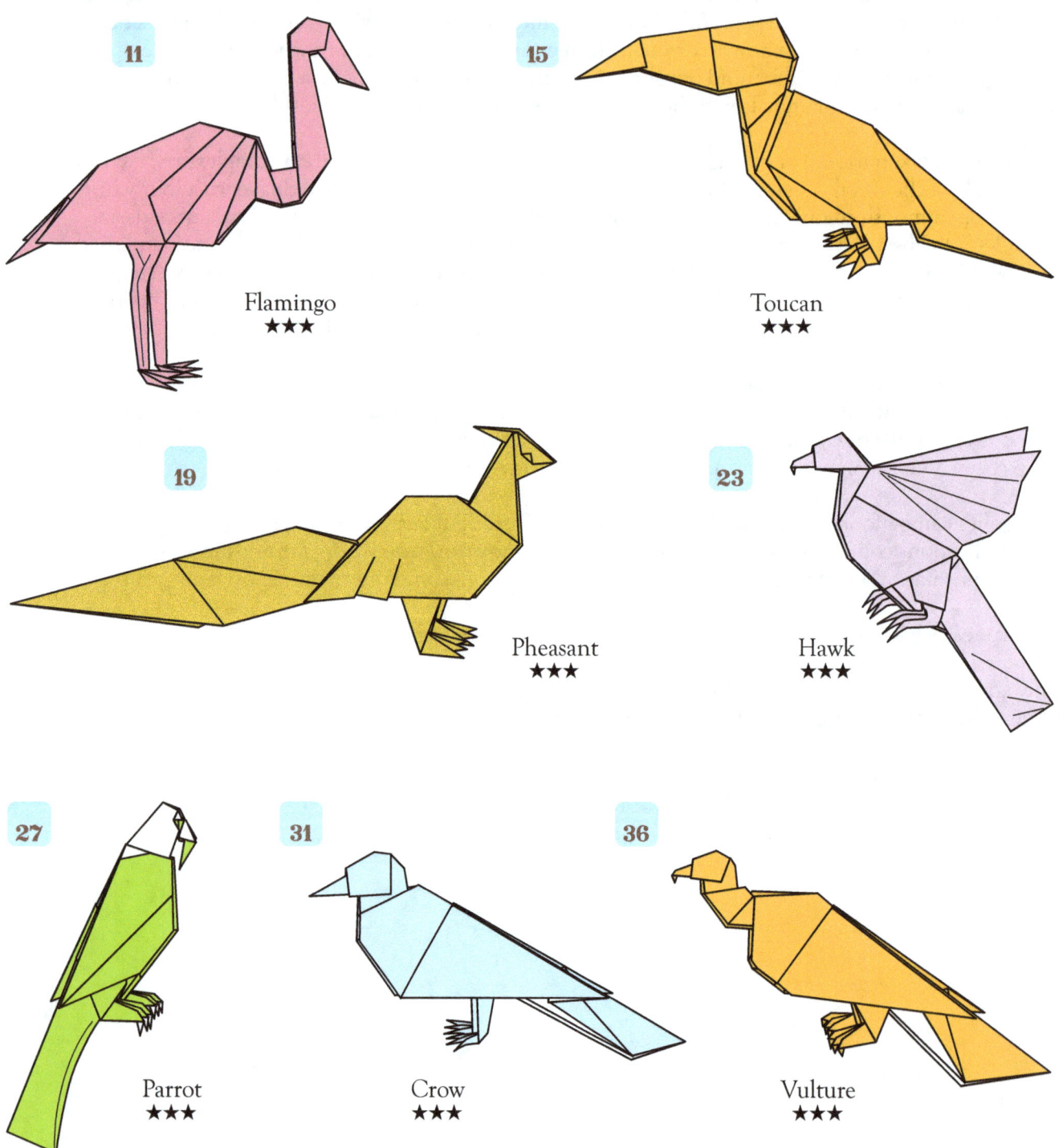

11 Flamingo ★★★

15 Toucan ★★★

19 Pheasant ★★★

23 Hawk ★★★

27 Parrot ★★★

31 Crow ★★★

36 Vulture ★★★

6 Origami Symphony No. 5

# Second Movement
## Andante: Woodwinds in the Woods

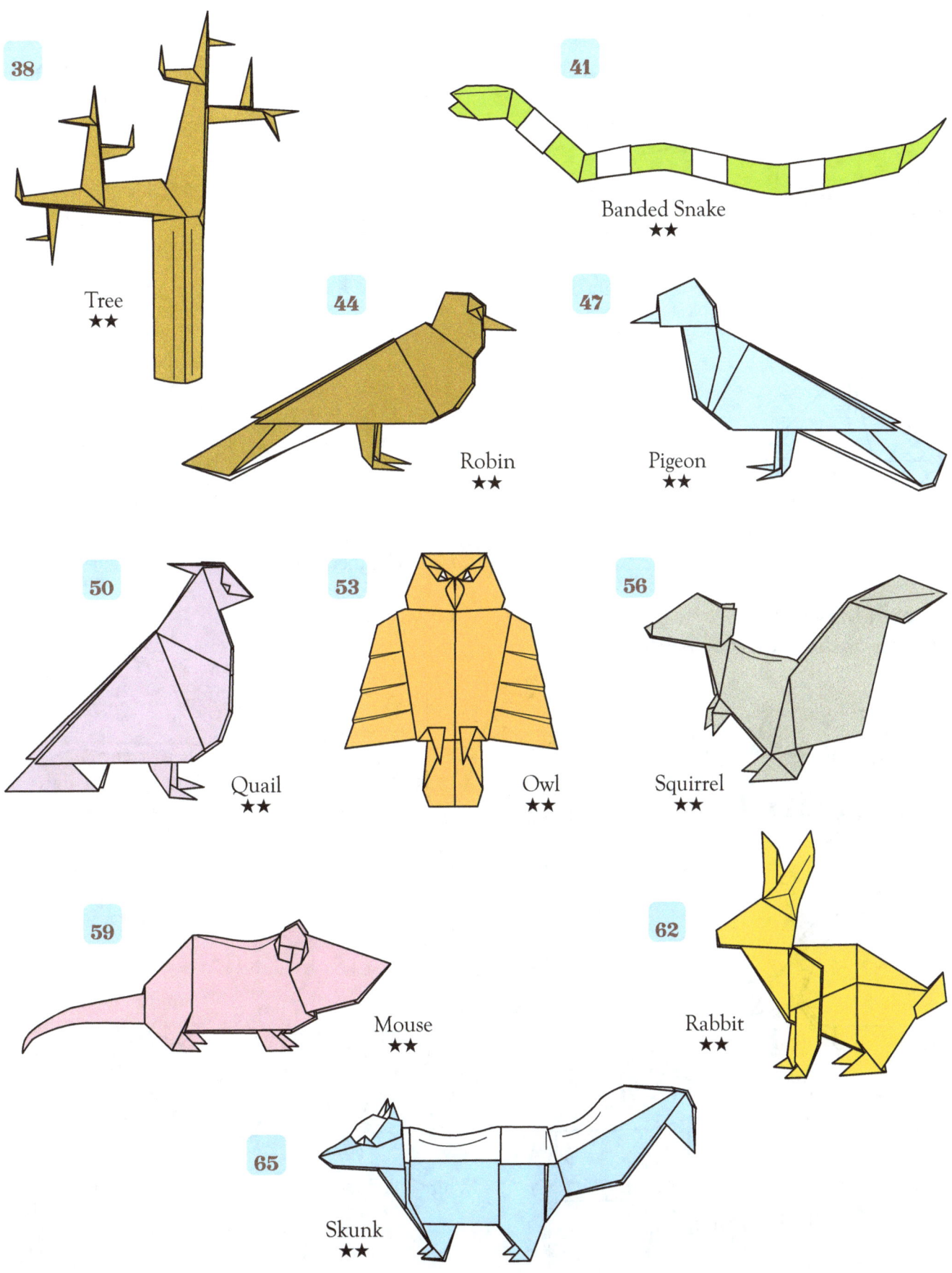

# Third Movement
## Minuet of Catalan Solids with a Trio of Sunken Quadruplet Solids

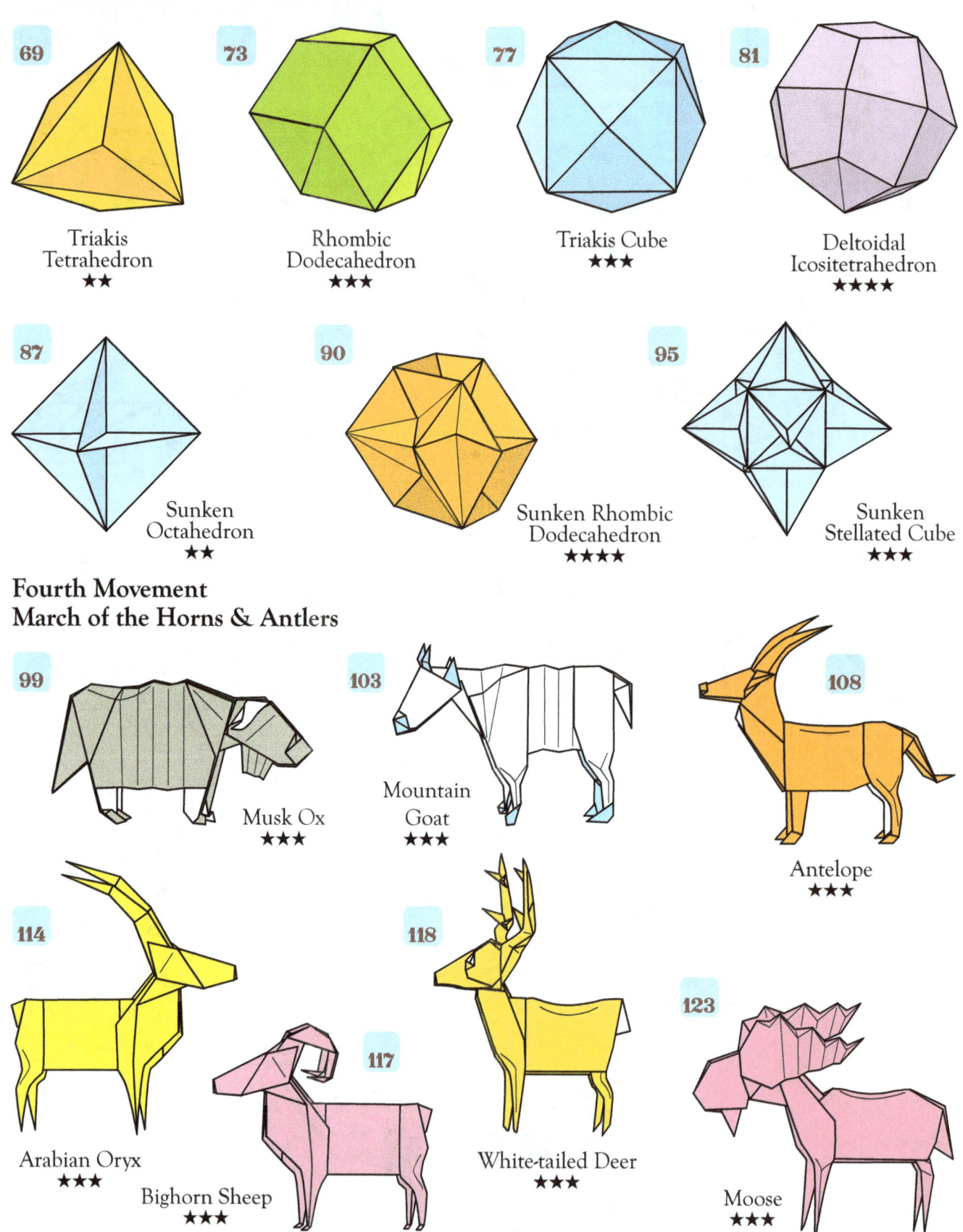

**69** Triakis Tetrahedron ★★

**73** Rhombic Dodecahedron ★★★

**77** Triakis Cube ★★★

**81** Deltoidal Icositetrahedron ★★★★

**87** Sunken Octahedron ★★

**90** Sunken Rhombic Dodecahedron ★★★★

**95** Sunken Stellated Cube ★★★

# Fourth Movement
## March of the Horns & Antlers

**99** Musk Ox ★★★

**103** Mountain Goat ★★★

**108** Antelope ★★★

**114** Arabian Oryx ★★★

**117** Bighorn Sheep ★★★

**118** White-tailed Deer ★★★

**123** Moose ★★★

8   *Origami Symphony No. 5*

# Symbols

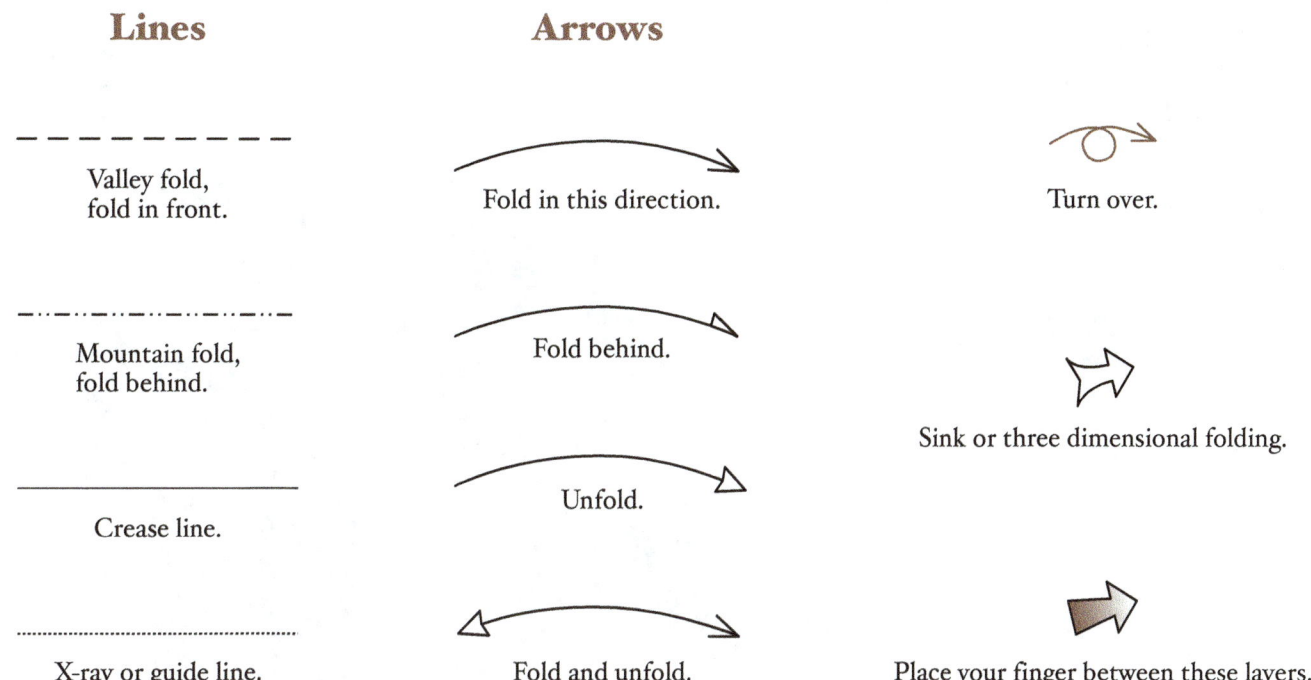

# Origami Bird Designs

Birds are elegant, colorful animals. They have wings, beaks, thin legs and maybe a fanned tail. Their bones are hollow and light. While mammals have muscular bulky legs and ears, birds have thin legs and no ear structure.

A bird can be flying, standing, or even standing with wings outstretched. For creating an origami bird, these three poses would take three independent designs. The bird in flight would have long wings with no feet, while the standing bird would have long legs with simple wings.

Compared to mammals or insects with great detail, I see birds as elegant and light animals. While I like to represent them with a certain amount of detail, I want to keep the folding less complex to highlight their elegance and lightness. It could be fun to include open beaks, wing textures and toes, but at some point the folding becomes bulky with too many steps, and their beauty is lost. Given these three poses (flying, standing, and standing with wings outstretched) requiring three independent designs, now add toes. There are now far more designs to represent the same bird. Now add an open beak, and other possible details, such as wing texture. It would be fun to design a dozen or so variations of one bird showing different details and positions, yet all in the same general style.

I have many bird designs which take about 20 steps or so. Wth their legs and wings in any pose, they express beauty and simplicity. By adding toes, perhaps ten or more steps would be required, along with more layers. Would these excesses keep the birds elegant and light? An origami bird without toes could be beautiful, but if done correctly, adding toes can make the designs magnificent. These are some thoughts to take into consideration.

# Origami Symphony No. 5

Origami Symphony No. 5 explores the complexities that come with folding birds with toes, reveals clever methods for the most familiar animals dwelling in the woods, discovers the least known Catalan Solids and sunken shapes that are out of this world, and concludes triumphantly with the challenges of horns and antlers. The symphony is unified by alluding to the woodwinds and horns of the orchestra.

A Flamingo opens the symphony. The detail of the toes foreshadows more complexities to come. The first movement, consisting of birds with toes, creates melodies with triplets. A similar looking Parrot from Origami Symphony No. 4 is now represented in splendor with added toes.

The woodwinds of the second movement are depicted as animals in the woods. This movement opens with a Tree, which is a transition from the first movement. The folding techniques to give the birds toes is used to give the Tree its branches. A hungry Banded Snake makes its entrance. With four white stripes of equal thickness, equally spaced throughout its body, the Snake only takes 21 steps. This highlights a new level of efficiency in the folding, as most of the models of this movement take fewer than 30 steps. The Snake and Skunk, along with a few horned mammals in the fourth movement, use color-change ideas for effect. A Robin, Pigeon, and Quail greet us, and a few small mammals gather 'round. The simplicity and peace from the winds in the woods reverberates throughout the movement.

From the most familiar of animals and origami subjects of the second movement, the minuet and trio of the third movement take us out of this world, to the least known geometric worlds of the Catalan Solids and Sunken Quadruplet Solids. Most of these models are so unfamiliar in the origami world that there are not even modular (using multiple sheets) representations of these Solids. As complex as these geometric shapes are, several take 30 or fewer steps, continuing with the efficient themes throughout this symphony. An interesting play of symmetry is revealed in this movement; while all the animals from the other movements use mirror-image symmetry in the folding, most of these shapes use square symmetry. Square symmetry means that the same folding patterns are used on the four sides of the square, which simplifies the folding process. For these challenging models, it is best to take your time, or they will turn into the origami equivalent of black holes.

The fourth movement brings us back to Earth on mountains, grasslands and the desert, as we meet mammals with horns and antlers. With a Musk Ox in the snow, a Mountain Goat in the mountains, and the Arabian Oryx in the desert, the horns and antlers challenge and reward us. A detailed Moose triumphantly closes the symphony.

With many styles and a wide variety of shapes, this symphony challenges the folder. Toes, horns, and antlers add elegance to detail, and the unusual Catalan Solids show how limitless origami subjects can be. The depths of the designs allow several of the otherwise complex models to be folded in under 30 steps, or far less than usual, which, though seeming to make the folding simpler, adds a majestic touch to the work. I hope this elaborate symphony is enjoyed many times over.

# First Movement

## Allegro: Triplets for Birds with Toes

Toes add a majestic touch to origami birds. With toes, the birds can balance better, perch better, reach for and carry their prey, dig and do much more. A common origami method of adding toes is through grafting, a method of adding a layer (or layers) to a known base, and the extra paper forms the toes. For the Flamingo, adding the extra parts to the bird base form both the toes and the long neck. Triplets await.

## Flamingo

The Flamingo is a tropical wading bird found in shallow lakes and lagoons. These social birds live in large colonies. At three to five feet tall, they only weigh four to eight pounds, which is perfect for flight. They sometimes fly hundreds of miles at night in search of another spot for food and water. They eat with their beaks upside-down as they scoop shrimp, algae, and crustaceans. Their diet contributes to the red and pink feather coloring. The Flamingo is very comfortable standing on one foot, and can even do so while sleeping.

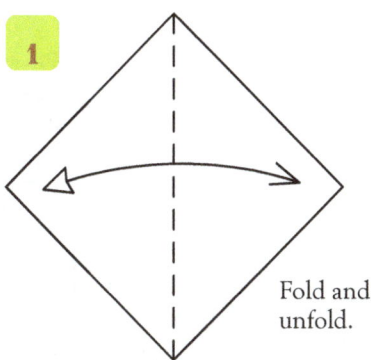

1. Fold and unfold.

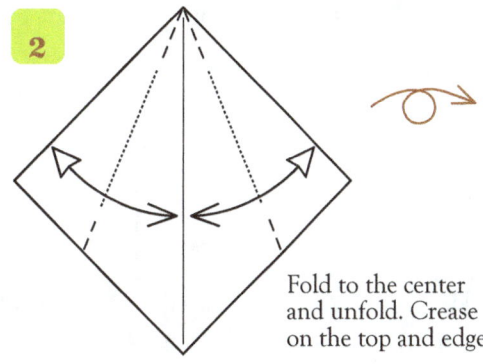

2. Fold to the center and unfold. Crease on the top and edges.

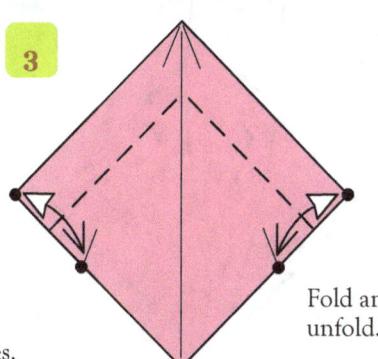

3. Fold and unfold.

*Flamingo* 11

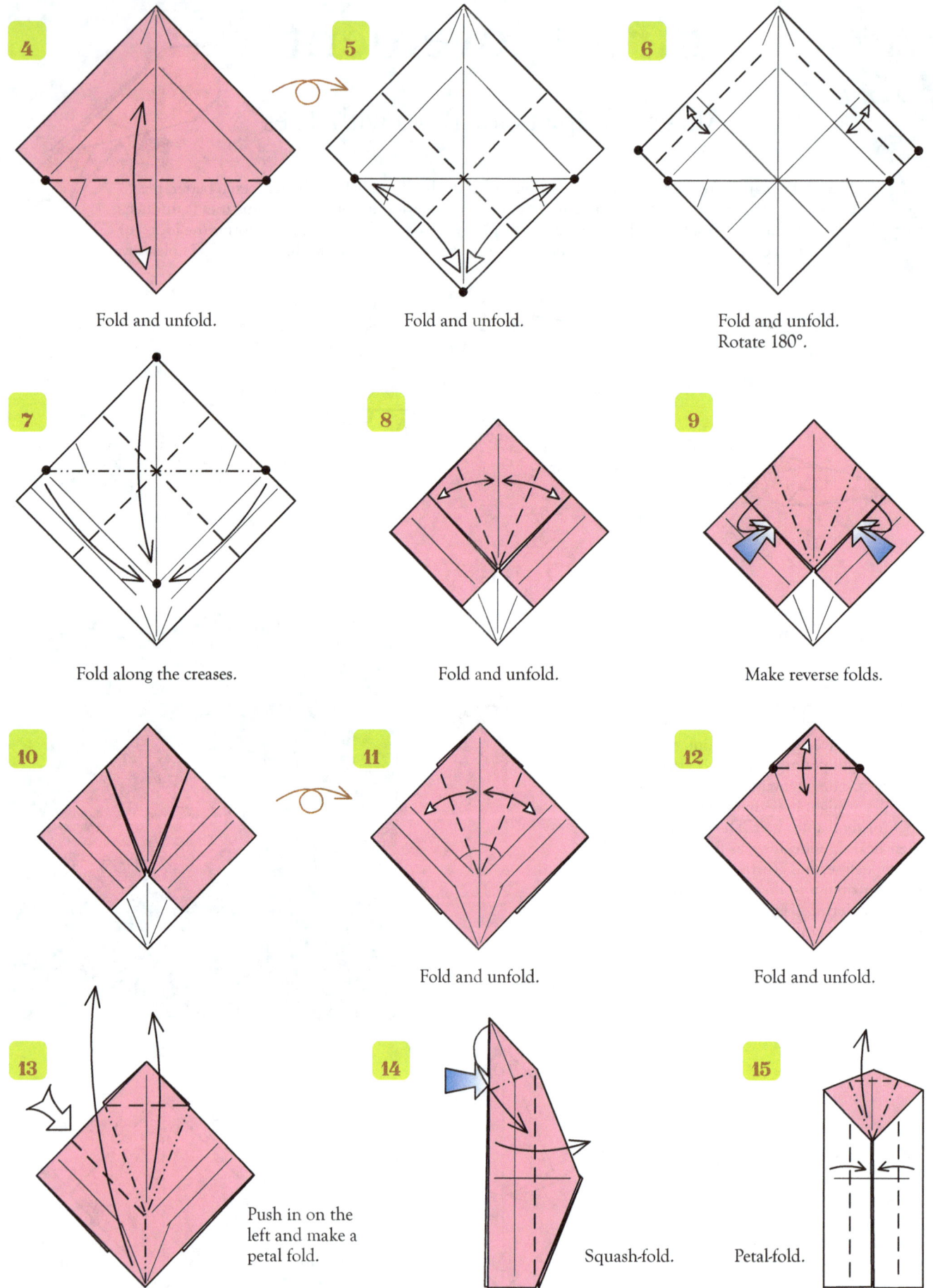

12  Origami Symphony No. 5

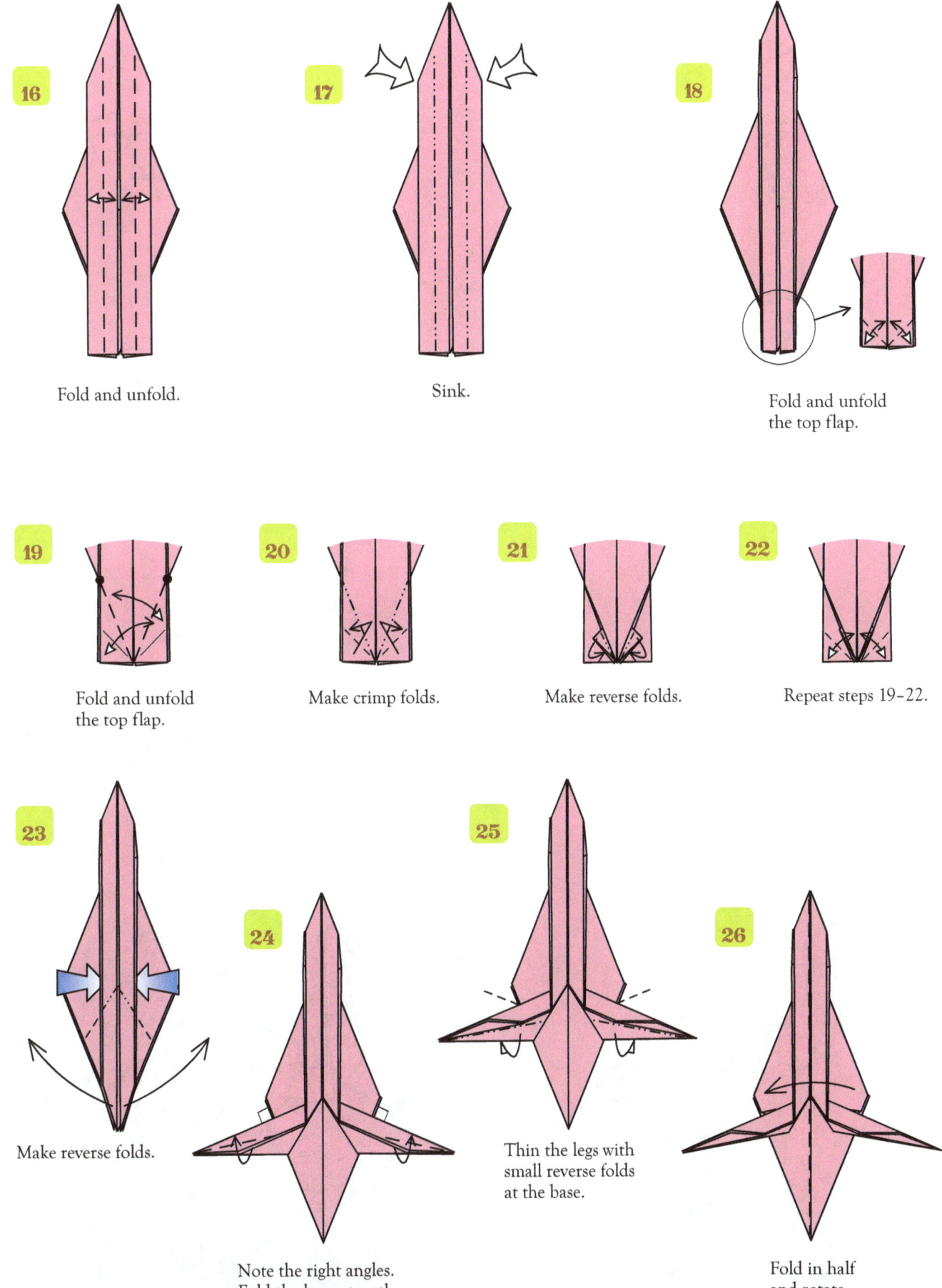

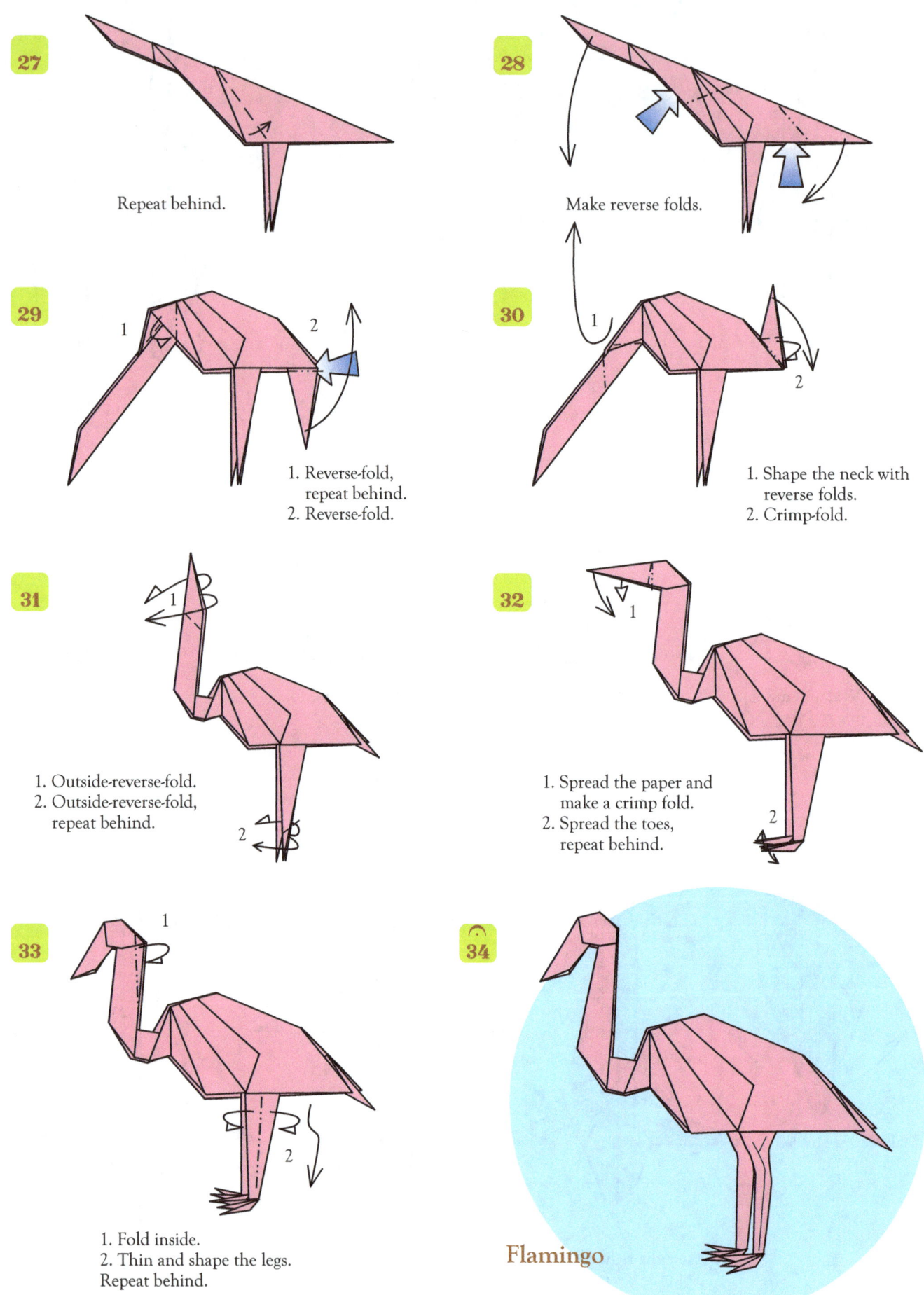

# Toucan

The Toucan can be found at the top of trees in tropical rain forests. Their colorful bills help to camouflage them in the trees. Though large, the bills are light and help cool them down. They stay in hollowed out trees and only fly for short distances. They feed on fruit, insects, and small lizards. Toucans are one of the noisiest birds. As pets, they are friendly and playful.

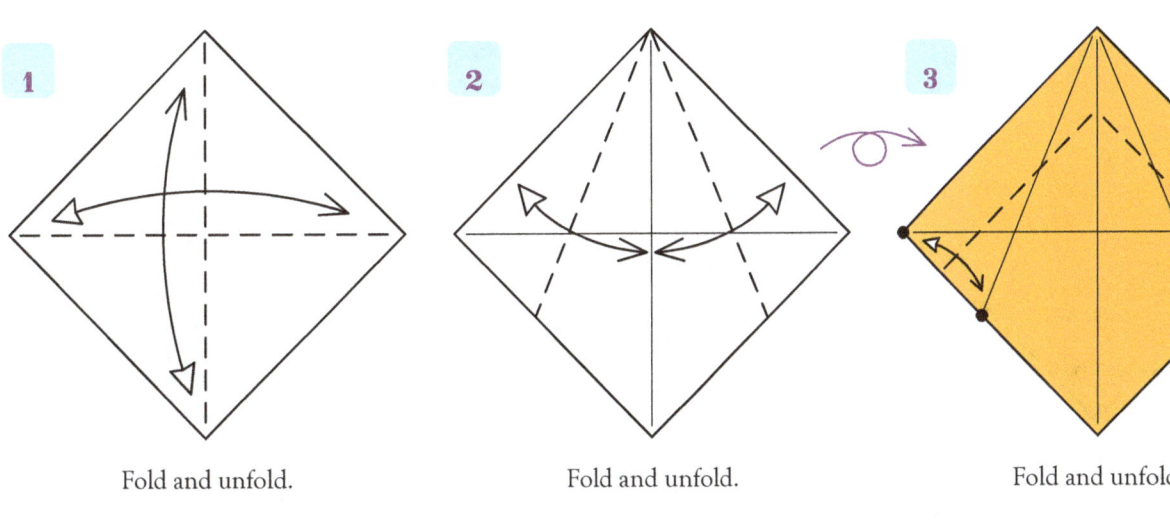

1. Fold and unfold.

2. Fold and unfold.

3. Fold and unfold.

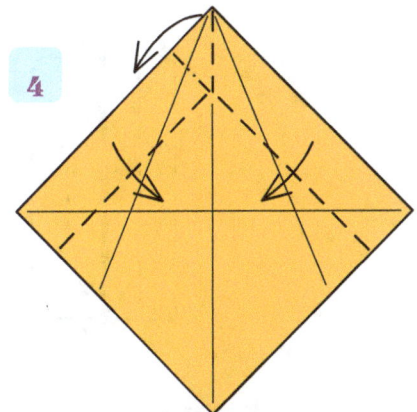

Rabbit-ear along the creases.

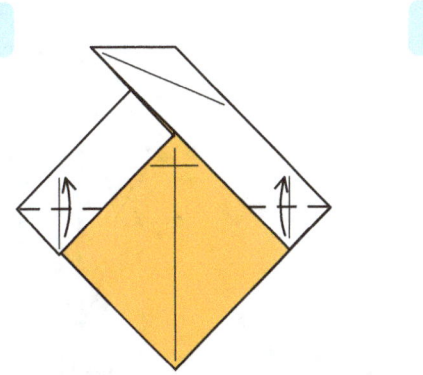

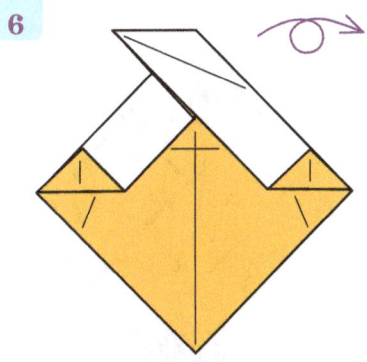

6. Rotate 180°.

Toucan 15

**7**

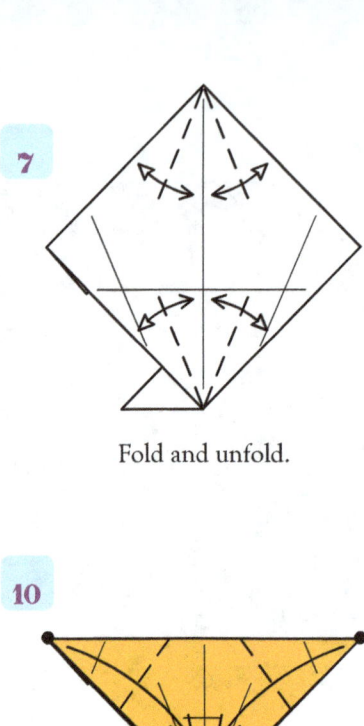

Fold and unfold.

**8**

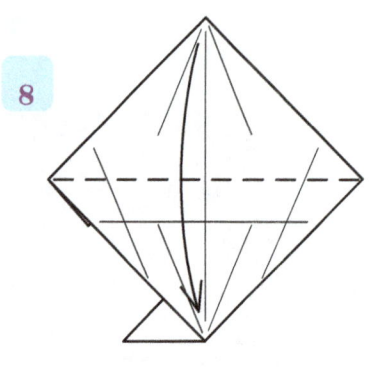

**9**

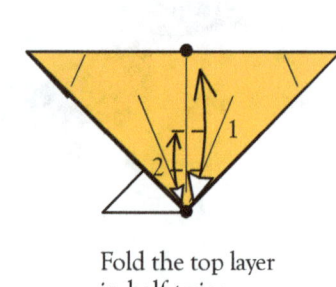

Fold the top layer in half twice.

**10**

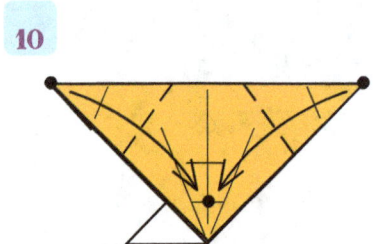

**11**

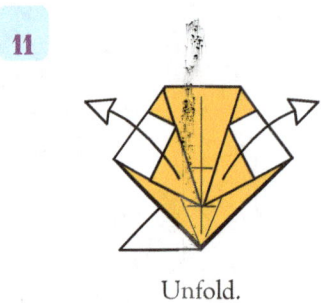

Unfold.

**12**

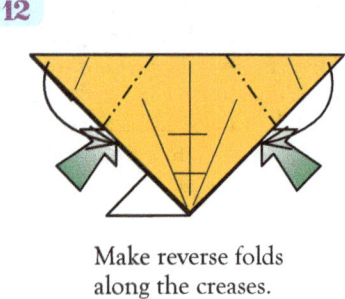

Make reverse folds along the creases.

**13**

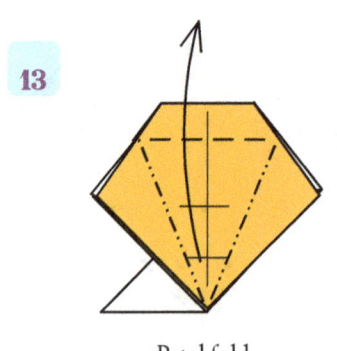

Petal-fold.

**14**

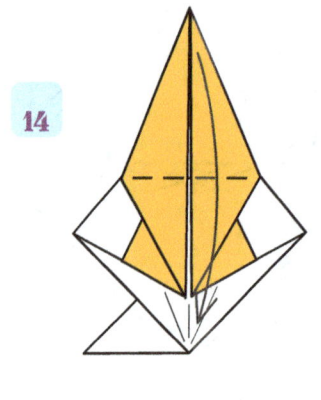

**15**

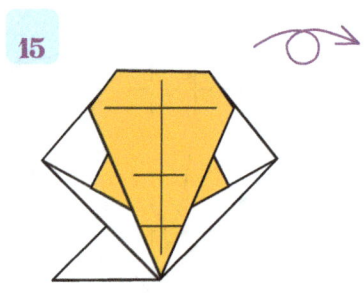

**16**

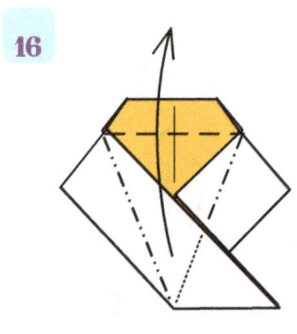

Petal-fold.

**17**

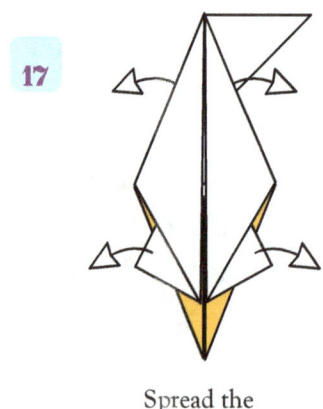

Spread the white flaps.

**18**

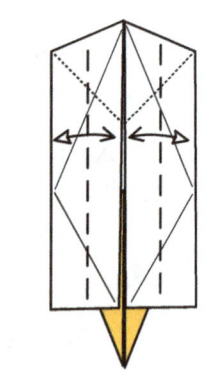

Fold to the center and unfold.

*Origami Symphony No. 5*

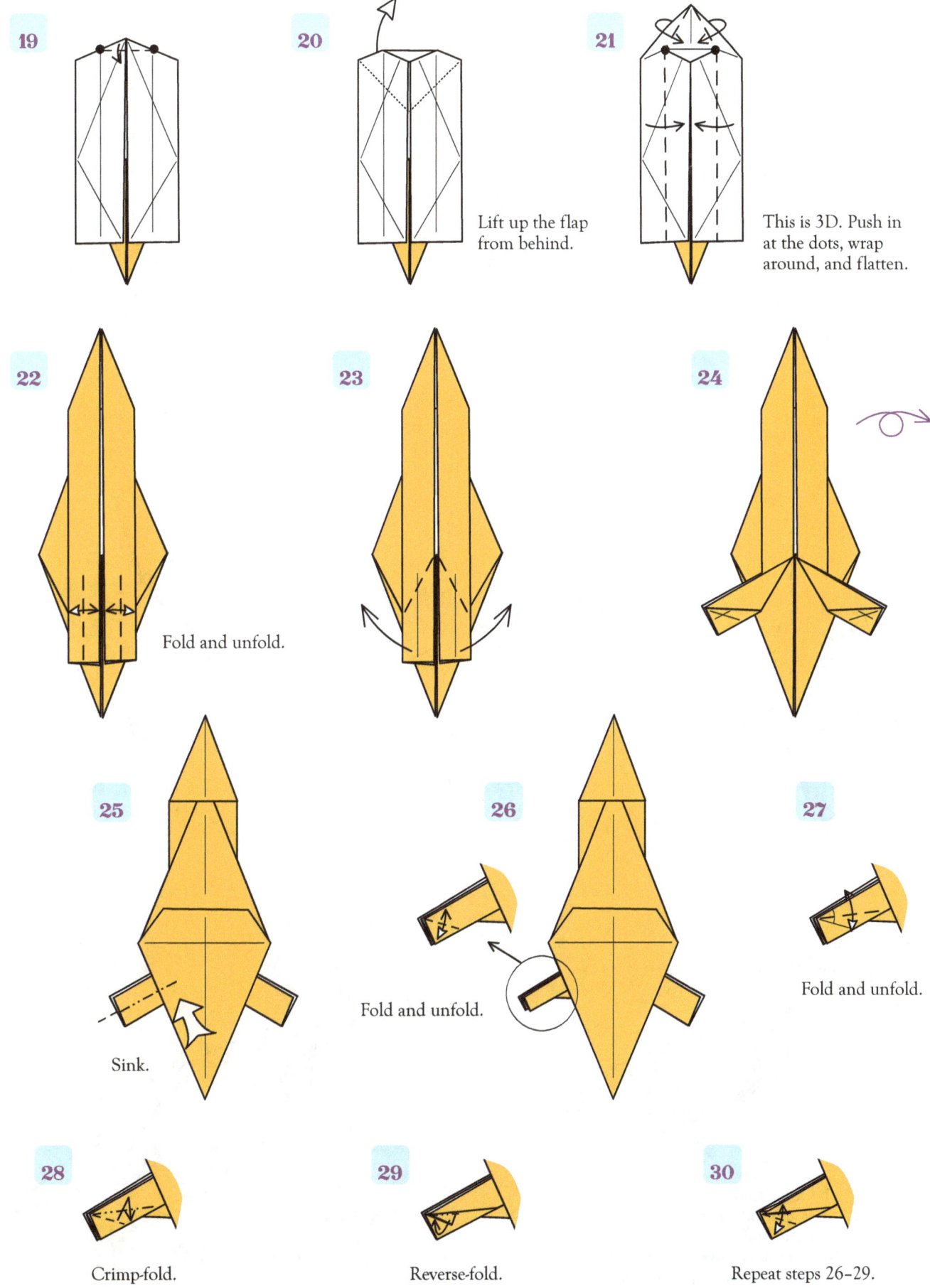

Toucan 17

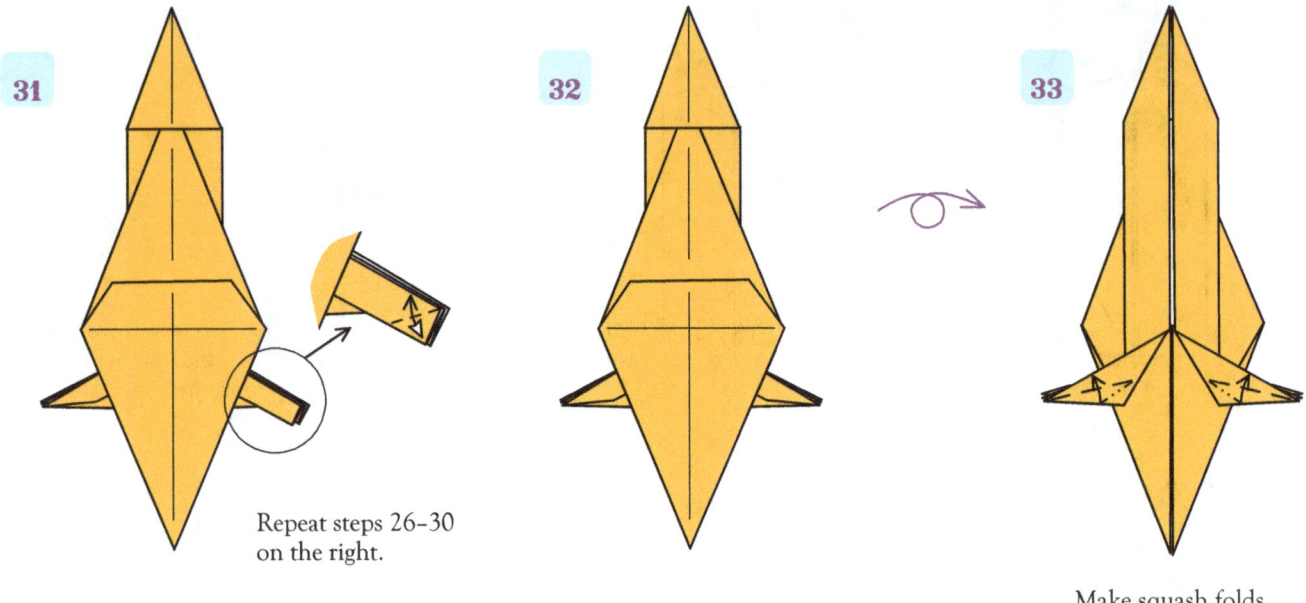

31 — Repeat steps 26–30 on the right.

32

33 — Make squash folds.

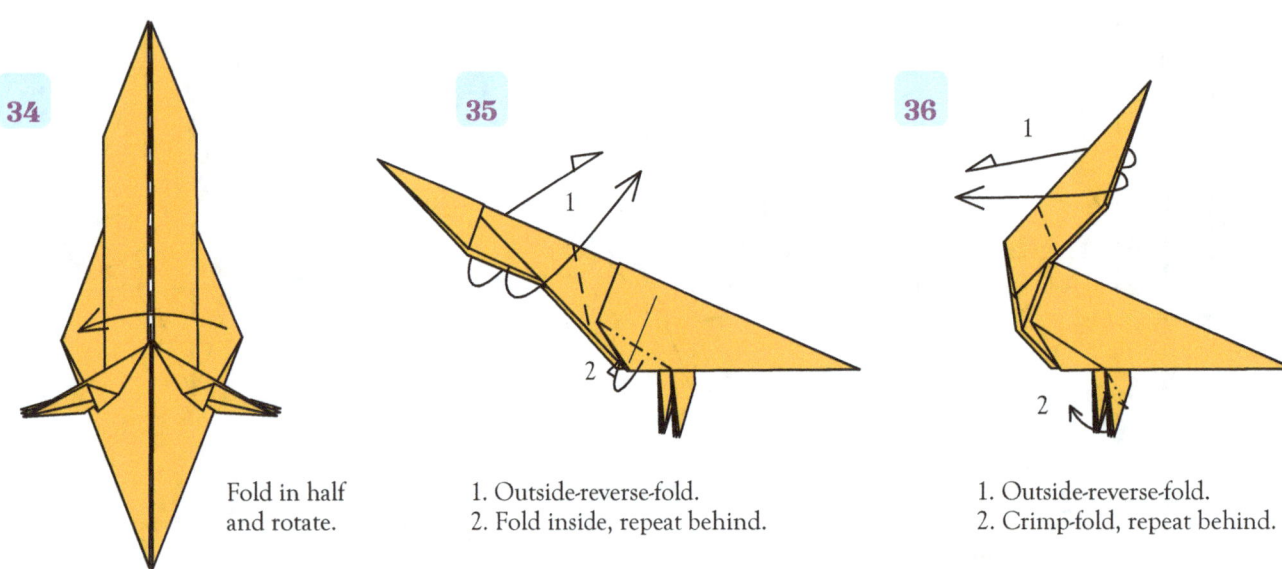

34 — Fold in half and rotate.

35
1. Outside-reverse-fold.
2. Fold inside, repeat behind.

36
1. Outside-reverse-fold.
2. Crimp-fold, repeat behind.

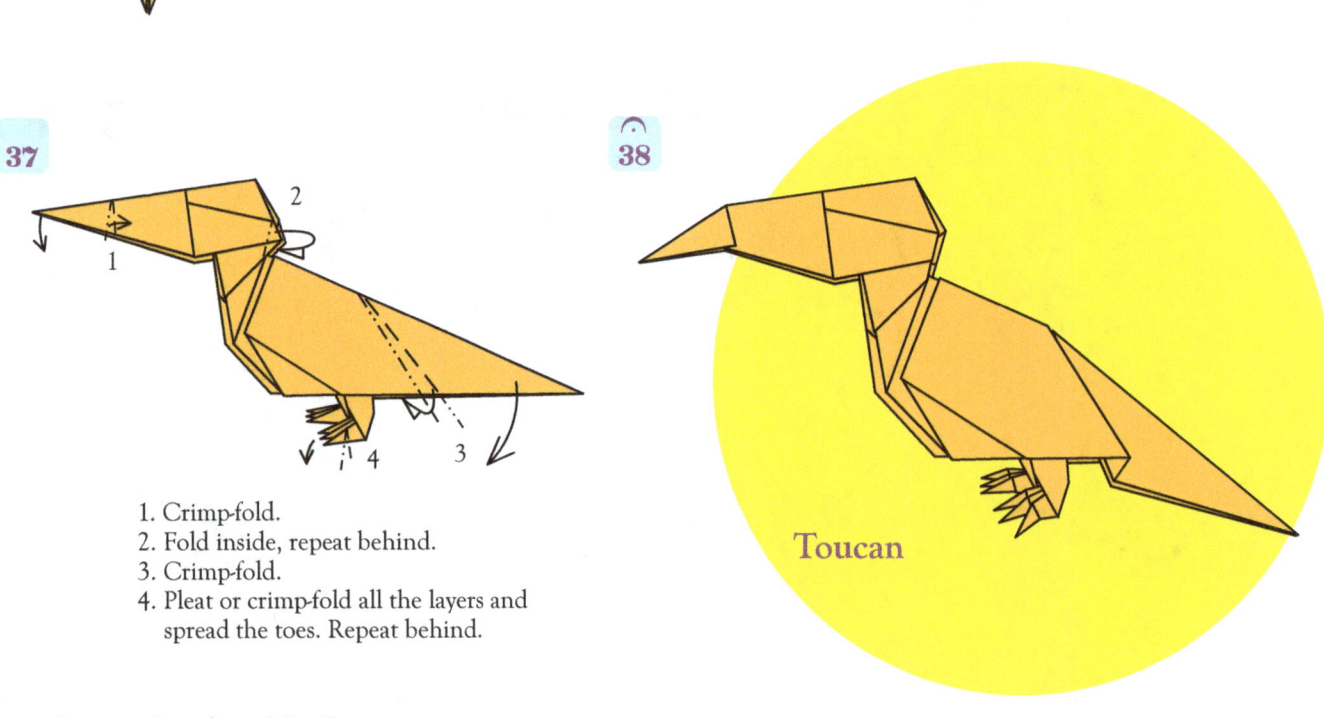

37
1. Crimp-fold.
2. Fold inside, repeat behind.
3. Crimp-fold.
4. Pleat or crimp-fold all the layers and spread the toes. Repeat behind.

38

Toucan

18  *Origami Symphony No. 5*

# Pheasant

At two to three feet long, Pheasants are long-tailed game birds with brilliant plumage. They live in forests, grasslands, and near farms where they dine on seeds, berries, fruits, insects, worms, and small reptiles. They have excellent vision and can swim well. Pheasants build nests on the ground and only fly for short distances. During the winter, they stay in the same place.

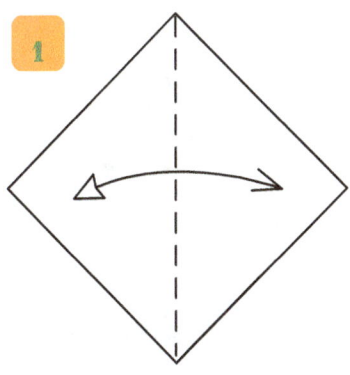

Fold and unfold.

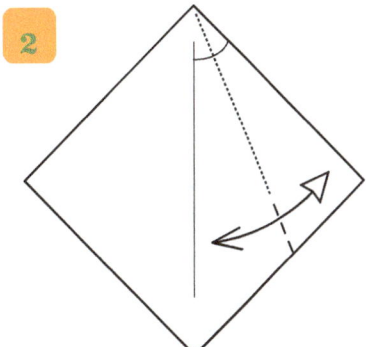

Fold and unfold by the edge.

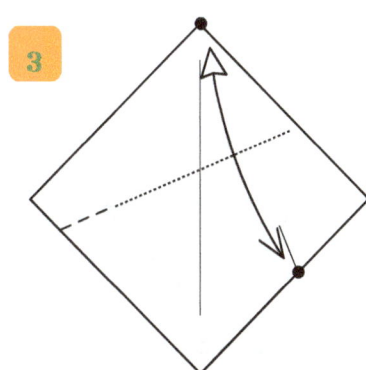

Fold and unfold by the edge.

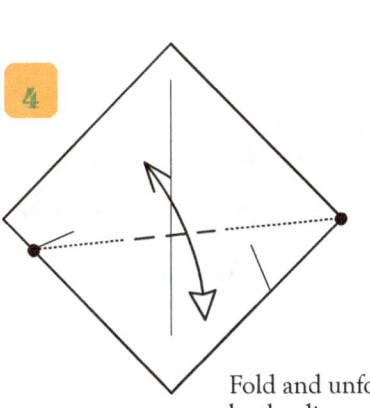

Fold and unfold by the diagonal.

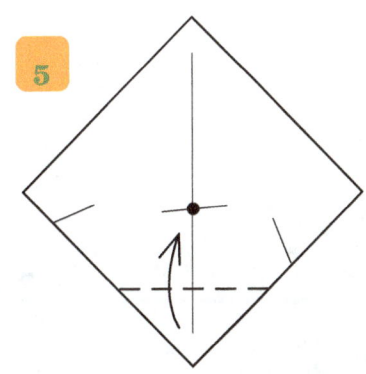

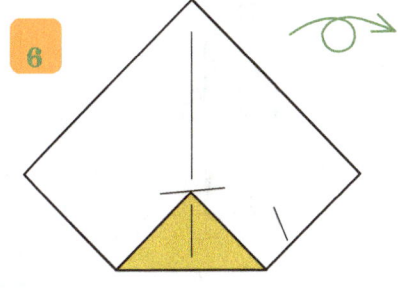

Rotate 180°.

*Pheasant* **19**

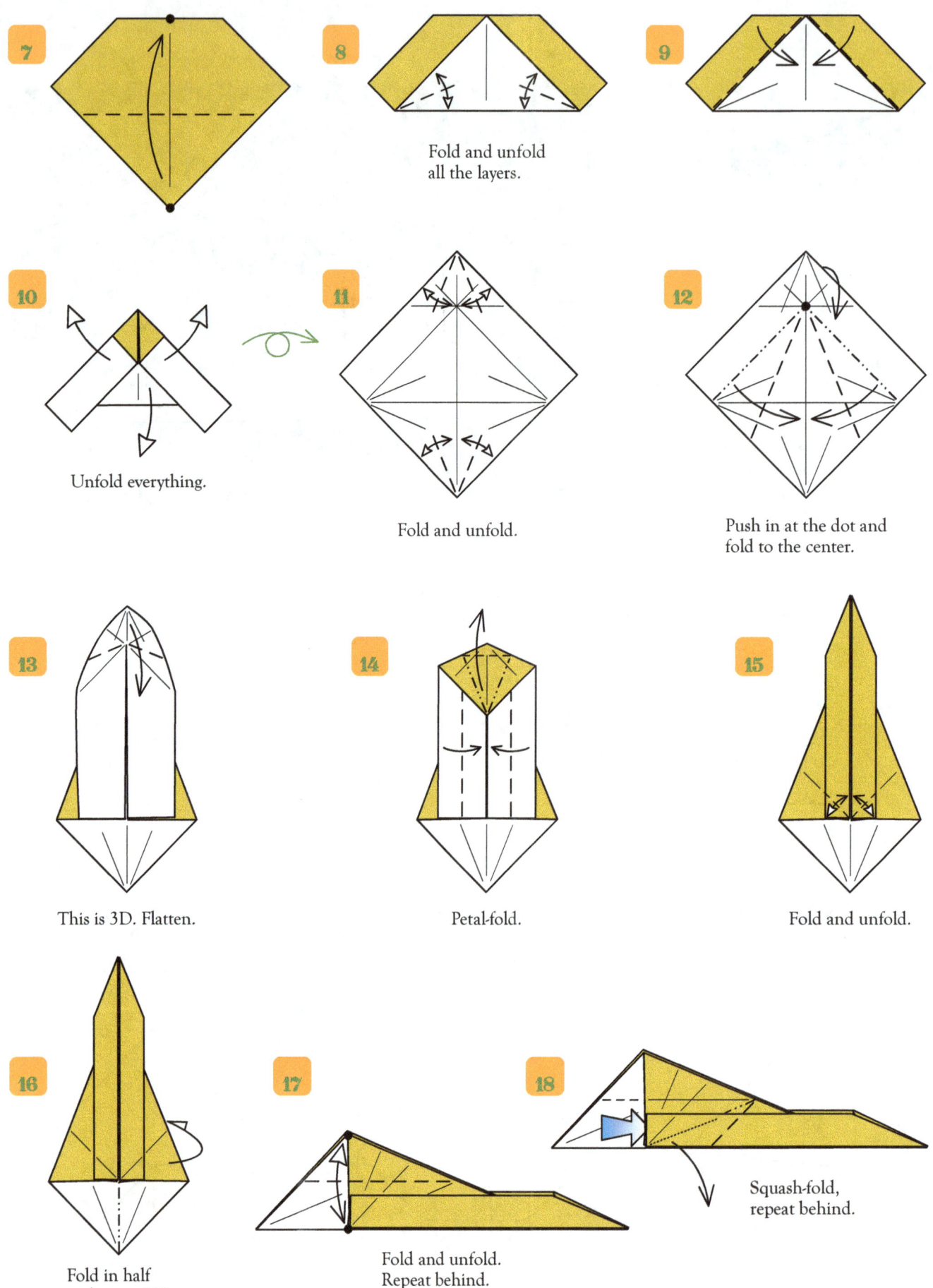

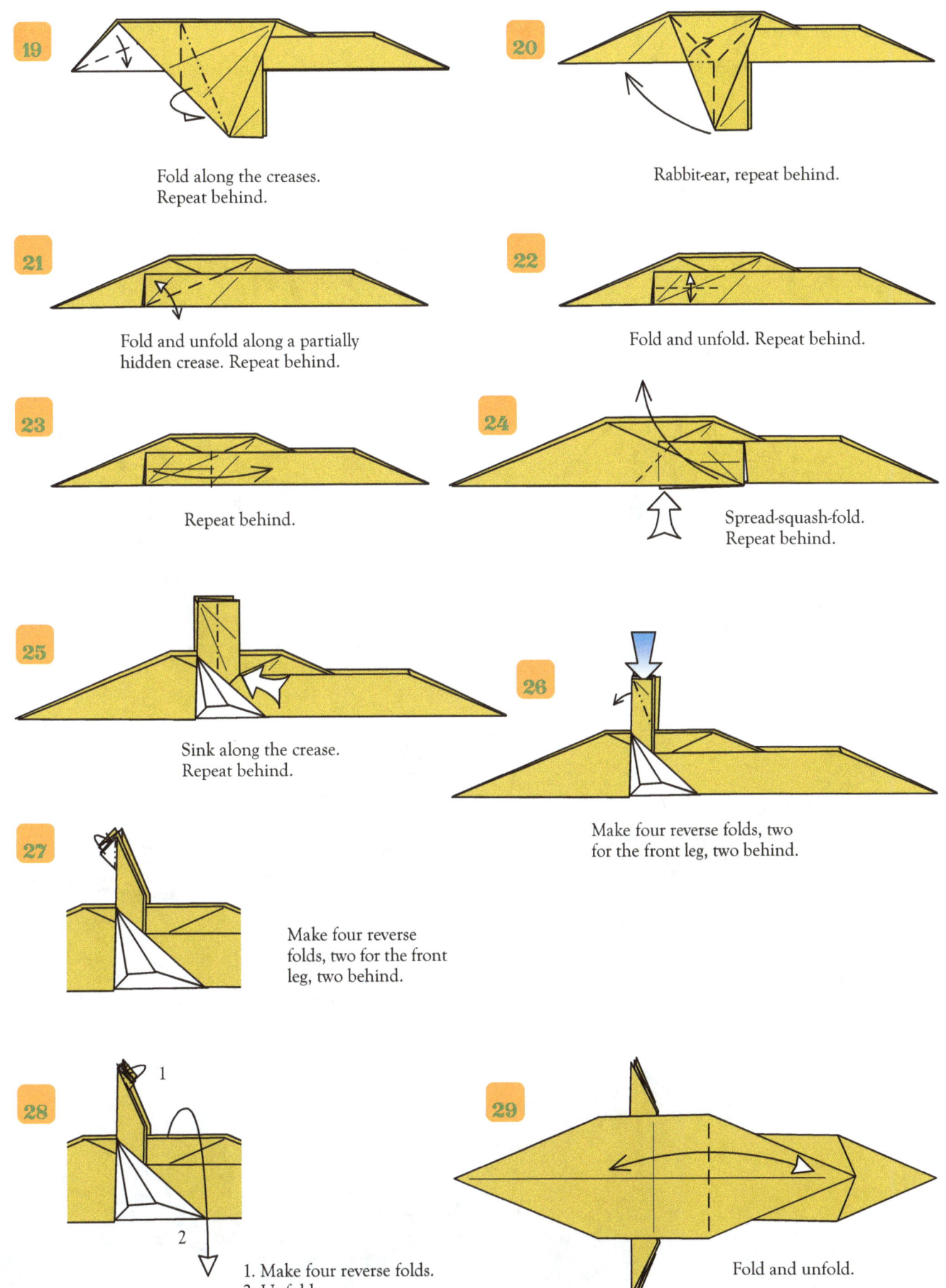

Pheasant

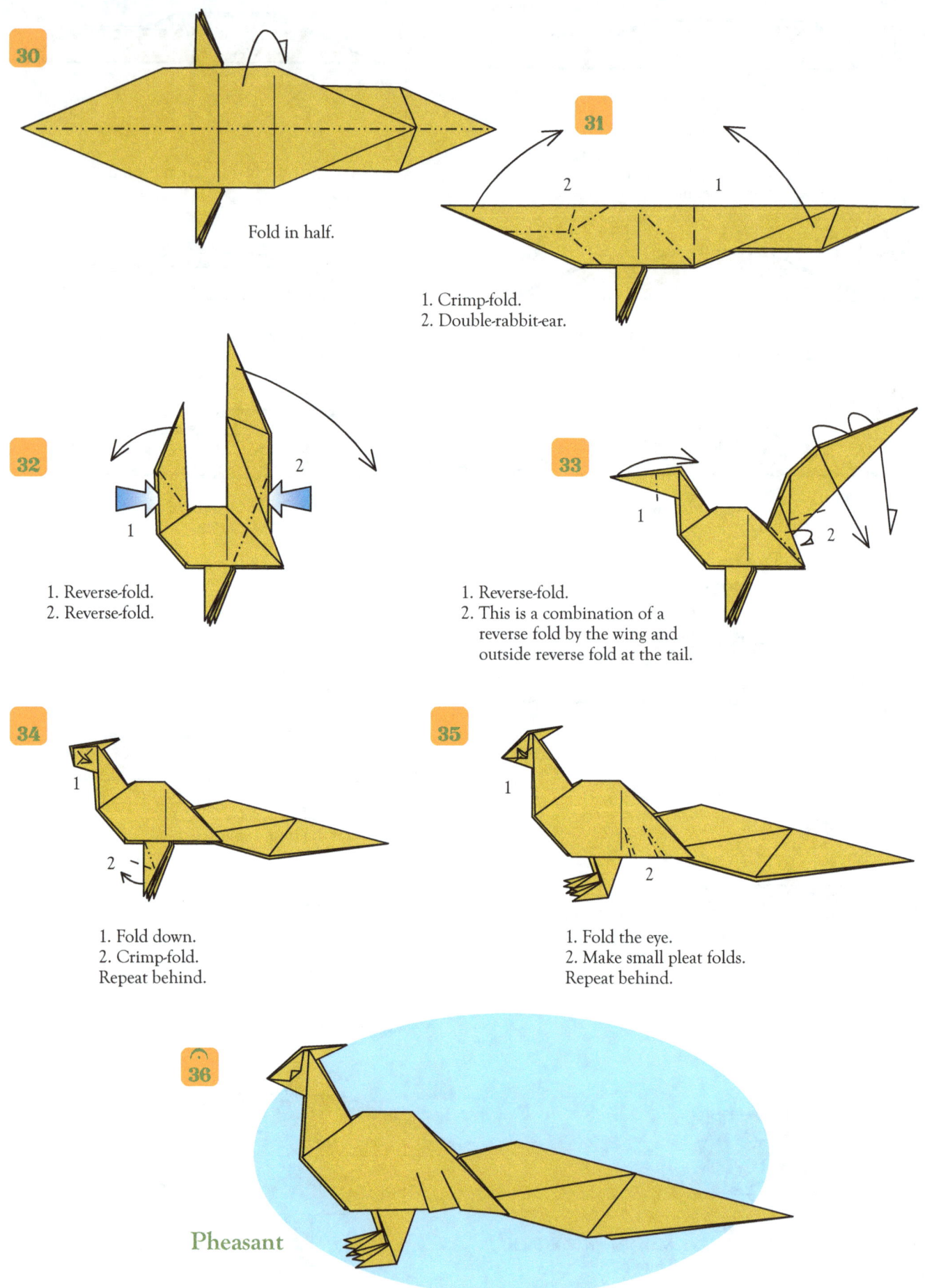

Pheasant

22 Origami Symphony No. 5

# Hawk

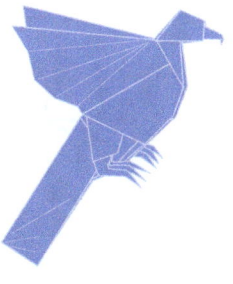

Hawks are very intelligent birds. They have sharp taloned feet and hooked beaks. Over 270 species are found in open fields, savannas, forests, and mountains. Their eyesight is incredible. They can see eight times more detail than humans, more colors, and even the magnetic field. Flying high above the ground, they spot their prey of frogs, snakes, squirrels, rabbits, and other small creatures. They dive down for their catch at over 150 miles per hour. During the winter, they migrate, flying over 1000 miles. They can build large nests of twigs and sticks high in the trees.

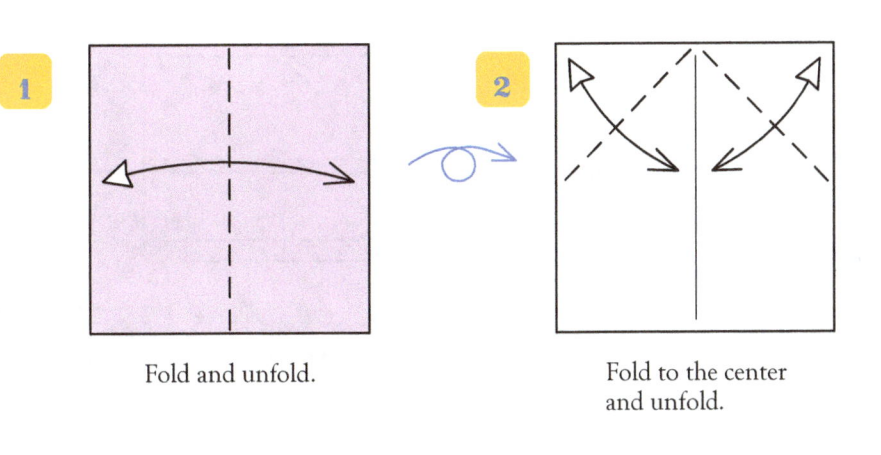

1. Fold and unfold.
2. Fold to the center and unfold.
3.

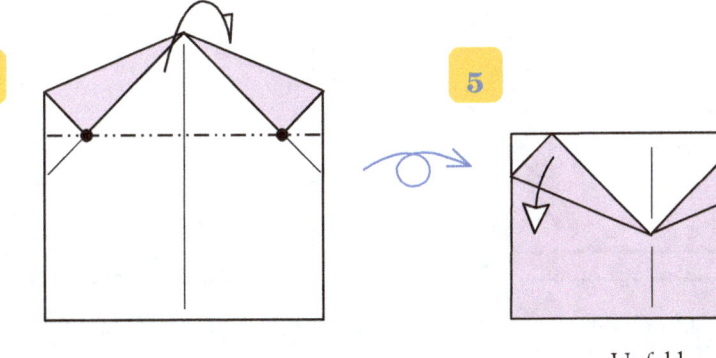

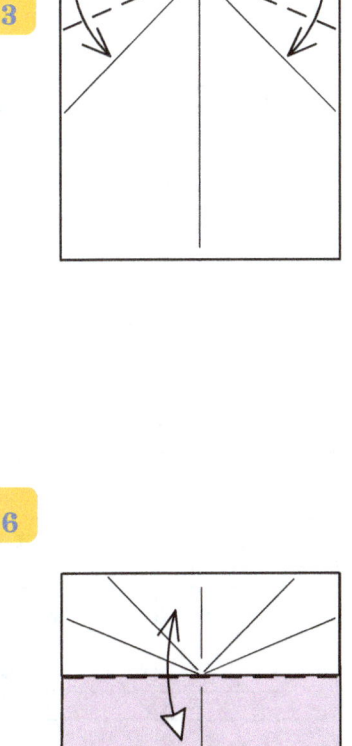

4.
5. Unfold.
6. Fold and unfold.

Hawk 23

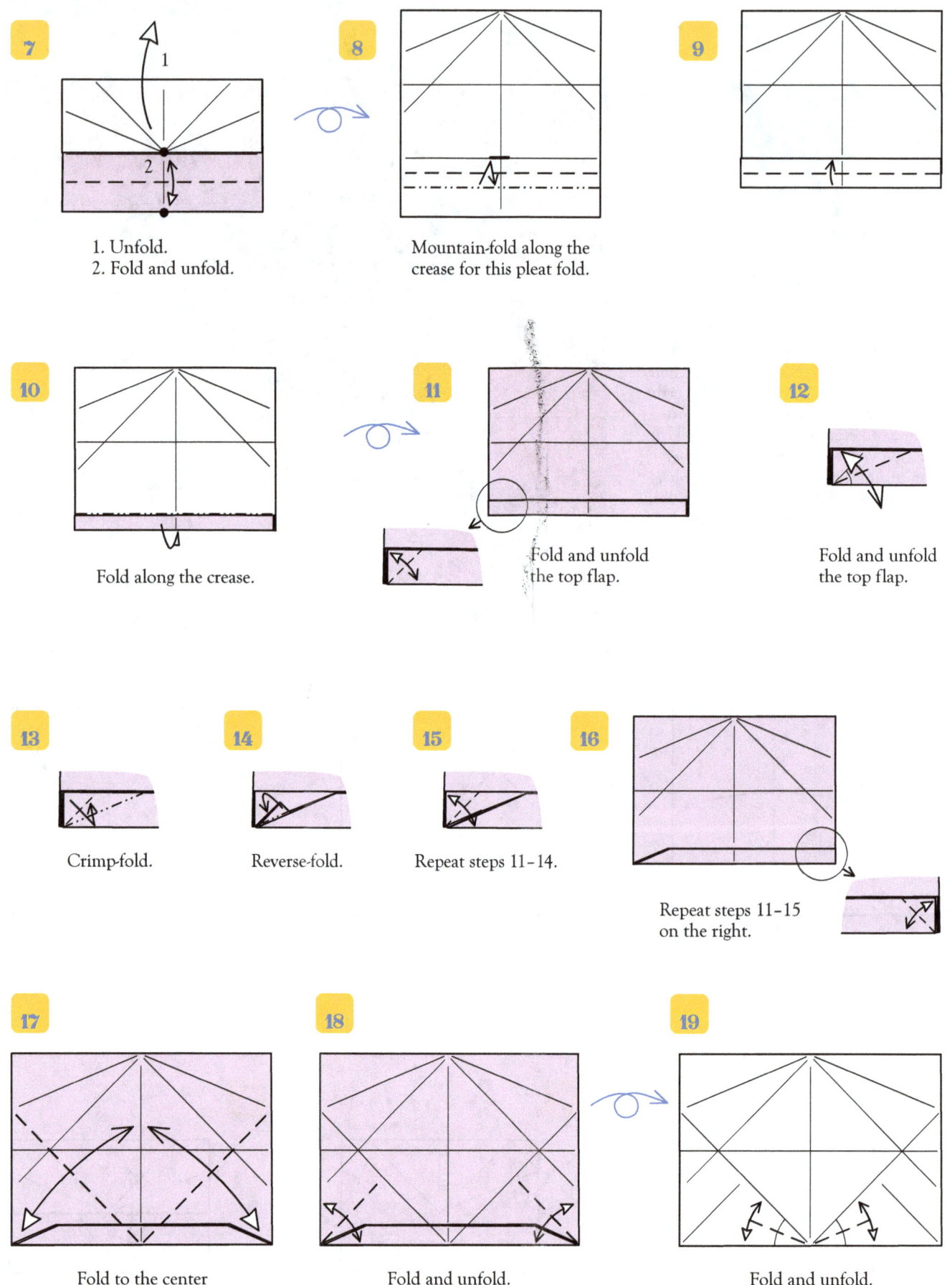

24  Origami Symphony No. 5

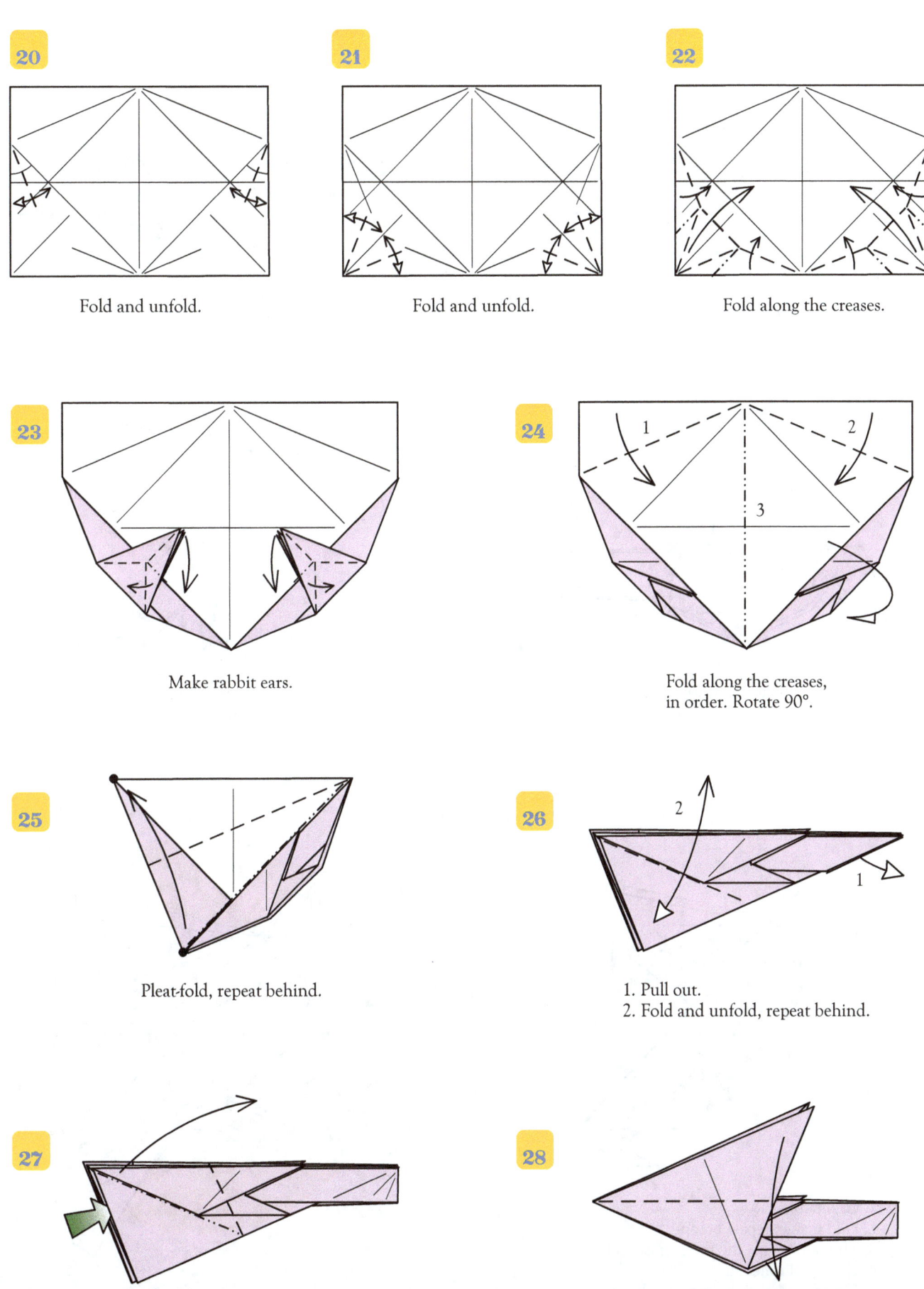

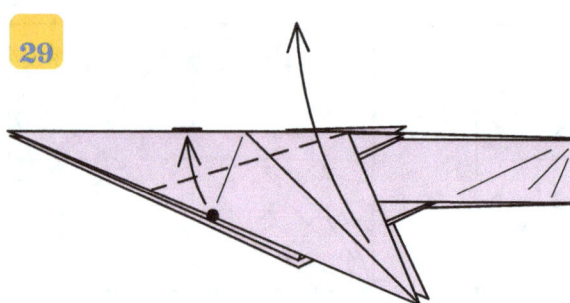

Repeat behind.

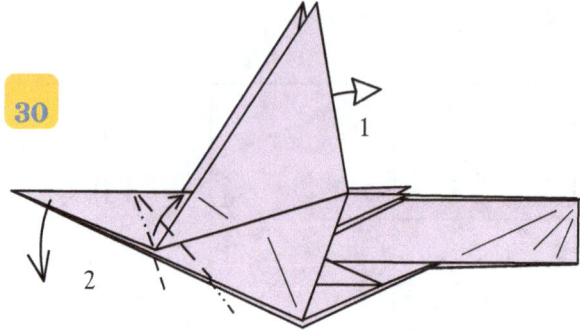

1. Pull out, repeat behind.
2. Crimp-fold.

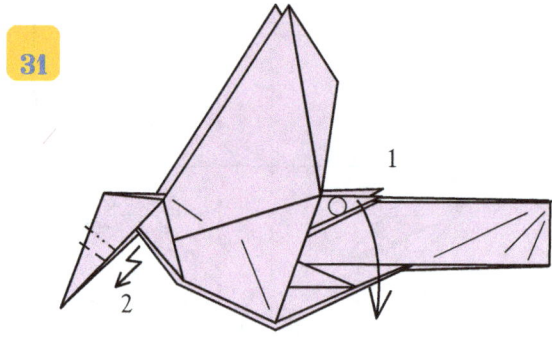

1. Hold the feet at the circle and slide the flaps down, repeat behind.
2. Crimp-fold.
Rotate.

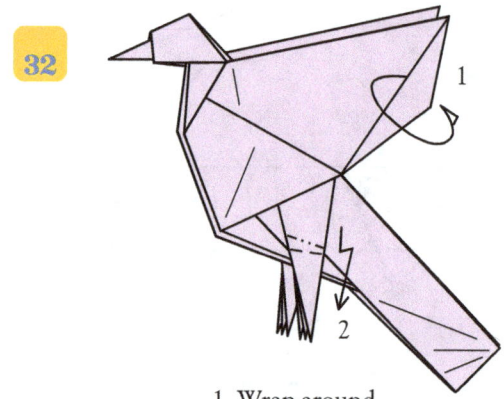

1. Wrap around.
2. Crimp-fold.
Repeat behind.

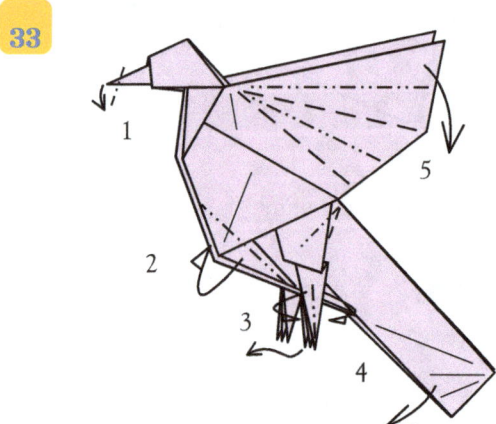

1. Crimp-fold.
2. Fold inside, repeat behind.
3. Thin and shape the toes, repeat behind.
4. Crimp-fold the tail.
5. Pleat-fold the wings, repeat behind.

Hawk

# Parrot

Parrots are colorful birds with strong, hooked beaks, which are perfect for cracking nuts. These intelligent birds are found in tropical and subtropical regions of South America, Africa, Australia, and New Zealand. These social birds feed on seeds, fruit, and insects. They are the only birds that can pick up food with their feet and feed themselves, as we would with our hands.

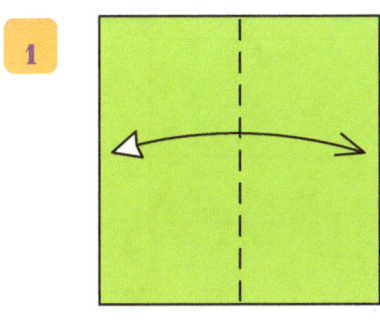

1. Fold and unfold.

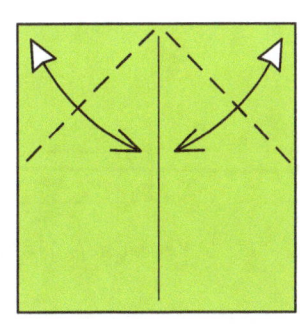

2. Fold to the center and unfold.

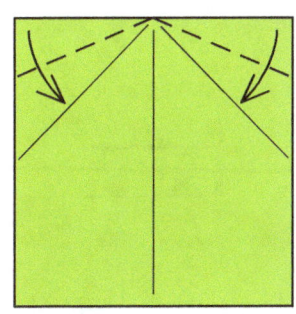

3.

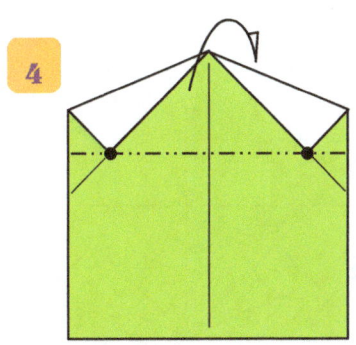

4.

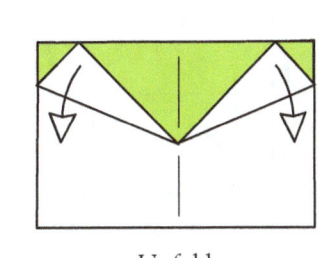

5. Unfold.

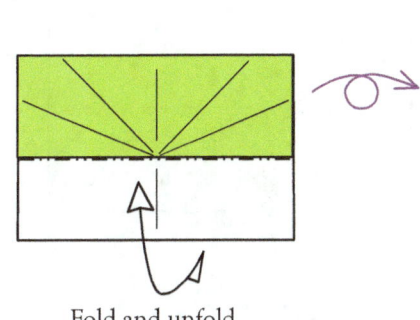

6. Fold and unfold.

*Parrot* **27**

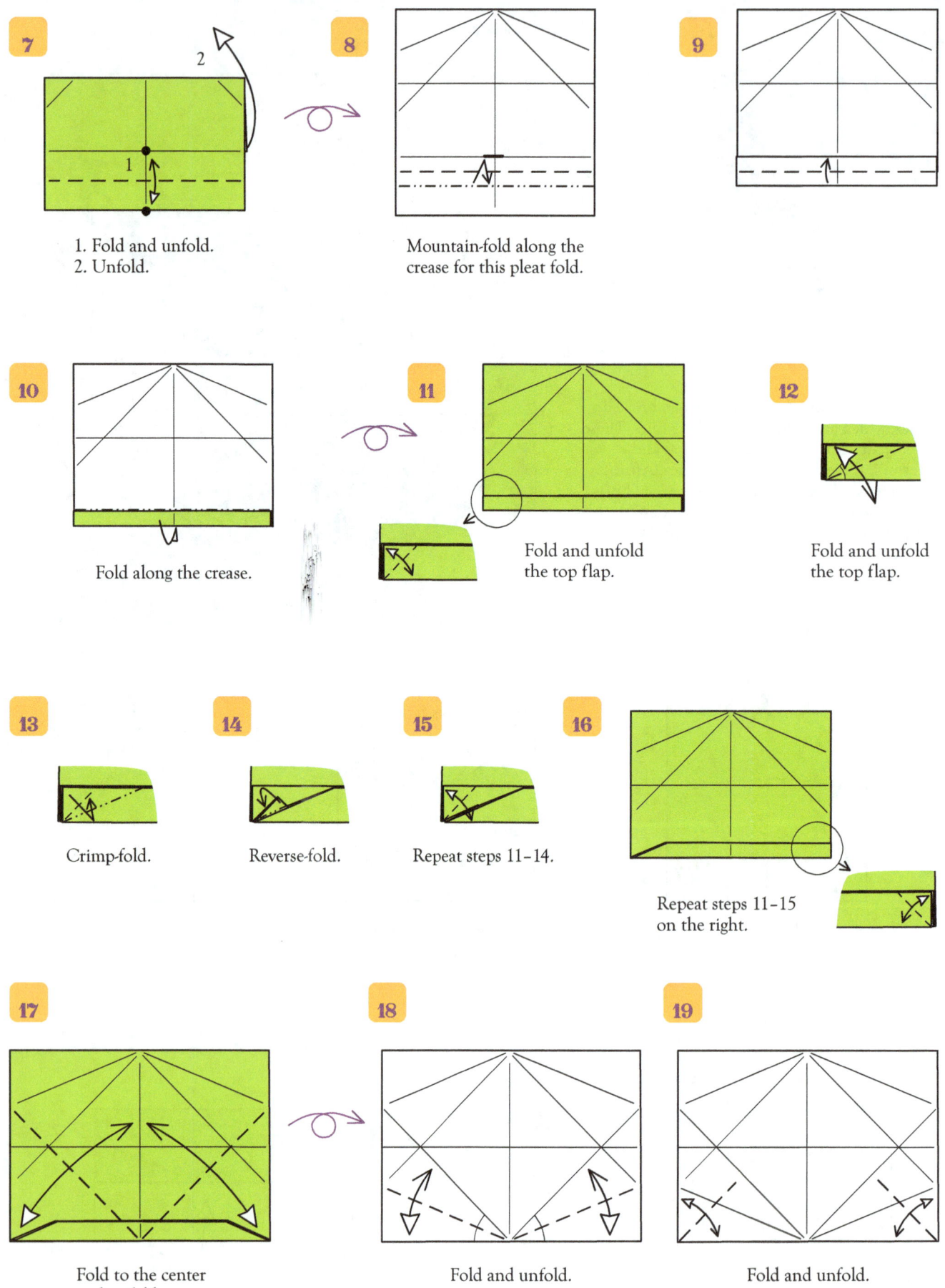

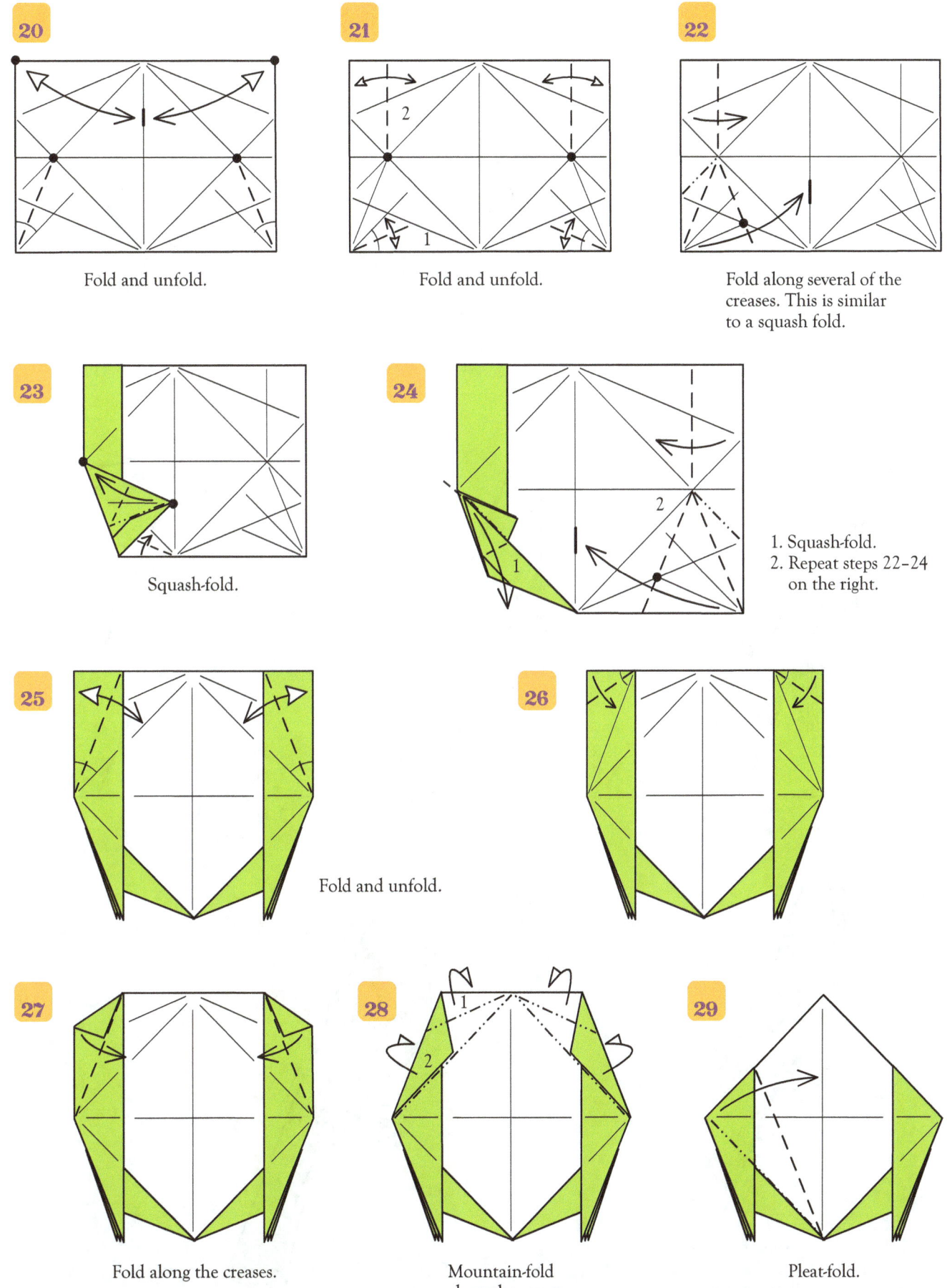

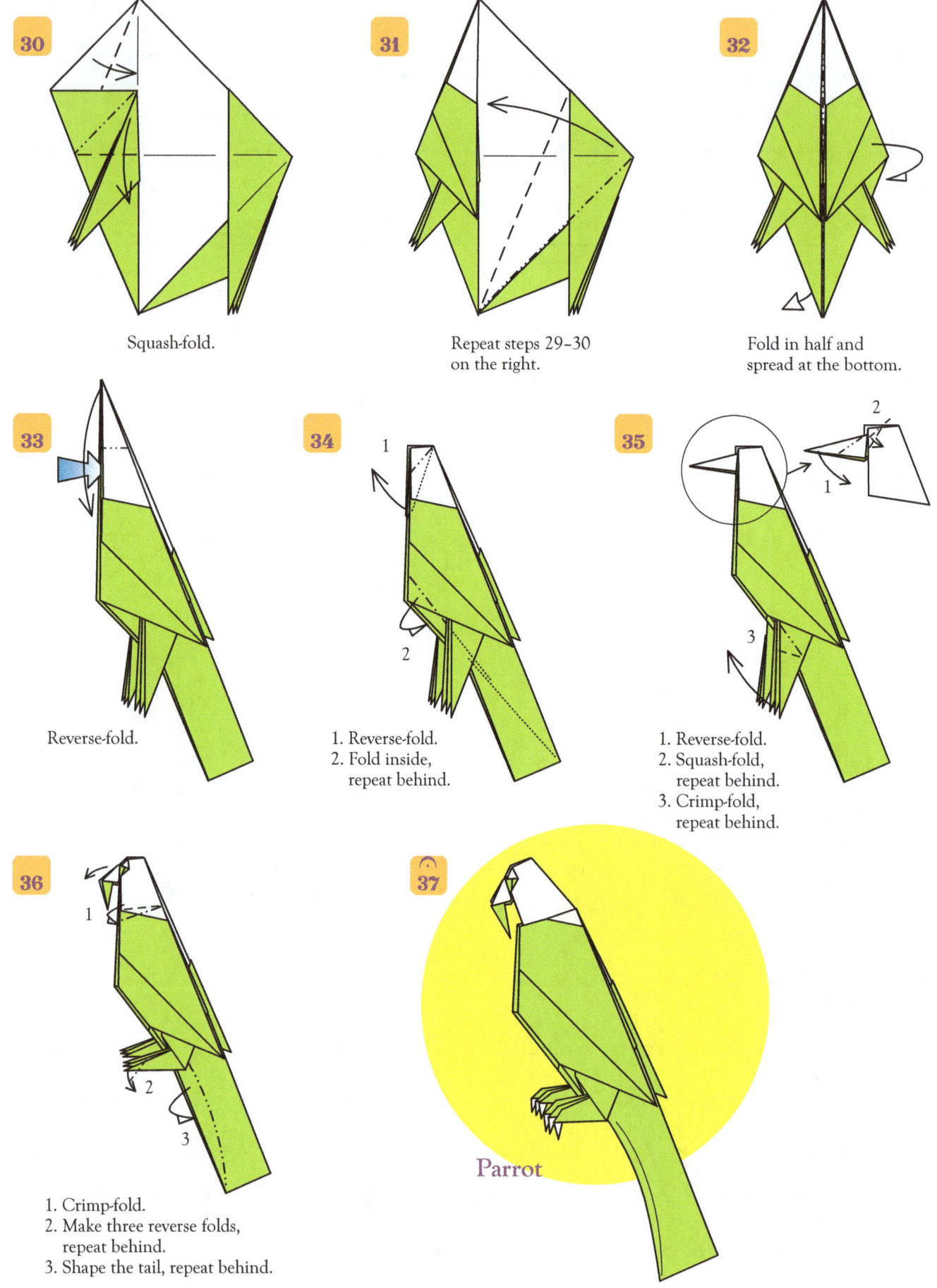

**30** Squash-fold.

**31** Repeat steps 29–30 on the right.

**32** Fold in half and spread at the bottom.

**33** Reverse-fold.

**34**
1. Reverse-fold.
2. Fold inside, repeat behind.

**35**
1. Reverse-fold.
2. Squash-fold, repeat behind.
3. Crimp-fold, repeat behind.

**36**
1. Crimp-fold.
2. Make three reverse folds, repeat behind.
3. Shape the tail, repeat behind.

**37** Parrot

30   Origami Symphony No. 5

# Crow

Crows are social black birds. They are extremely intelligent. They make tools to get food, they can recognize themselves in the mirror, and have even been known to enjoy sledding on cup lids. Found all over the world in forests, mountains, grasslands, deserts and elsewhere, they eat all kinds of foods including fruits, mice, and human leftovers.

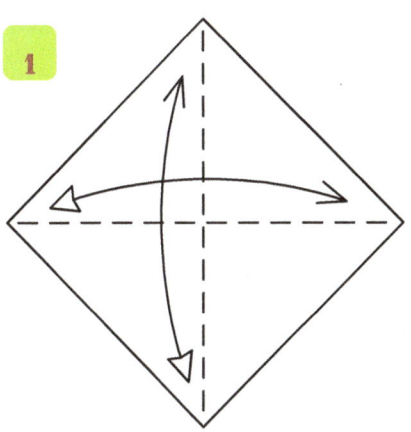

1. Fold and unfold.

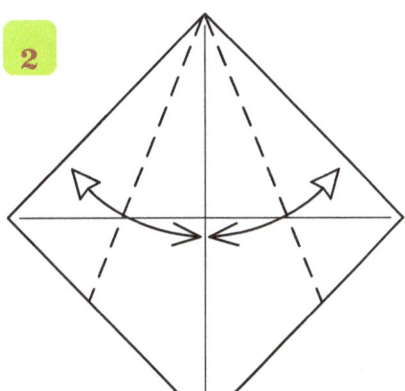

2. Fold and unfold.

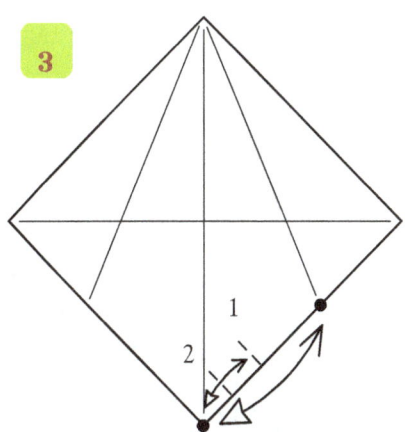

3. Fold and unfold twice.

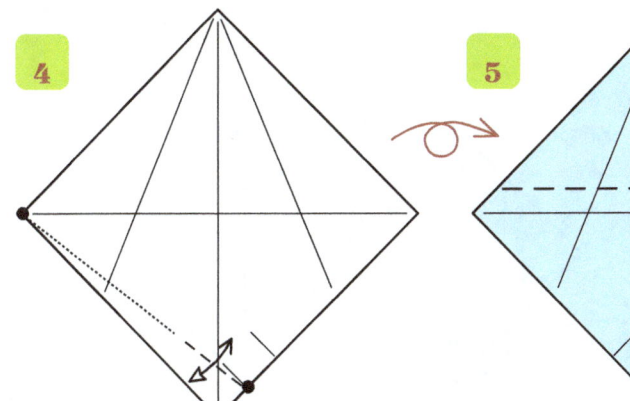

4. Fold and unfold on the diagonal.

5.

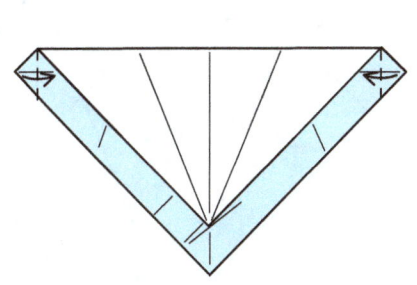

6.

Crow 31

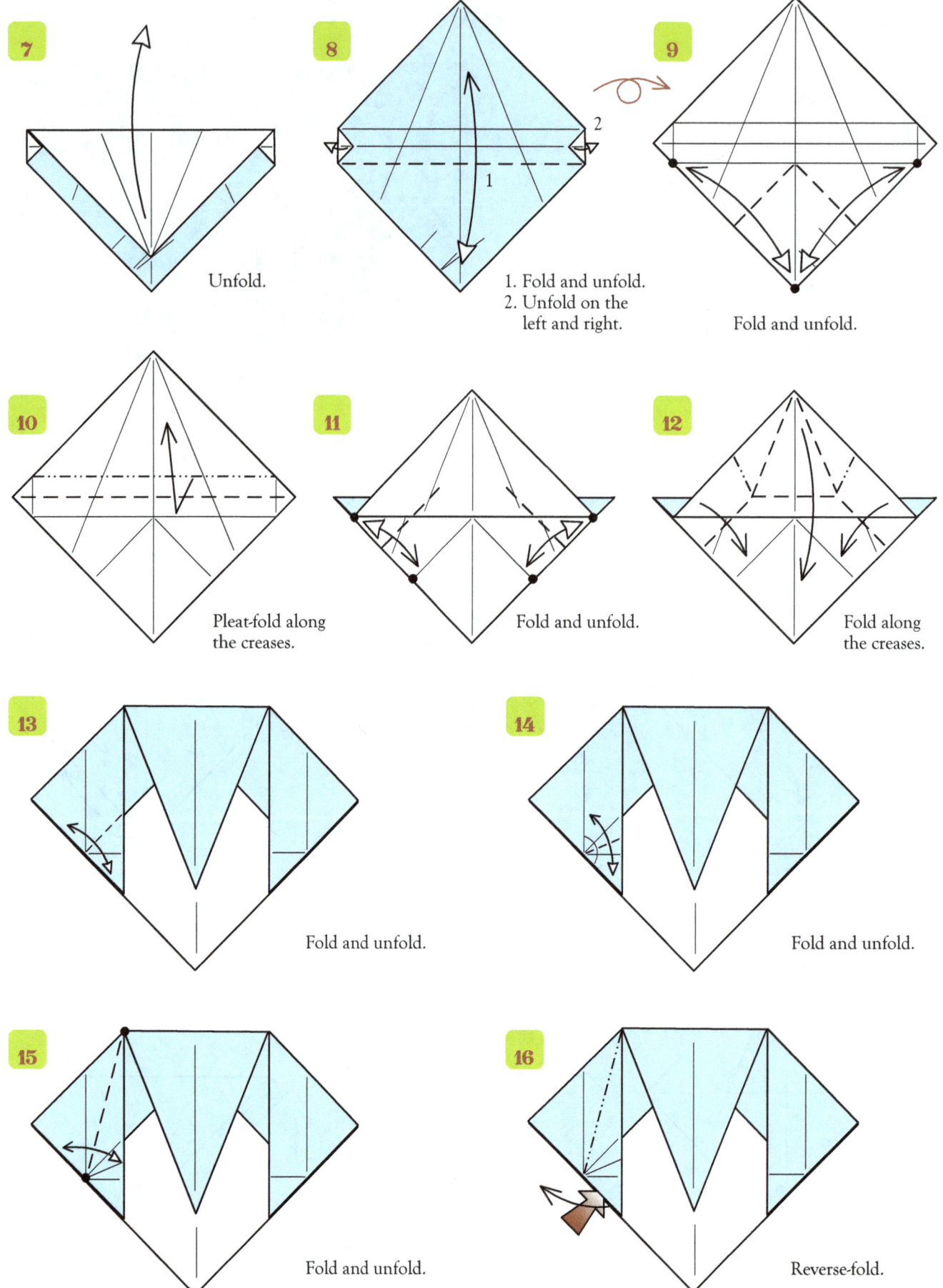

32  Origami Symphony No. 5

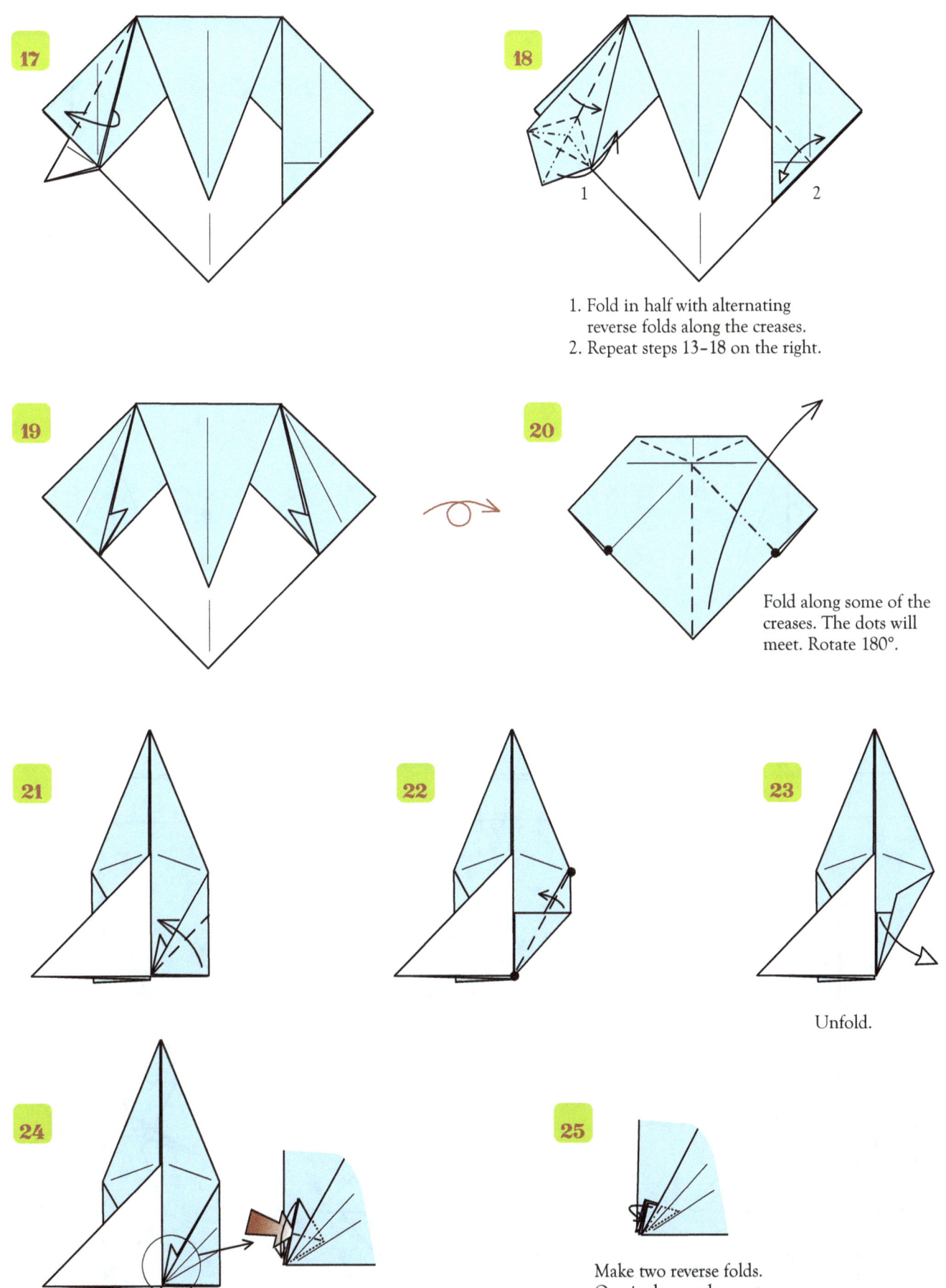

1. Fold in half with alternating reverse folds along the creases.
2. Repeat steps 13–18 on the right.

Fold along some of the creases. The dots will meet. Rotate 180°.

Unfold.

Reverse-fold.

Make two reverse folds. One is shown, the next one is right below it.

Crow 33

Crimp-fold along the creases.

Reverse-fold.

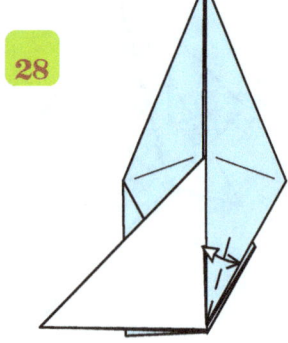

Fold and unfold all but the bottom layers.

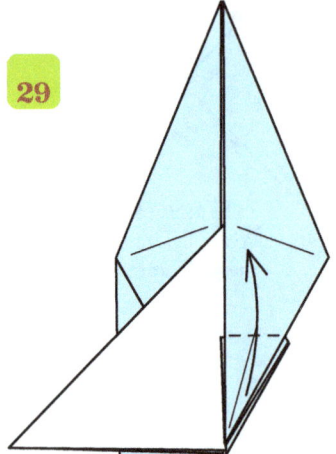

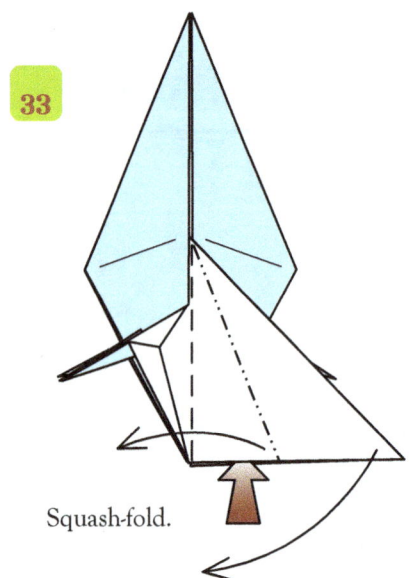

Fold along the creases to form the leg.

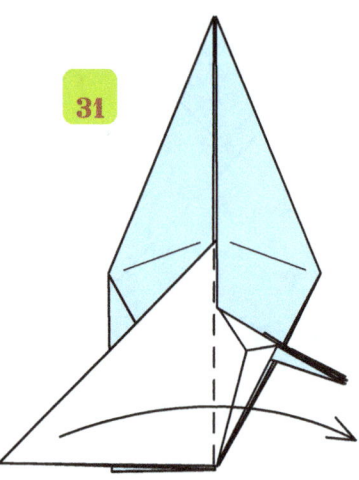

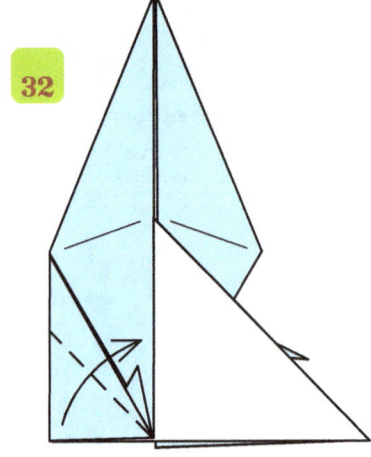

Repeat steps 21–30 on the left.

Squash-fold.

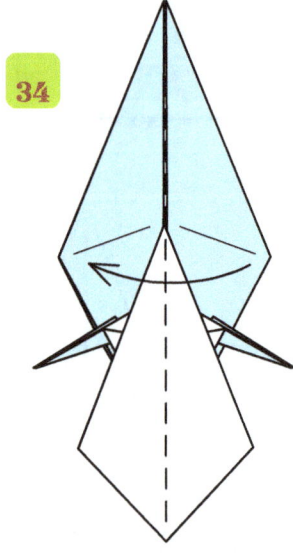

Fold in half and rotate.

**34** Origami Symphony No. 5

**35**

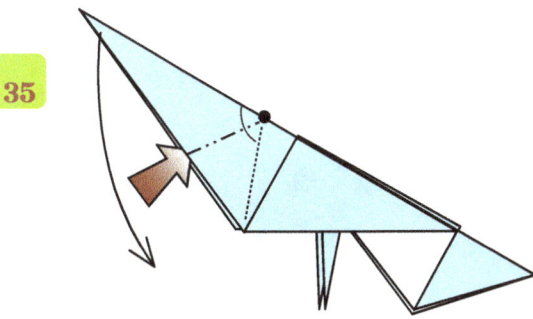

Reverse-fold.

**36**

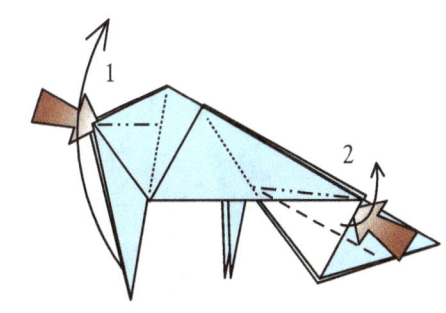

1. Reverse-fold.
2. This is similar to a reverse fold. Begin under the wing. Repeat behind.

**37**

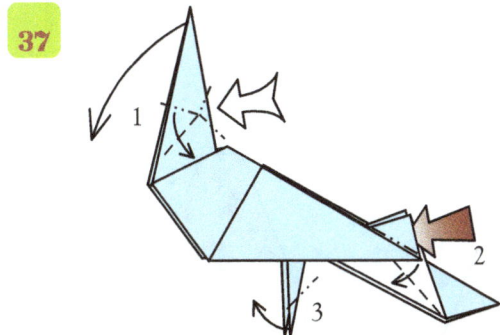

1. Push in on the right and make a crimp fold.
2. Reverse-fold, repeat behind.
3. Reverse-fold, repeat behind. Place your finger after the second flap, so the toes can separate from this reverse fold.

**38**

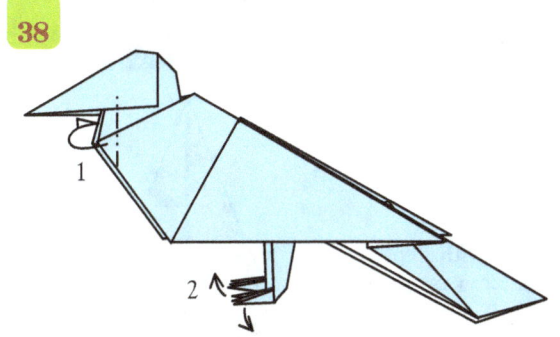

1. Fold inside.
2. Spread the toes. Repeat behind.

**39**

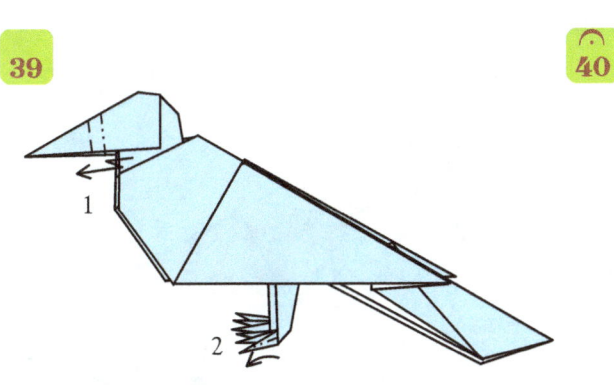

1. Crimp-fold.
2. Thin and curl the toes, repeat behind.

**40**

Crow

# Vulture

Vultures are large, social birds. Found in grasslands and mountains, they glide for hours with their strong wings, searching for food. When one Vulture finds the food, others follow. They feed mainly on dead animals, and can even digest rotten meat and bones. By doing so, they are eco-friendly by cleaning up the area. Upon eating, they bathe themselves to keep clean, and soar again.

Begin with step 28 of the Crow on page 34.

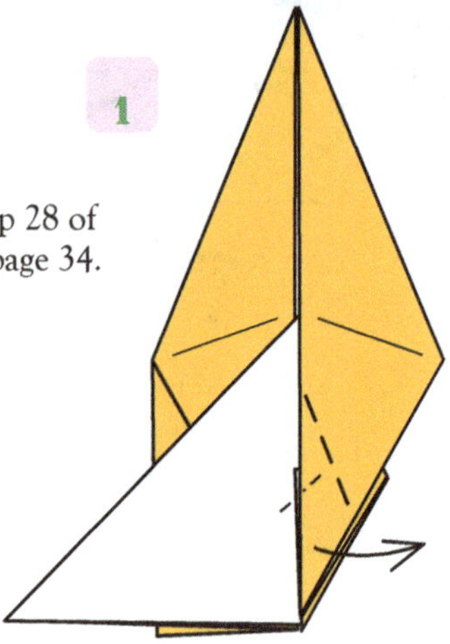

1. Make a small squash fold.

2. 

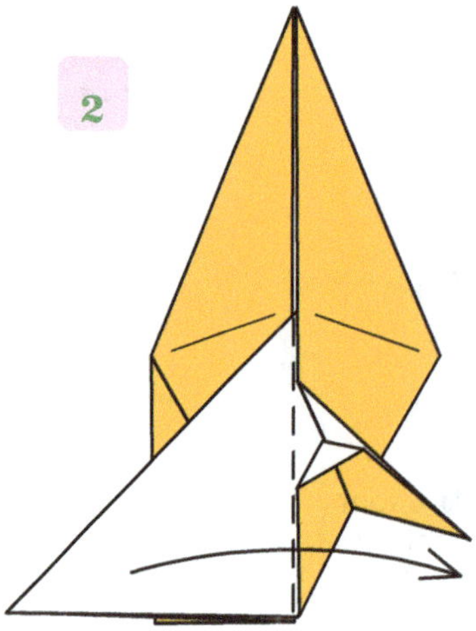

3. 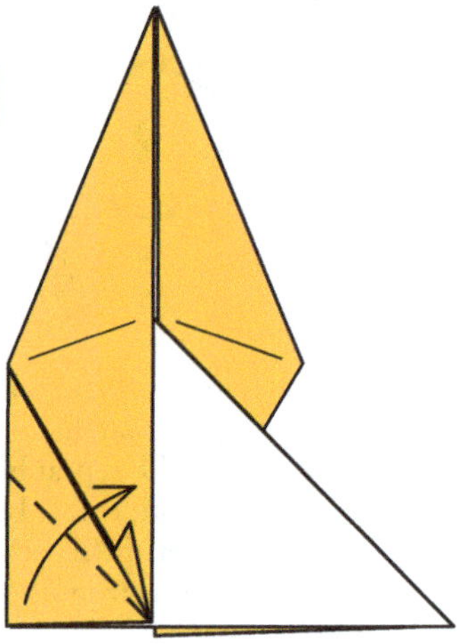 Repeat steps 21–28 of the Crow and step 1 of the Vulture, on the left.

4. Squash-fold.

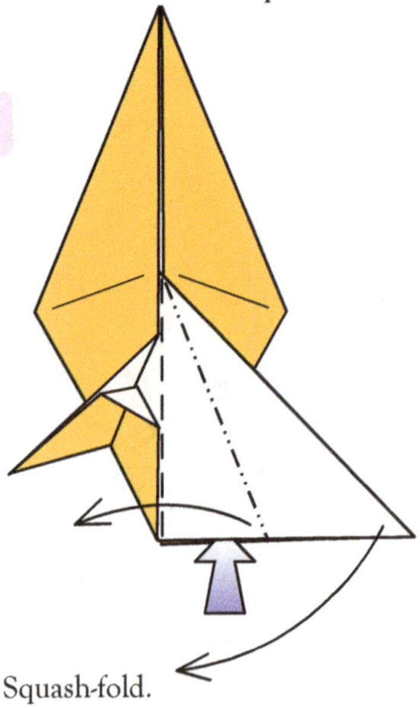

5. Fold in half and rotate.

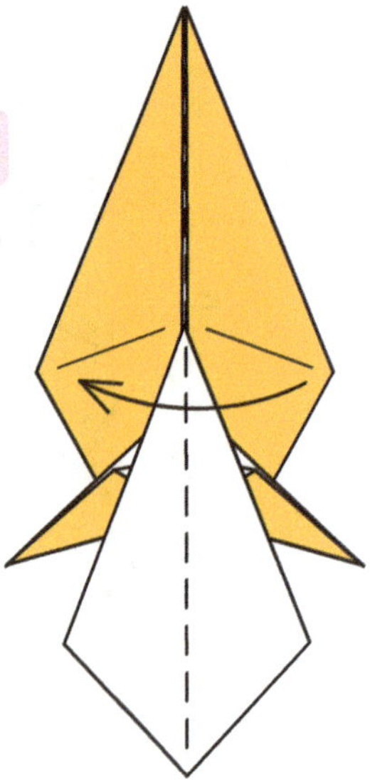

6. Reverse-fold.

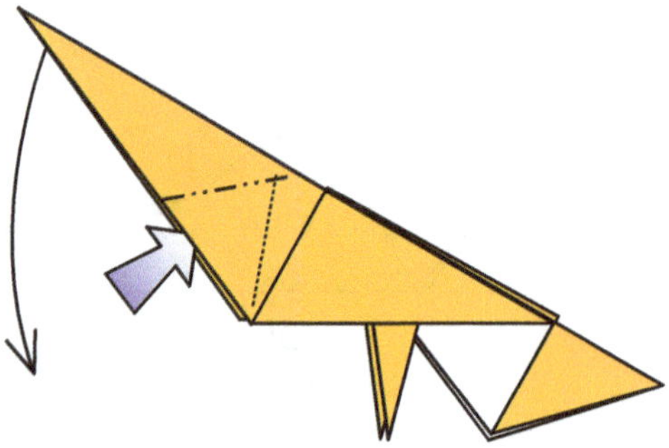

36  Origami Symphony No. 5

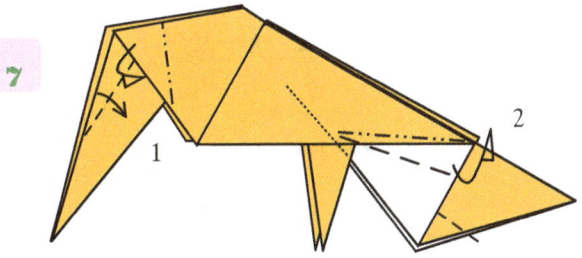

1. Reverse-fold.
2. This is similar to a reverse fold. Begin under the wing. Repeat behind.

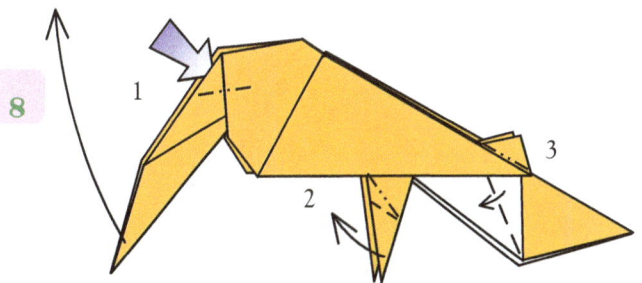

1. Reverse-fold.
2. Reverse-fold, repeat behind.
3. Reverse-fold, repeat behind.

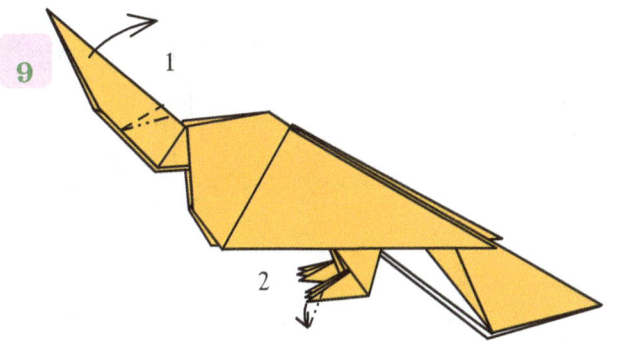

1. Crimp-fold.
2. Make three small reverse folds, repeat behind.

1. Push in on the right and make a crimp fold.
2. Fold inside, repeat behind.

Make a crimp fold and reverse fold.

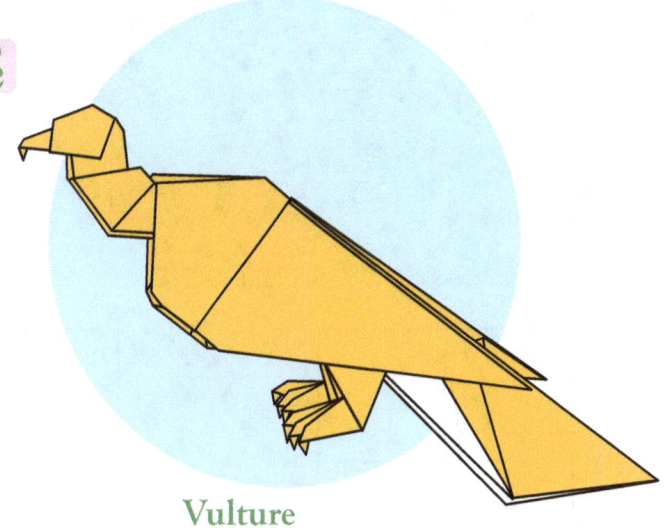

Vulture

Vulture 37

# Second Movement

## Andante: Woodwinds in the Woods

The Woods are filled with life. Every little creature has a song and a scamper. Put them all together and listen as the Wind creates a symphonic masterpiece. Walk slowly through the woods, watch and listen as the squirrels and rabbits play, the robin hops around, and the skunk tries to hide.

## Tree

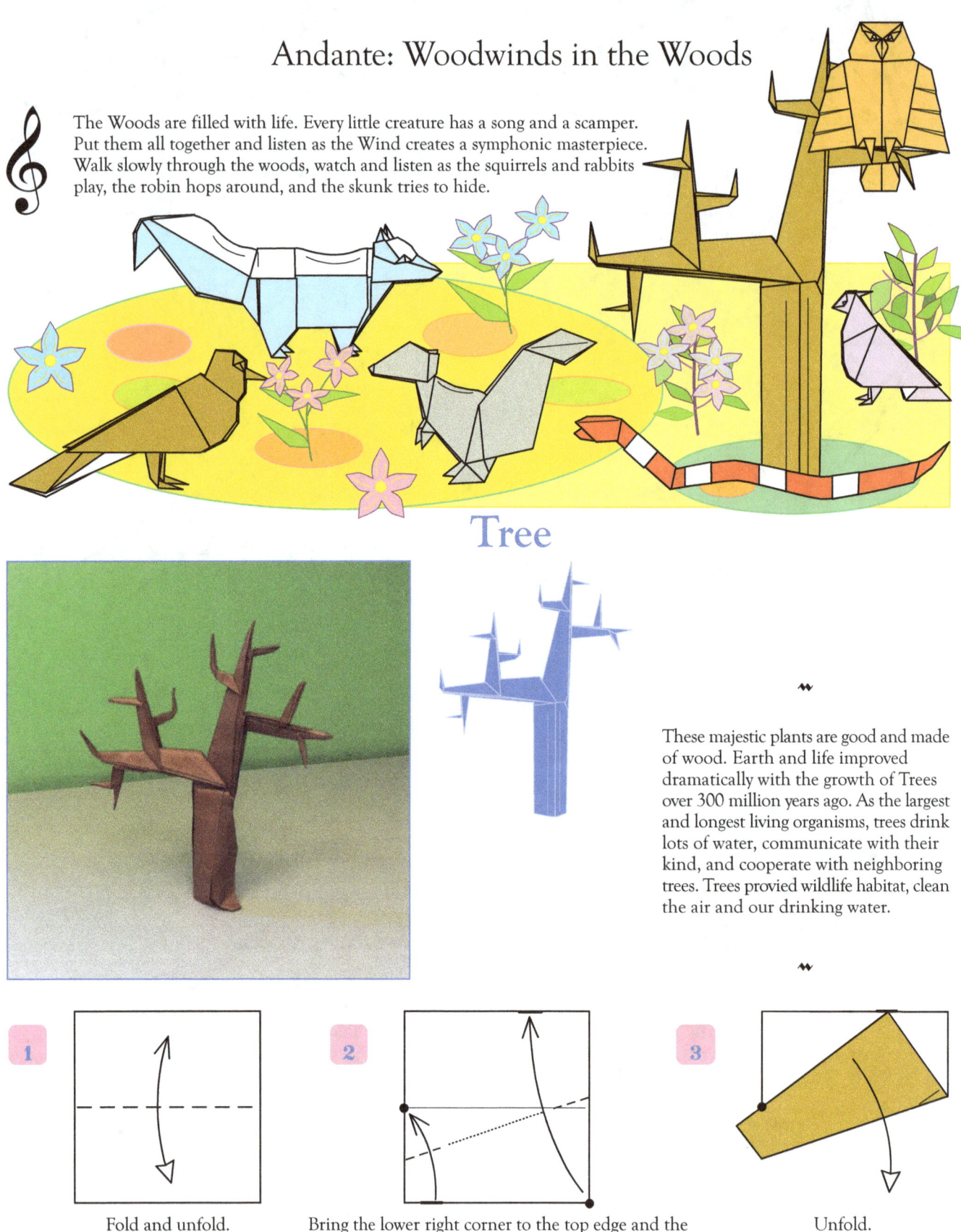

These majestic plants are good and made of wood. Earth and life improved dramatically with the growth of Trees over 300 million years ago. As the largest and longest living organisms, trees drink lots of water, communicate with their kind, and cooperate with neighboring trees. Trees provied wildlife habitat, clean the air and our drinking water.

1. Fold and unfold.
2. Bring the lower right corner to the top edge and the bottom edge to the left center. Crease on the edges.
3. Unfold.

38 Origami Symphony No. 5

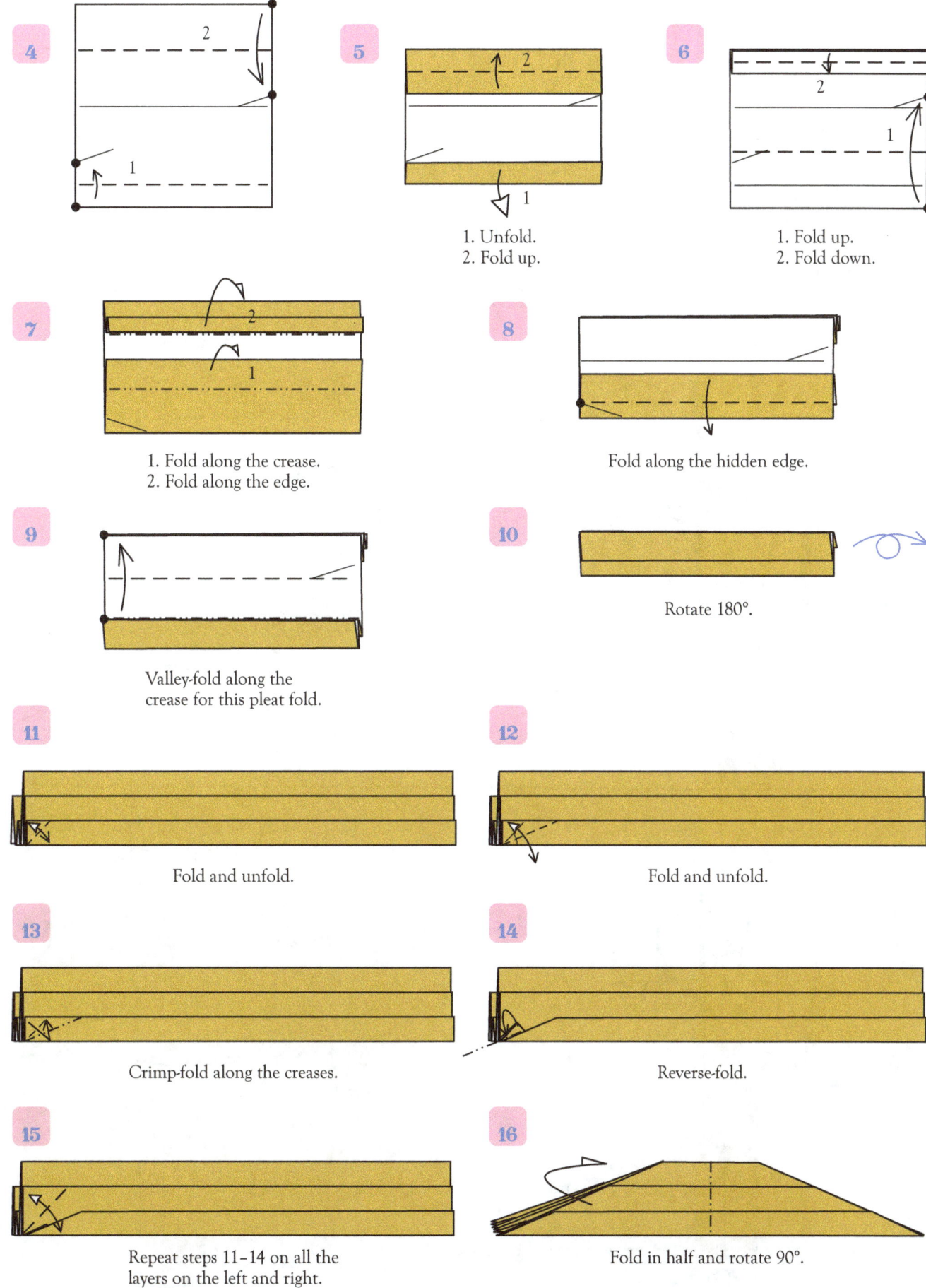

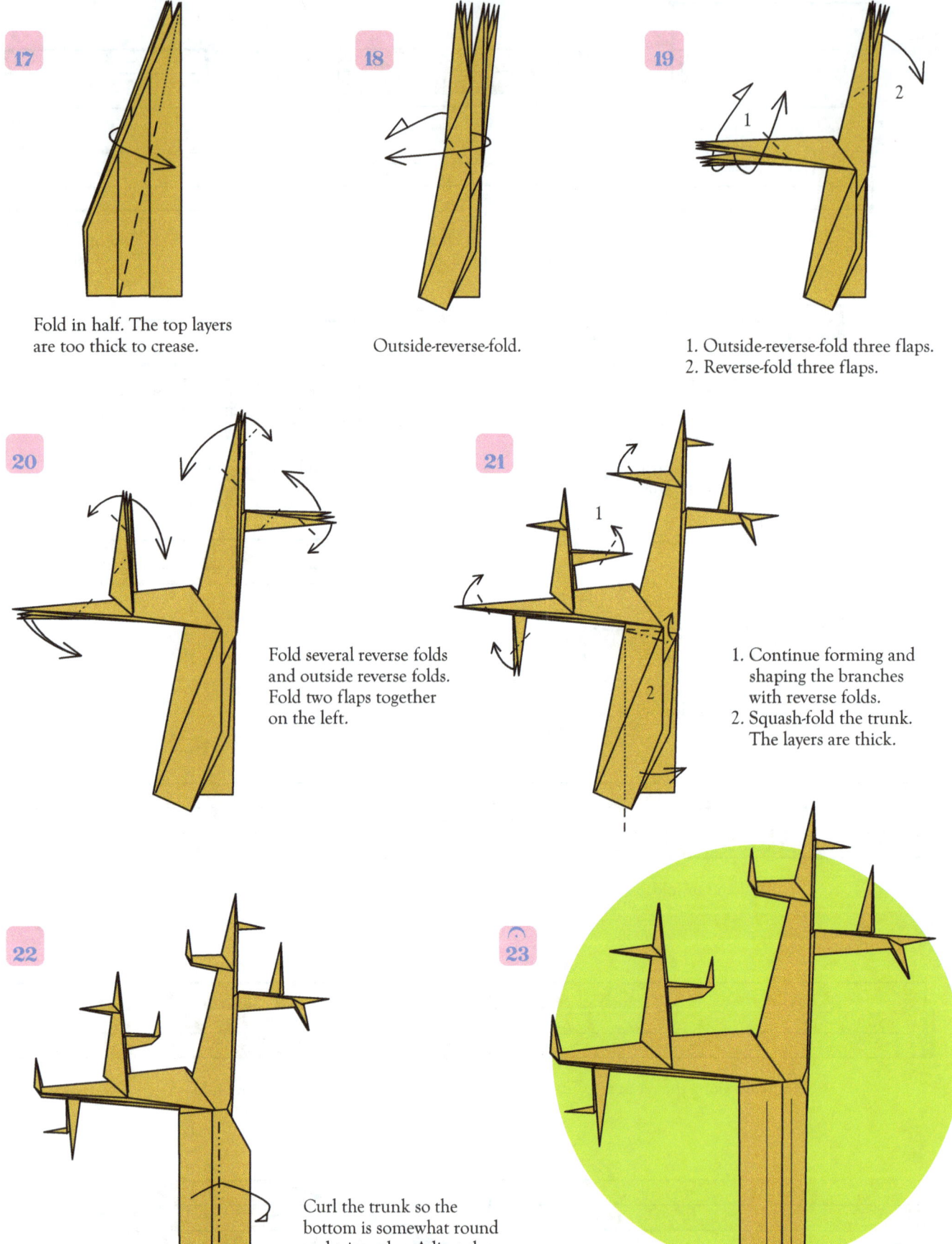

40 Origami Symphony No. 5

# Banded Snake

With over 3,000 species, Snakes can live up to 170 years. Found in forests, deserts, swamps, and grasslands, Snakes vary in size from four inches to thirty feet long. Though they do not see or hear well, they use their forked tongue to smell and find prey. They eat meat, which they swallow whole, but it can take days to digest. In a typical year, they would only need six to thirty meals. Through evolution, the small legs did not help and finally disappeared.

1. Fold and unfold.

2. Bring the lower right corner to the top edge and the bottom edge to the left center. Crease on the edges.

3. Unfold.

4. 
   1. Fold up.
   2. Fold and unfold on the right.

5. 
   1. Fold up.
   2. Fold and unfold on the right.

6. Unfold everything and rotate 180°.

Banded Snake 41

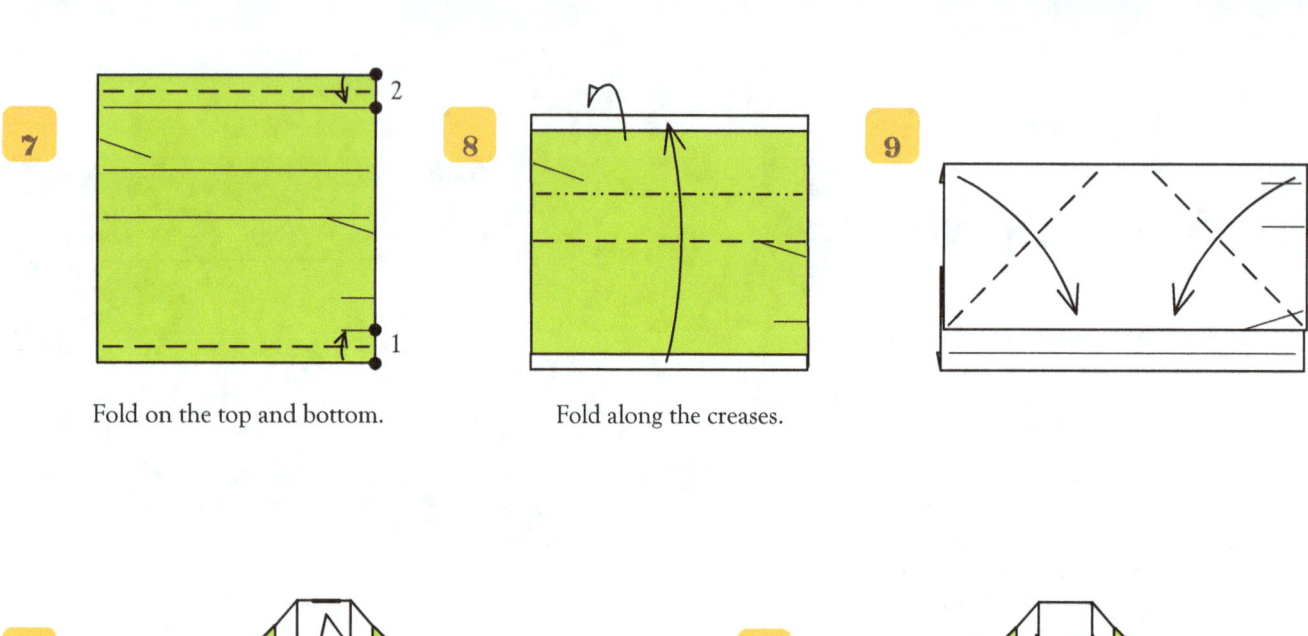

**7** Fold on the top and bottom.

**8** Fold along the creases.

**9**

**10** 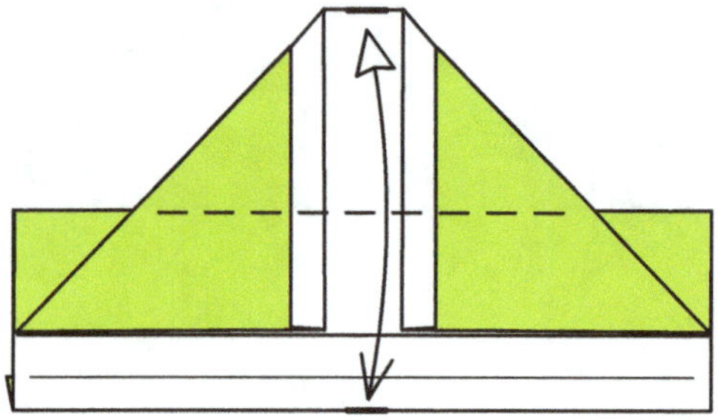 Fold and unfold.

**11** Make reverse folds along the crease.

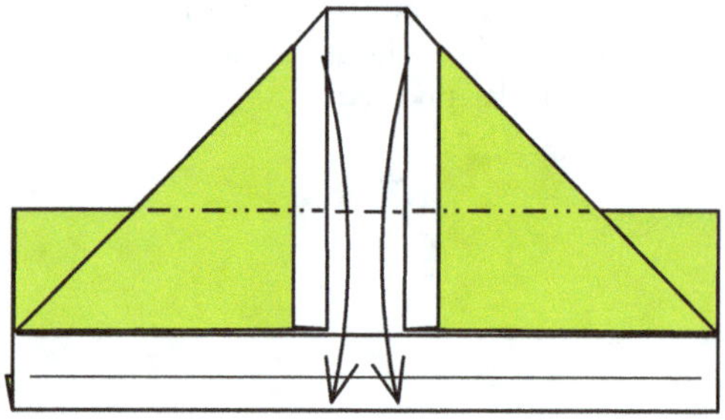

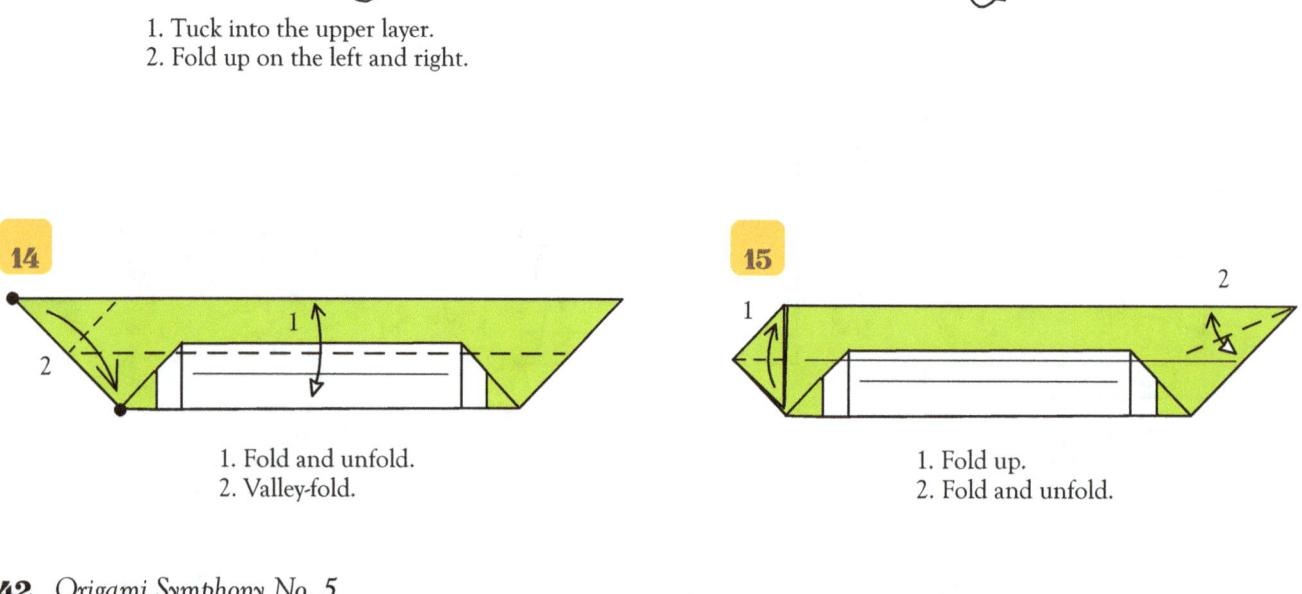

**12** 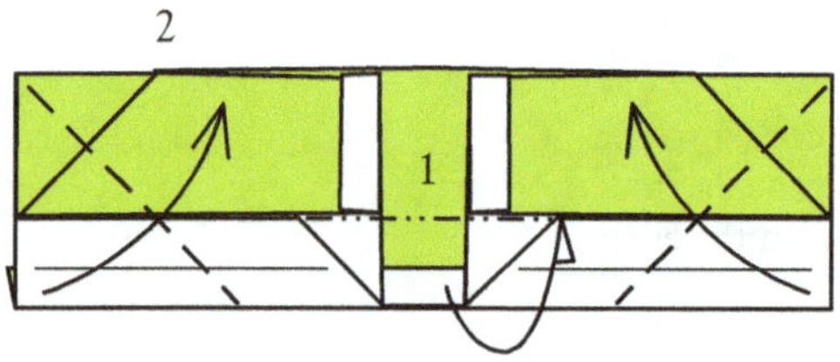
1. Tuck into the upper layer.
2. Fold up on the left and right.

**13**

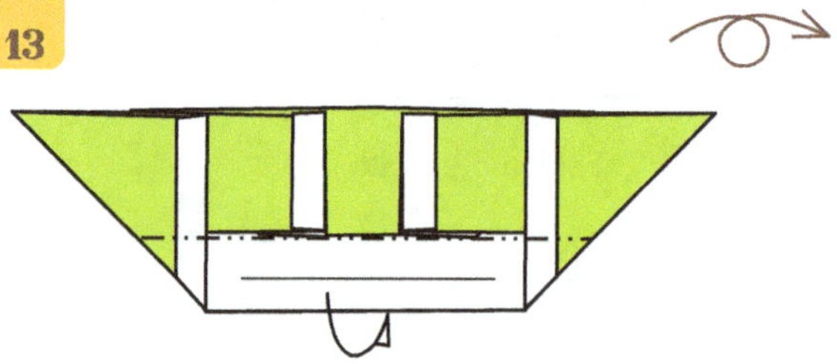

**14**
1. Fold and unfold.
2. Valley-fold.

**15**
1. Fold up.
2. Fold and unfold.

42   Origami Symphony No. 5

**16**

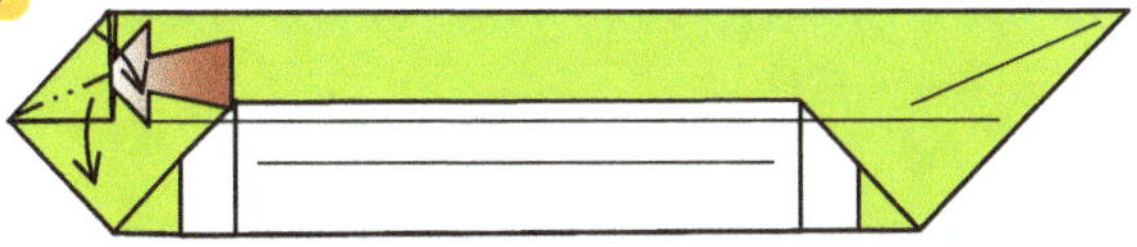

Squash-fold.

**17**

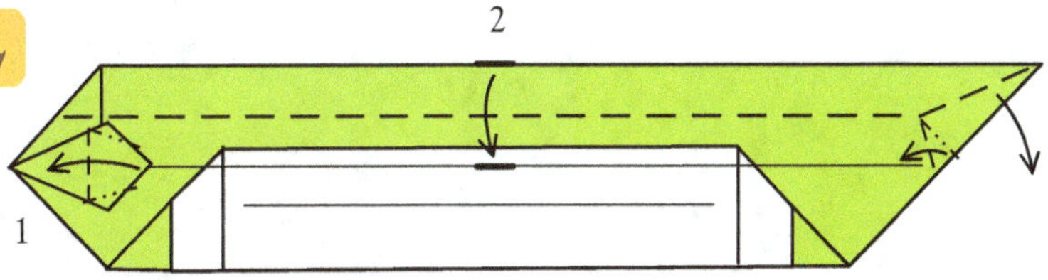

1. Petal-fold.
2. Fold to the center and rabbit-ear on the right.

**18**

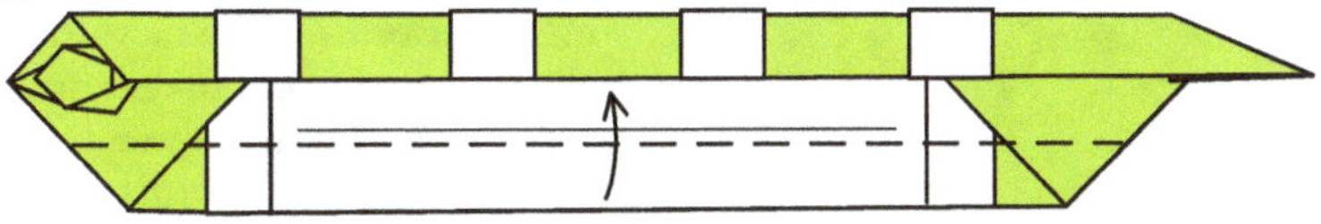

**19**

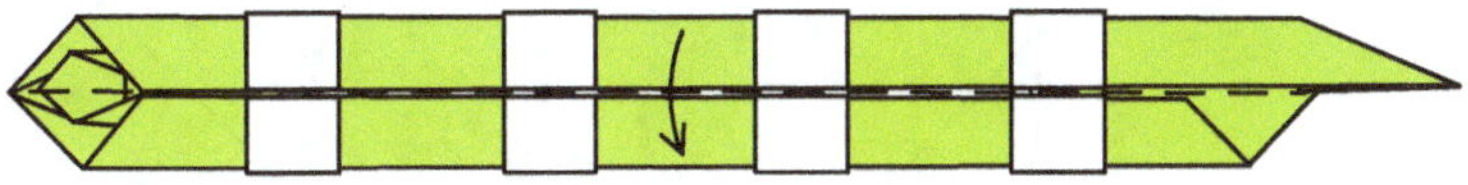

Fold in half.

**20**

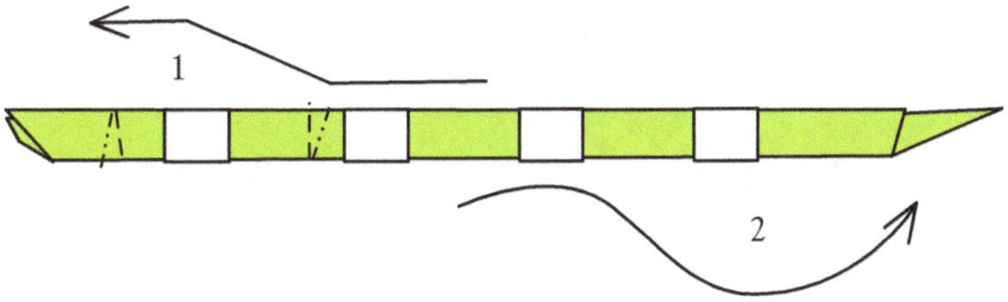

1. Make crimp folds and open the mouth.
2. Curl and shape the snake.
You can shape the snake in many ways.

**21**

**Banded Snake**

Banded Snake **43**

# Robin

As a symbol of spring, The Robin can be seen running and hopping in yards aroud much of North America. The male robin sings "Cheer-up, cheerily, cheer-up, cheer-up, cheerily". As the early bird gets the worm, Robins feed on earthworms in the morning. They also dine on insects, spiders, fruits and wild berries, but have been known to get drunk from the berries.

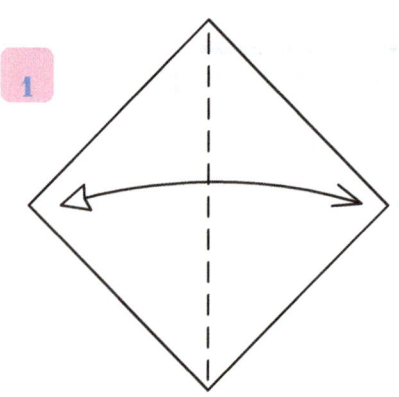

Fold and unfold.

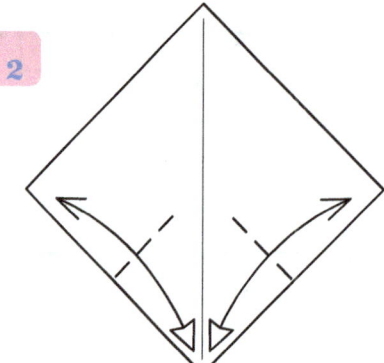

Fold and unfold.

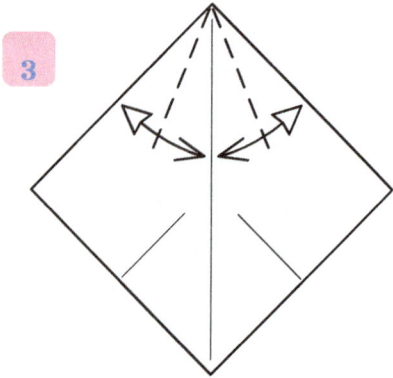

Fold and unfold.

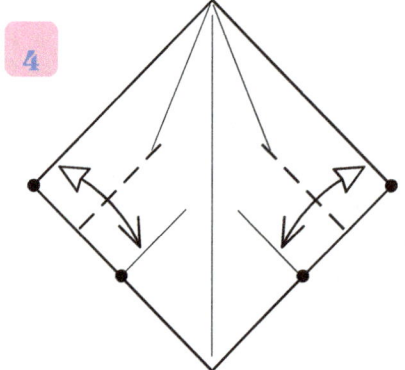

Fold and unfold.

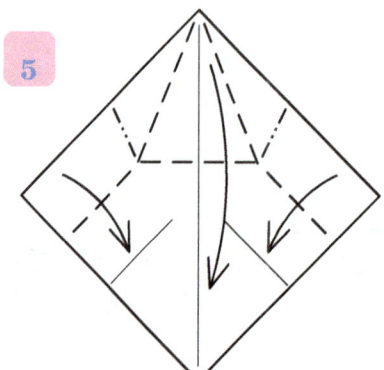

Fold along the creases.

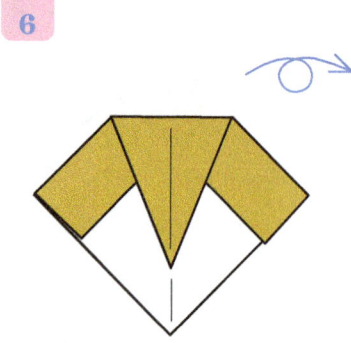

44 Origami Symphony No. 5

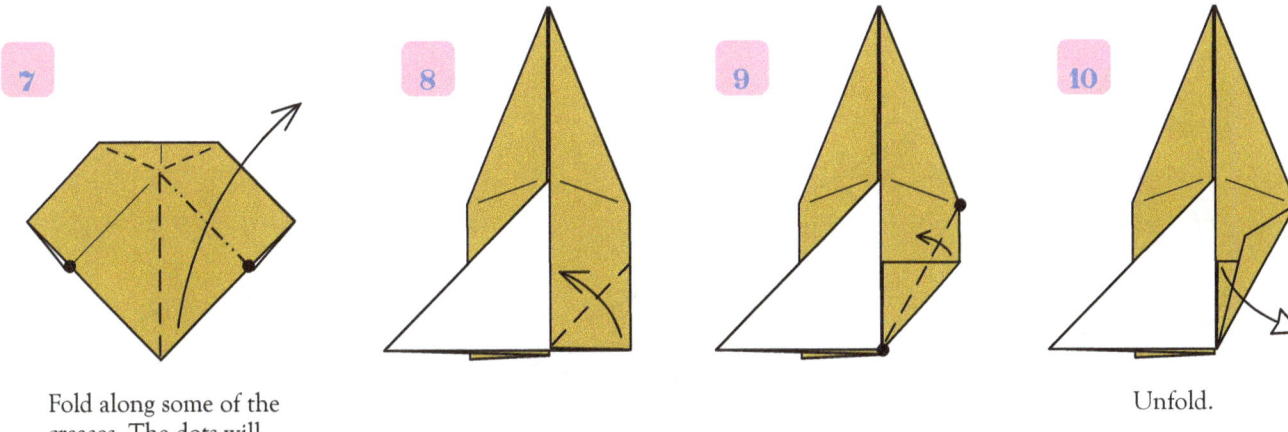

7. Fold along some of the creases. The dots will meet. Rotate 180°.

10. Unfold.

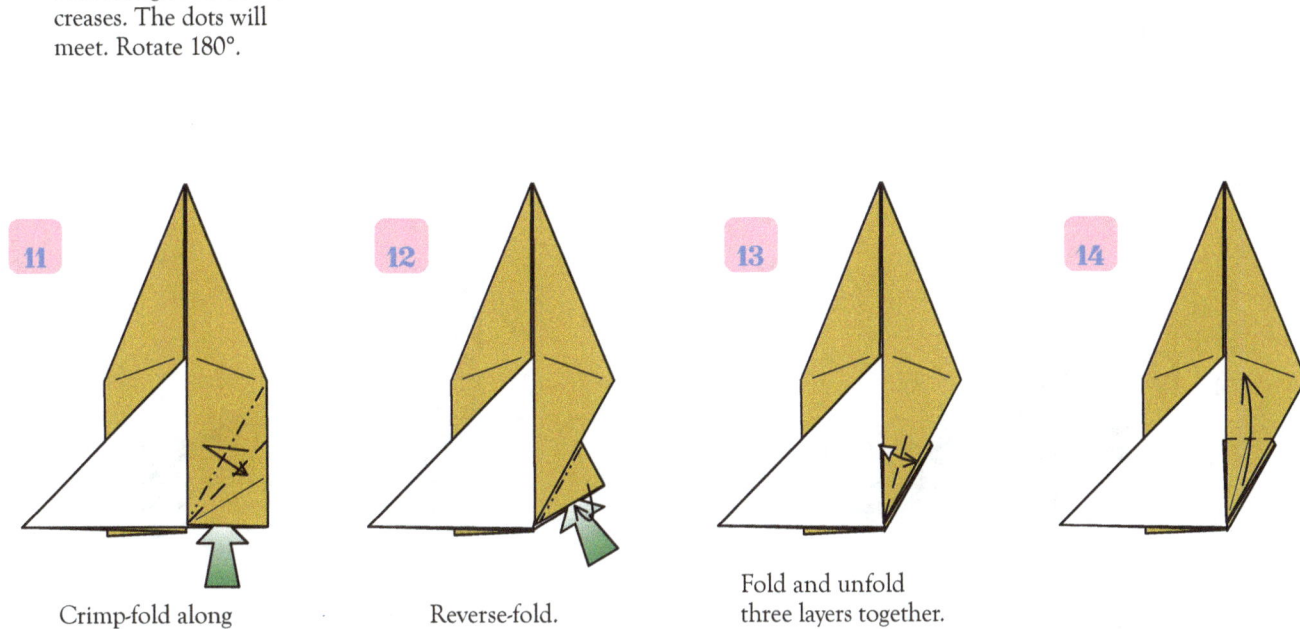

11. Crimp-fold along the creases.

12. Reverse-fold.

13. Fold and unfold three layers together.

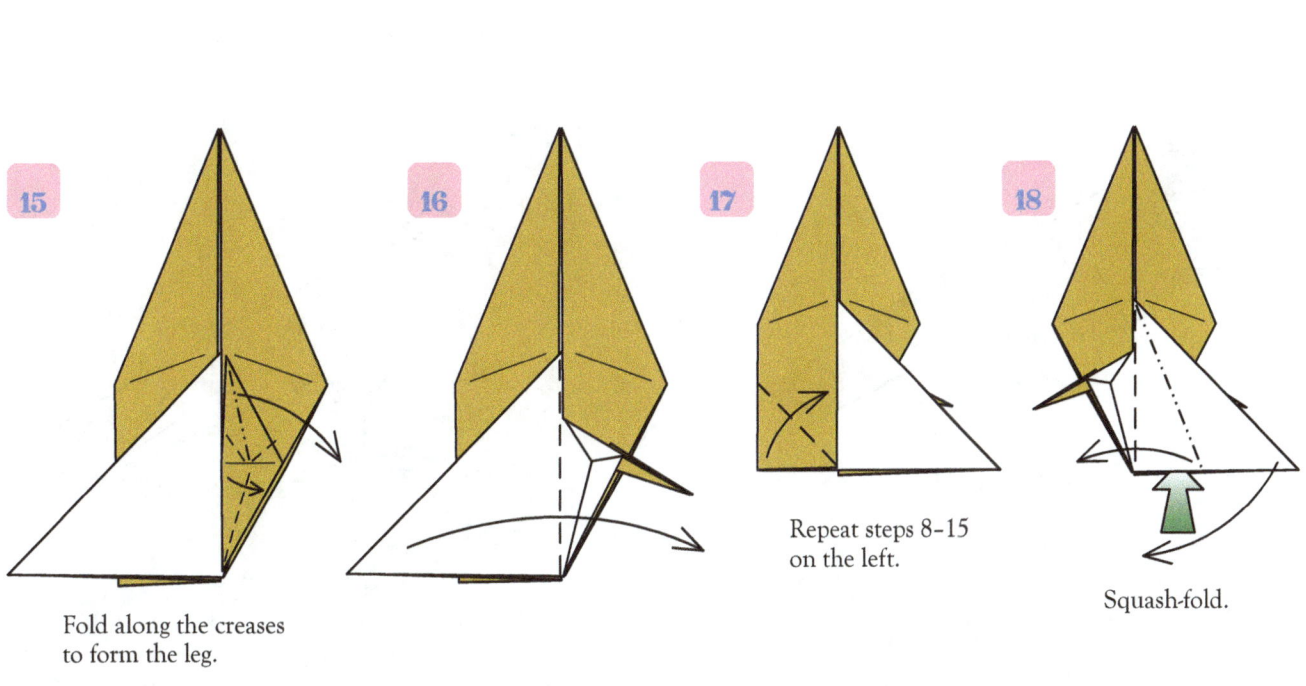

15. Fold along the creases to form the leg.

17. Repeat steps 8–15 on the left.

18. Squash-fold.

Robin **45**

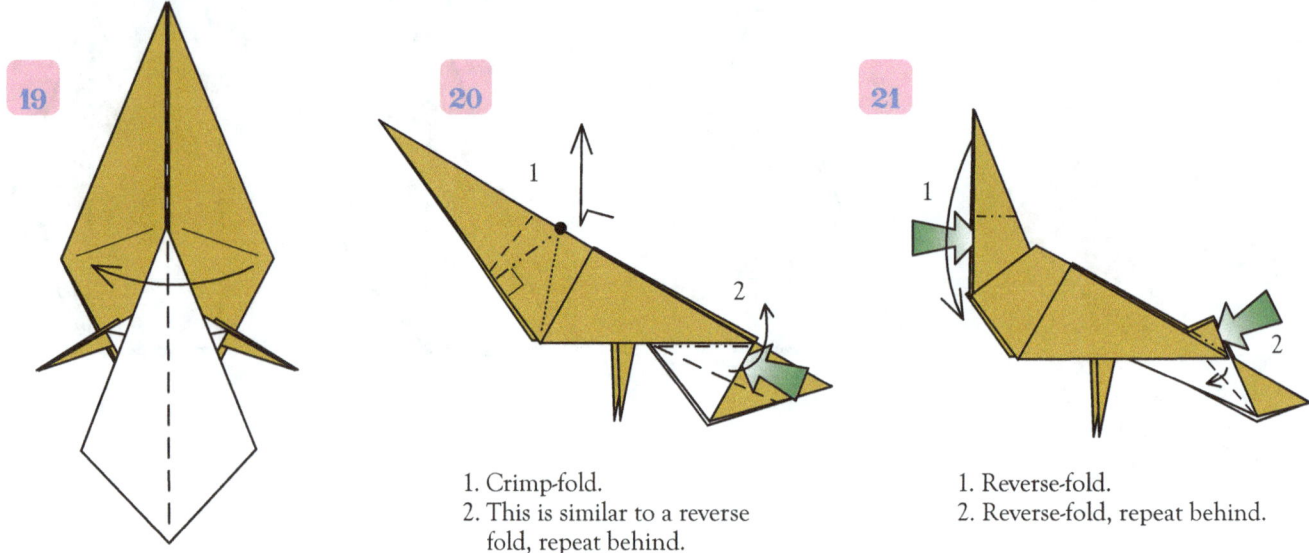

**19.** Fold in half and rotate.

**20.**
1. Crimp-fold.
2. This is similar to a reverse fold, repeat behind.

**21.**
1. Reverse-fold.
2. Reverse-fold, repeat behind.

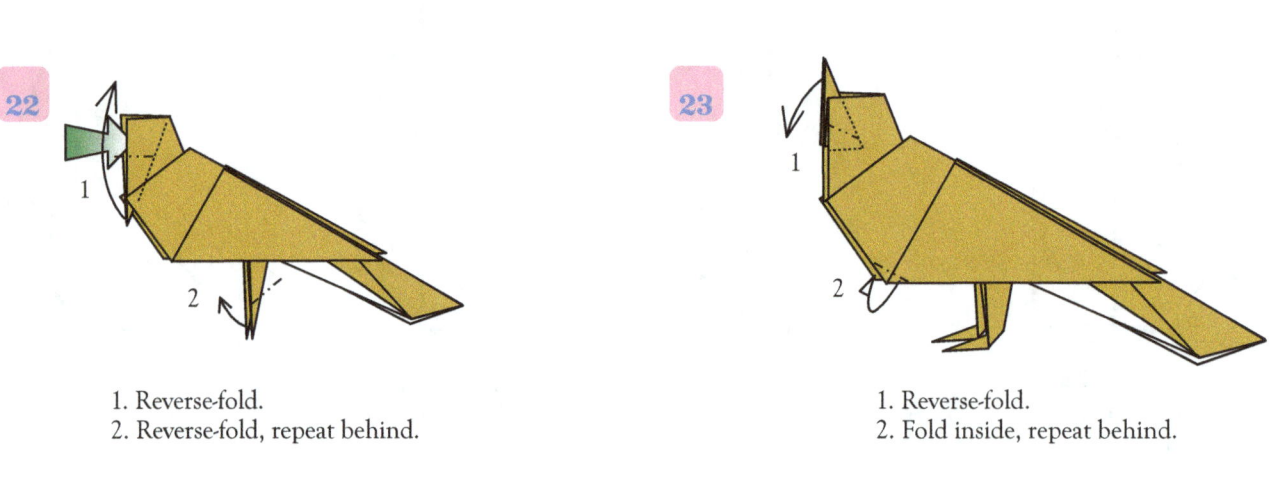

**22.**
1. Reverse-fold.
2. Reverse-fold, repeat behind.

**23.**
1. Reverse-fold.
2. Fold inside, repeat behind.

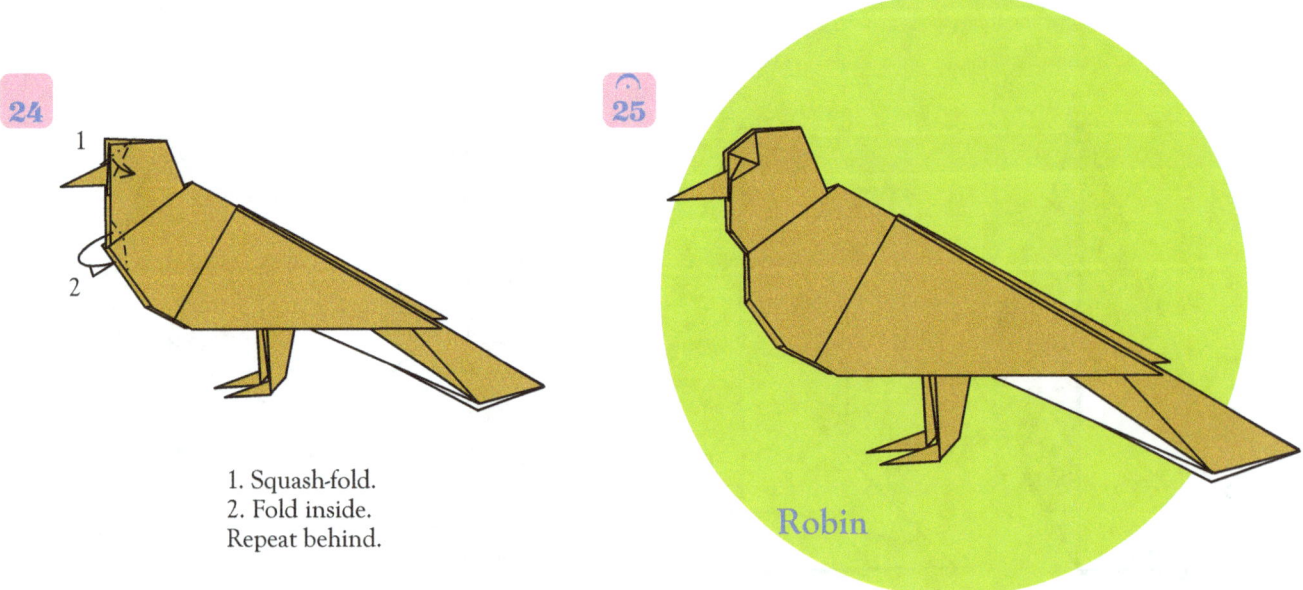

**24.**
1. Squash-fold.
2. Fold inside. Repeat behind.

**25.** Robin

46   Origami Symphony No. 5

# Pigeon

Pigeons are one of the most intelligent birds. They understand space and time, recognize themselves in the mirror, can identify the letters of our alphabet, and can even do simple arithmetic. Famous Pigeons have been known to save the day during wars. As we experience colors through our three cones, Pigeons have five cones, allowing for unimaginable colors and finer discrimination. While they feed on worms, insects, vegetables and berries, they especially enjoy our garbage. They thrive in cities and interact with humans more than any other wild animal.

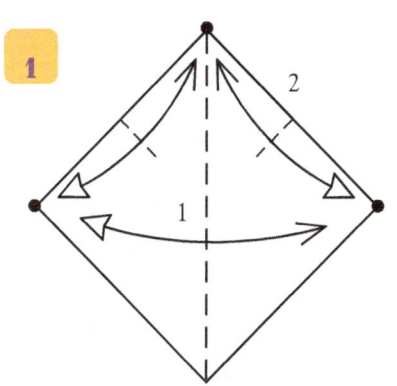

1. Fold and unfold.
2. Fold and unfold on the edge.

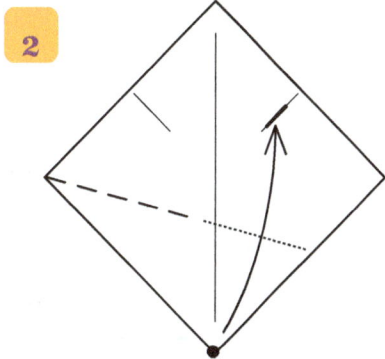

Bring the dot to the line.

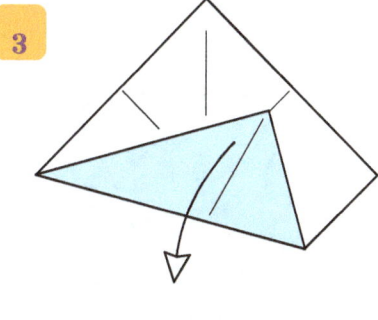

Unfold.

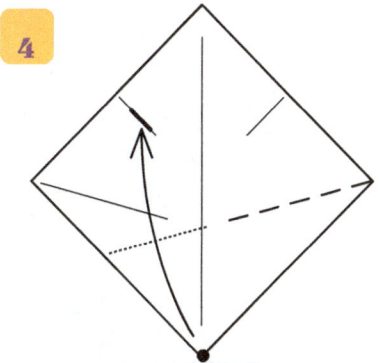

Repeat steps 2-3 on the right.

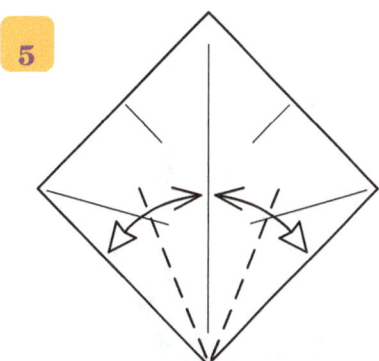

Fold to the center and unfold.

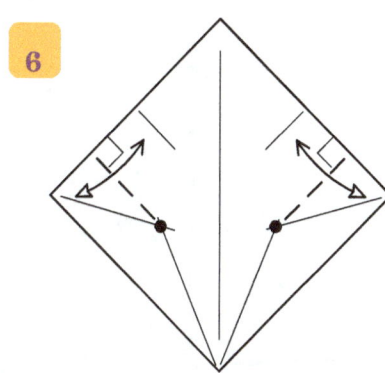

Fold and unfold. Rotate 180°.

*Pigeon* **47**

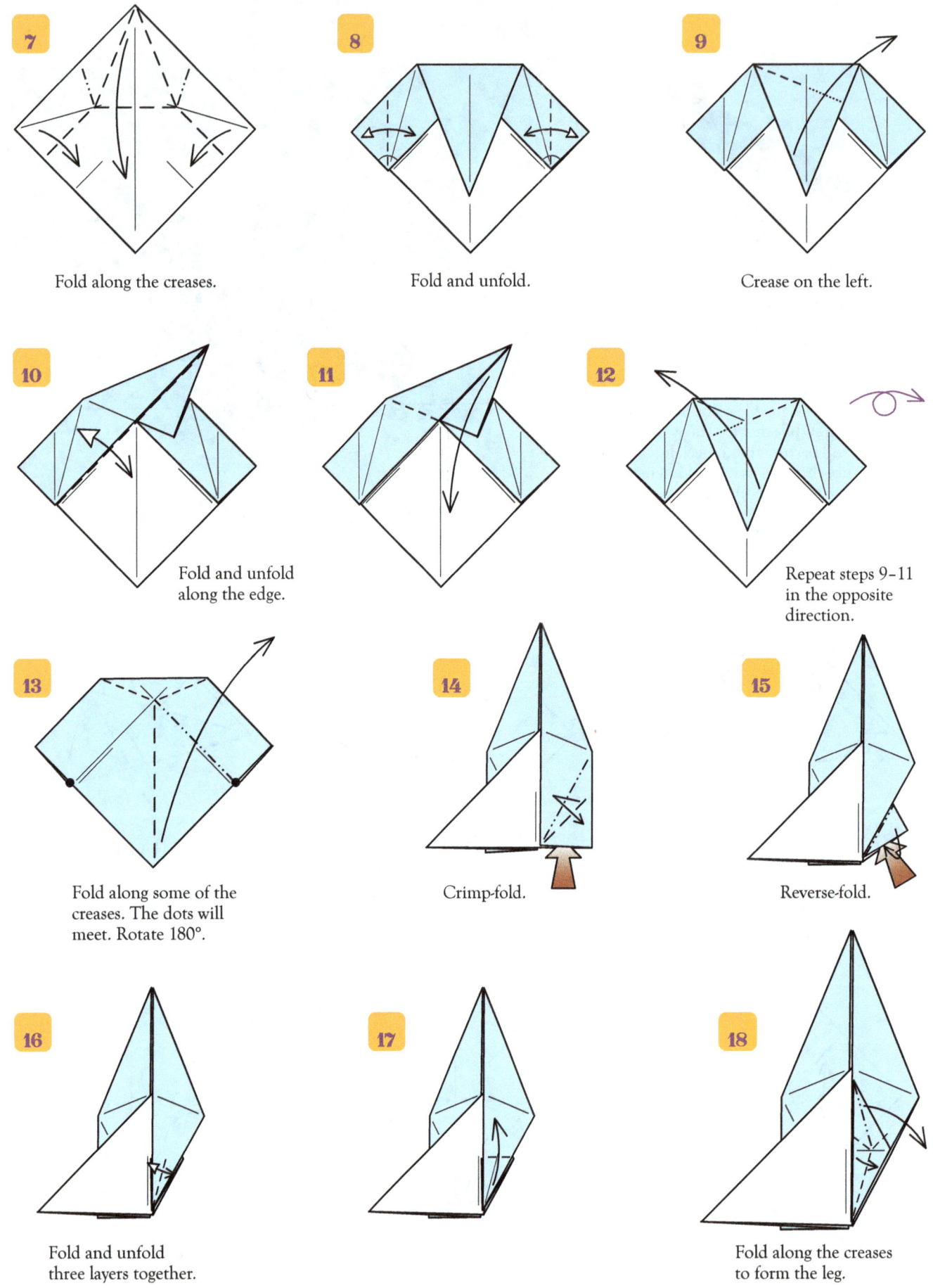

48  Origami Symphony No. 5

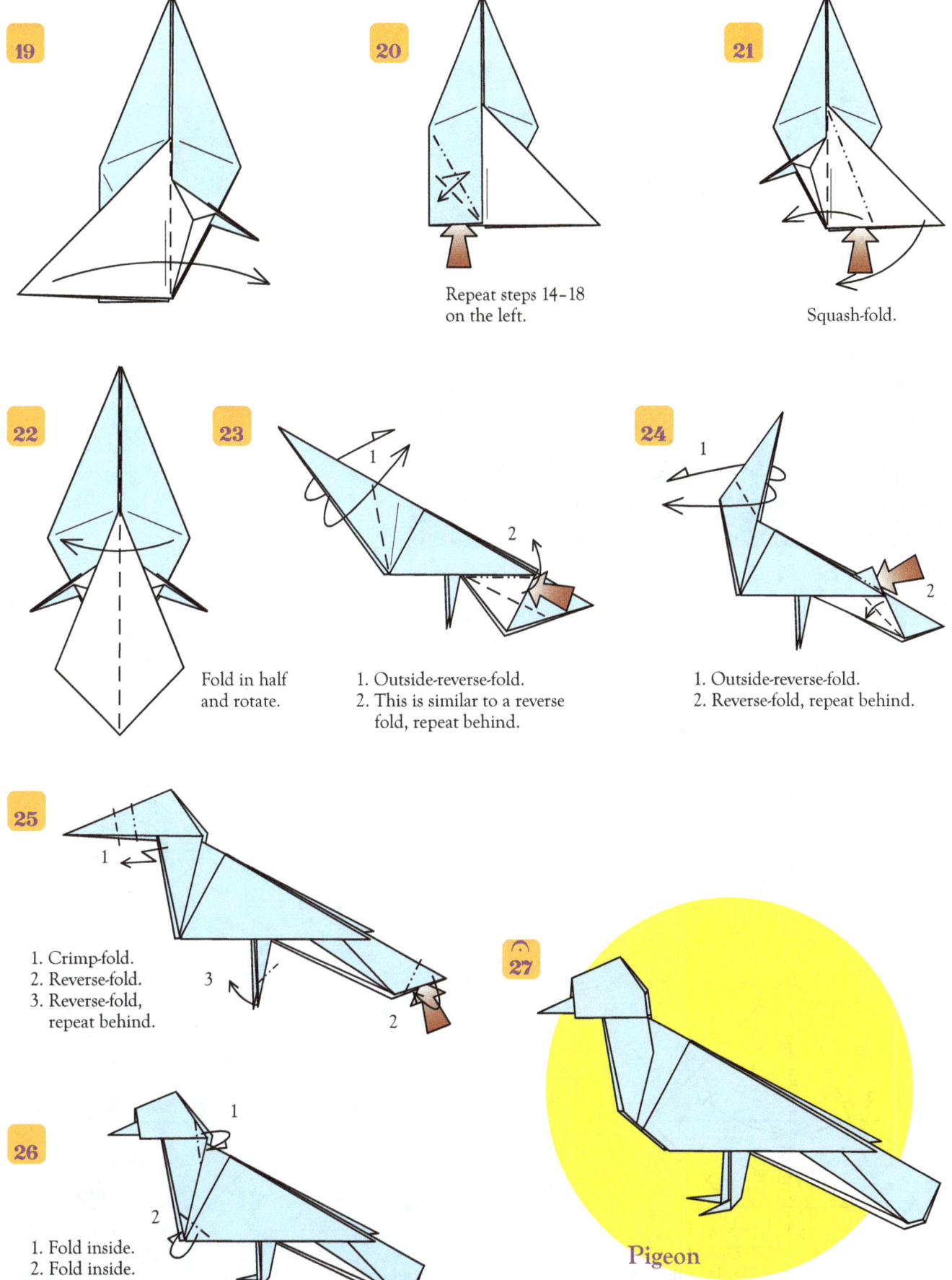

Pigeon 49

# Quail

Quails are small, stocky birds in the pheasant family. They spend most of their lives in small areas in the woodlands and only fly for short distances. Their high pitched chirps sound like "weep for me". Many Quails have decorative plumes on their heads. They feed on worms, insects, grass seeds, and berries.

1. Fold and unfold.

2. Fold and unfold on the edge.

3. 

4. 
   1. Unfold.
   2. Fold to the center and unfold.

5. Fold and unfold.

6. Fold and unfold in the center.

50 Origami Symphony No. 5

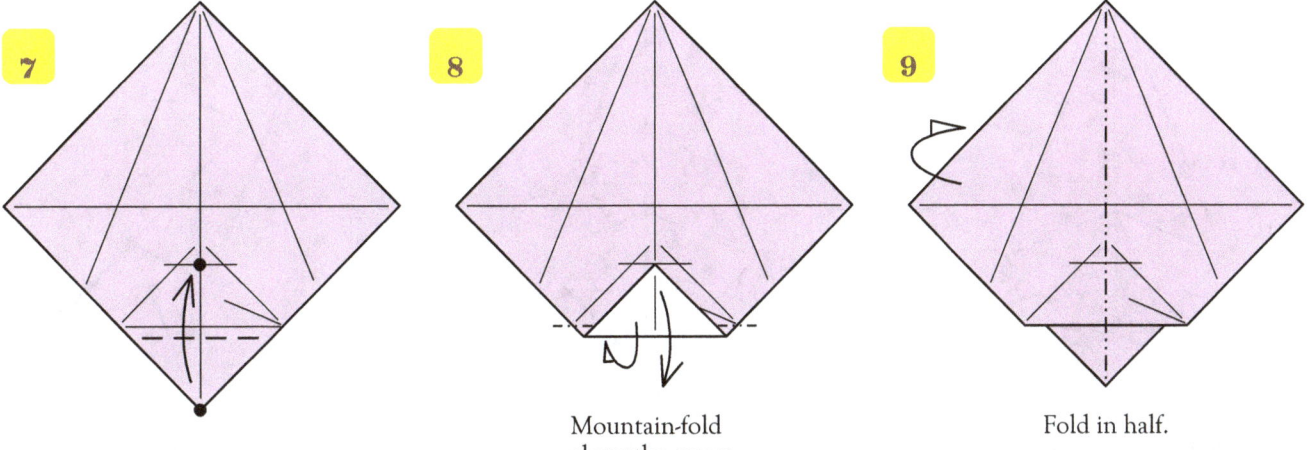

Mountain-fold along the crease.

Fold in half.

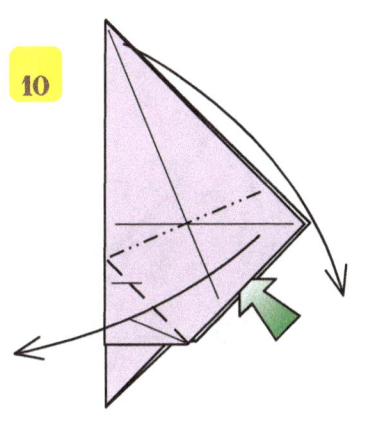

Valley-fold along the crease for this squash fold. Rotate.

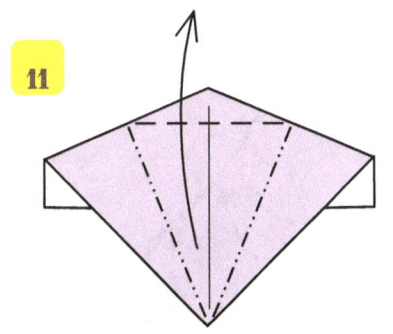

Petal-fold along the creases.

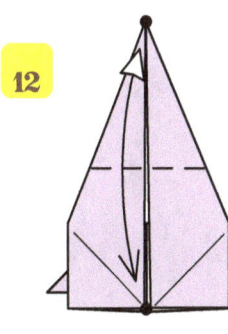

Fold and unfold.

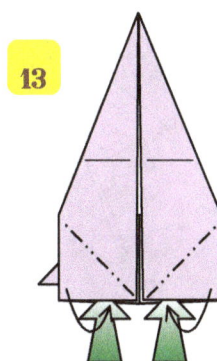

Make reverse folds.

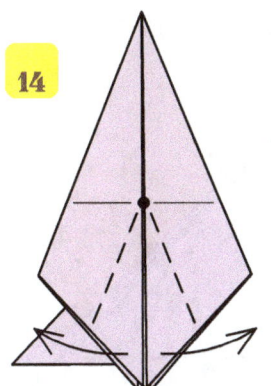

Make squash folds.

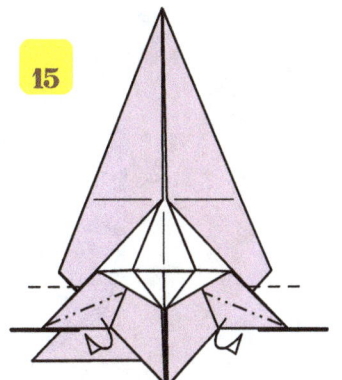

Note the legs line up on the bold horizontal line. Thin the legs with reverse folds.

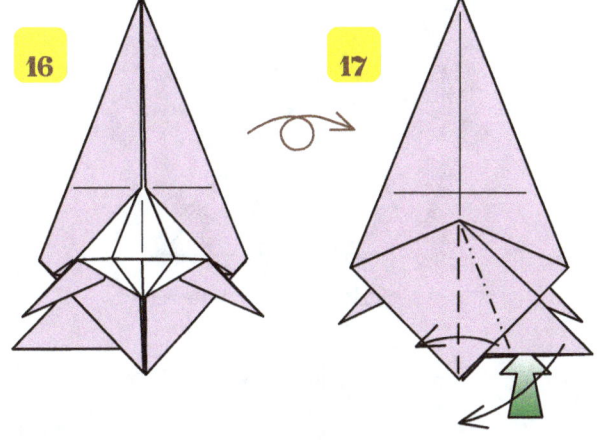

Squash-fold.

*Quail* 51

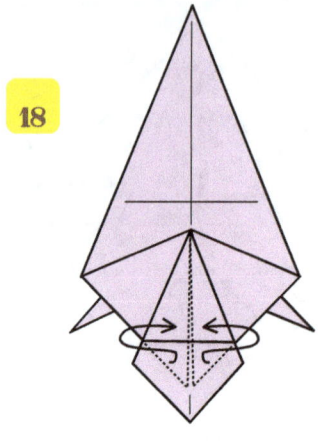

18

Pull out from inside and wrap around.

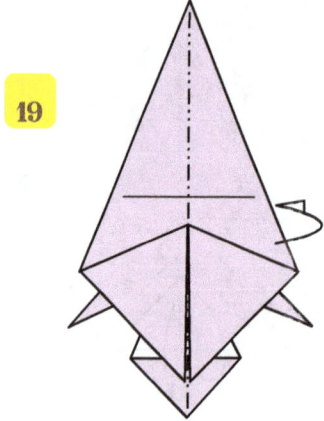

19

Fold in half and rotate.

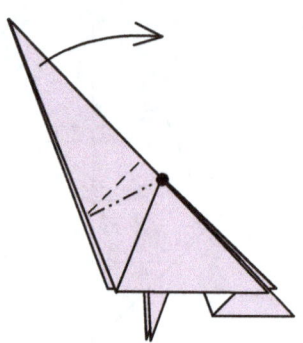

20

Valley-fold along the crease for this crimp fold.

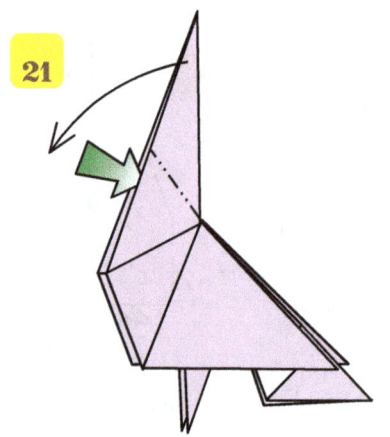

21

Reverse-fold.

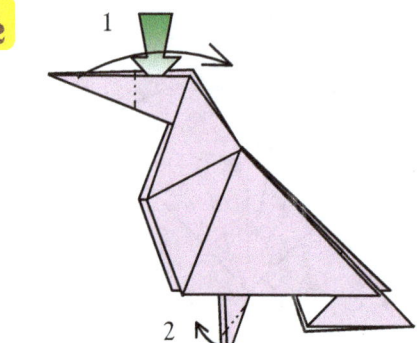

22

1. Reverse-fold.
2. Reverse-fold, repeat behind.

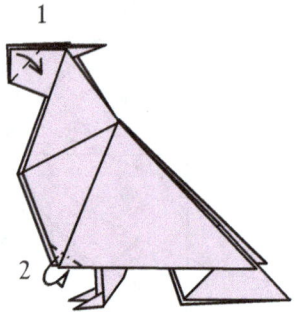

23

1. Fold down.
2. Fold inside.
Repeat behind.

24

1. Fold the eye.
2. Fold inside.
Repeat behind.

25

Quail

51  *Origami Symphony No. 5*

# Owl

Owls are intelligent and social birds. The 250 species range in size from five inches to three feet tall. They catch insects, rodents, and reptiles with their sharp talons and beaks. The shape of their round, flat head provides Owls with exceptional hearing. They can hear mice under the snow and swoop down for the catch. Owls stay in holes of tree trunks or vacant nests, but are not good at building nests.

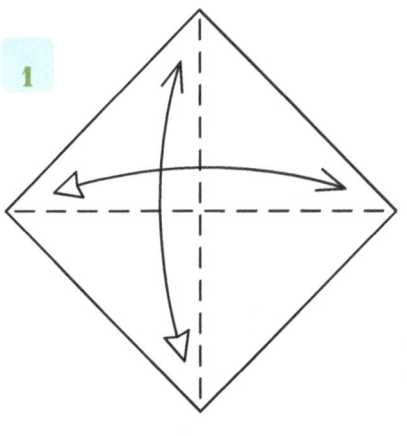

1. Fold and unfold.

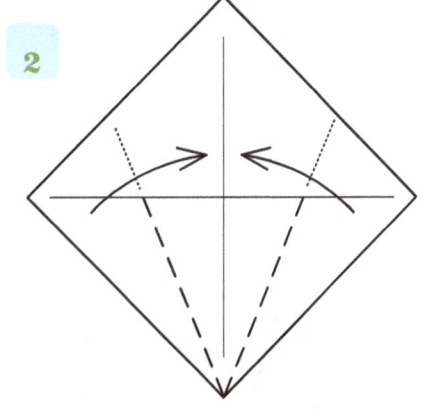

2. Fold to the center.

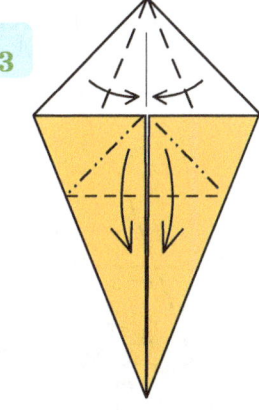

3. Squash folds.

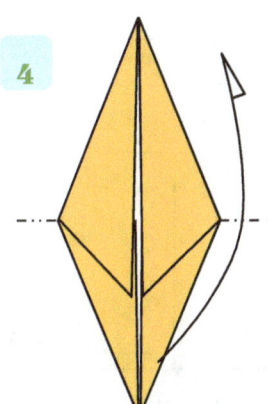

4.

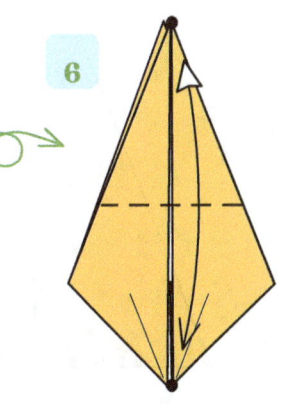

5. Fold and unfold.

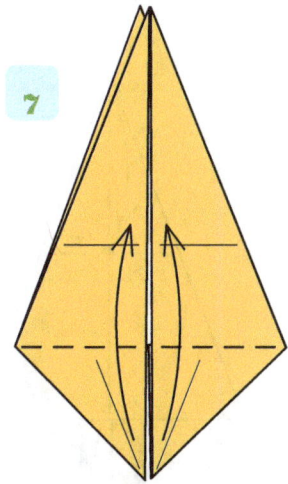

6. Fold and unfold.

7.

Owl 53

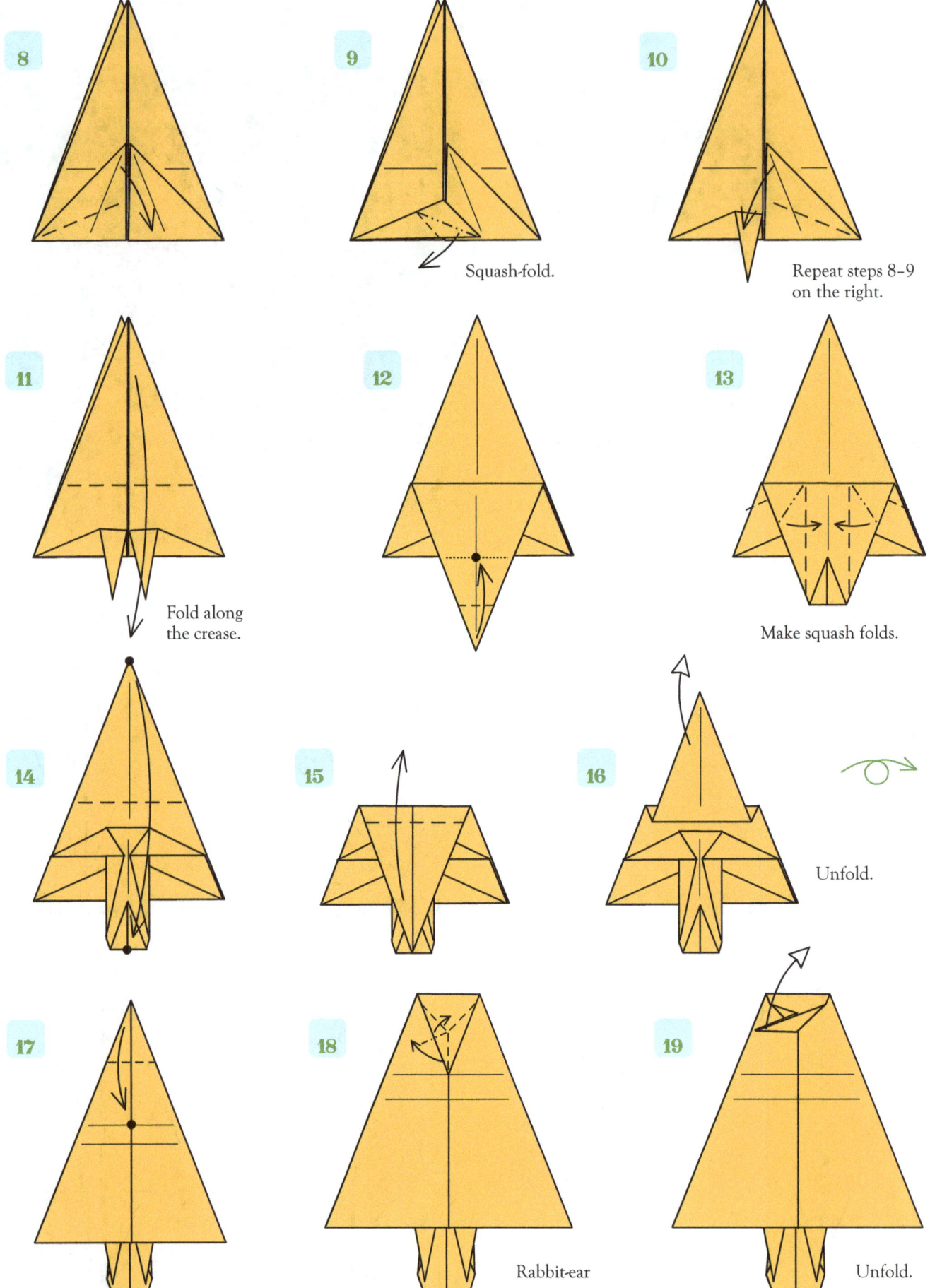

54  Origami Symphony No. 5

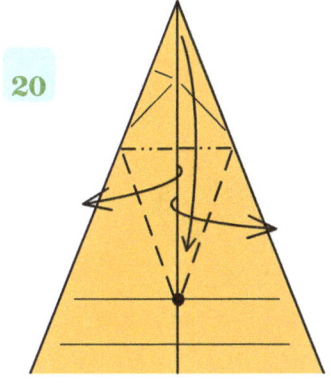

**20**

Spread while folding down.

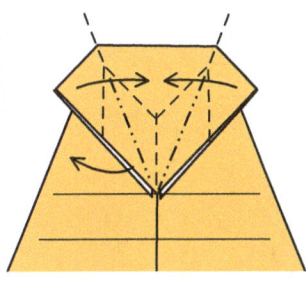

**21**

This is a combination of reverse folds. Fold along the creases.

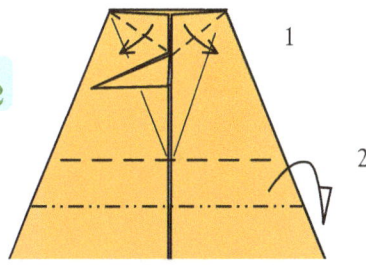

**22**

1. Make valley folds.
2. Pleat-fold along the creases.

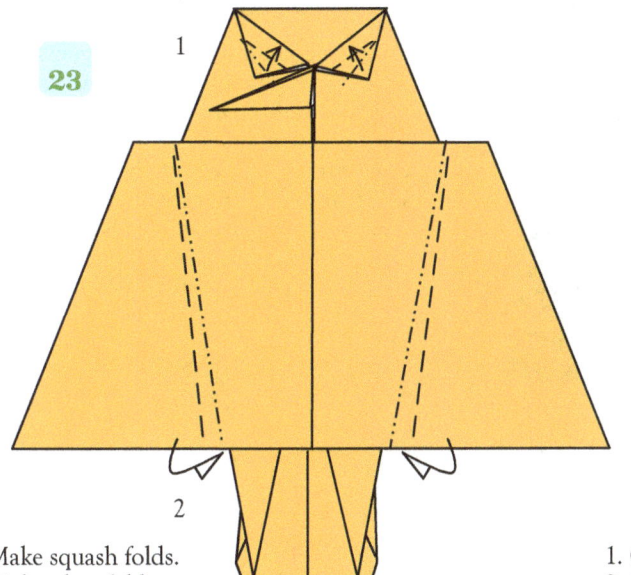

**23**

1. Make squash folds.
2. Make pleat folds.

**24**

1. Outside-reverse-fold.
2. Shape the neck and wings.
3. Make pleat folds.

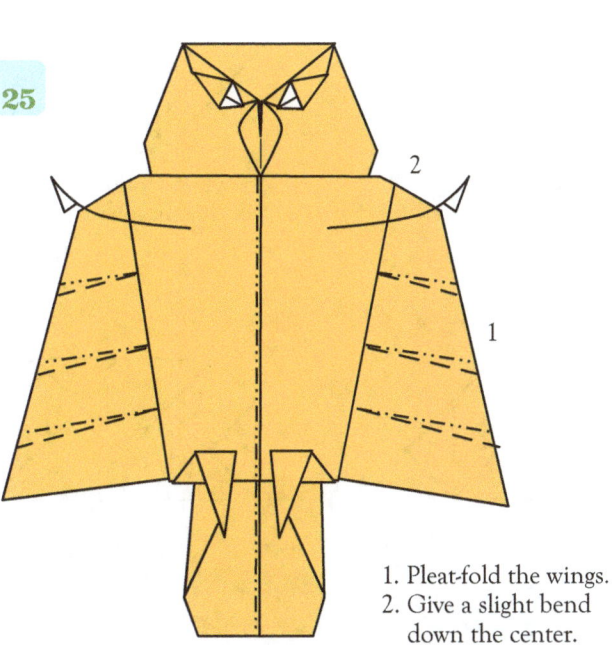

**25**

1. Pleat-fold the wings.
2. Give a slight bend down the center.

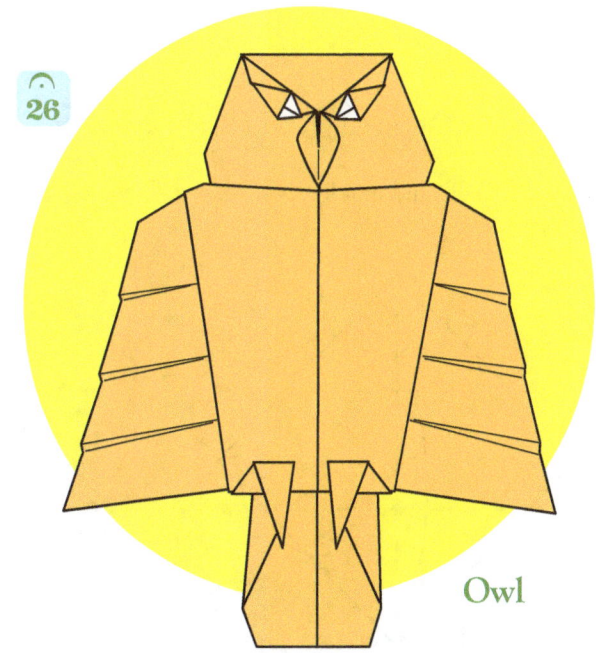

**26**

Owl

Owl **55**

# Squirrel

Jumping from branch to branch and scampering all around us, Squirrels are one of the few animals that do not hide from us. Squirrels are intelligent and communicate with high pitched chirps and tail movements. To prepare for the cold, they hide acorns and other foods into the ground throughout a wide area. Some squirrels watch others, to steal their food, while other squirrels pretend to hide their nuts and seeds, to fool the thieves. Meanwhile, much of their hoard is forgotten, and become new trees. They have a keen sense of smell and the eyes are placed so they can see behind.

1. Fold and unfold.

2. Fold and unfold on the edge.

3. Fold and unfold on the diagonal.

4.

5.

6. Unfold.

56  Origami Symphony No. 5

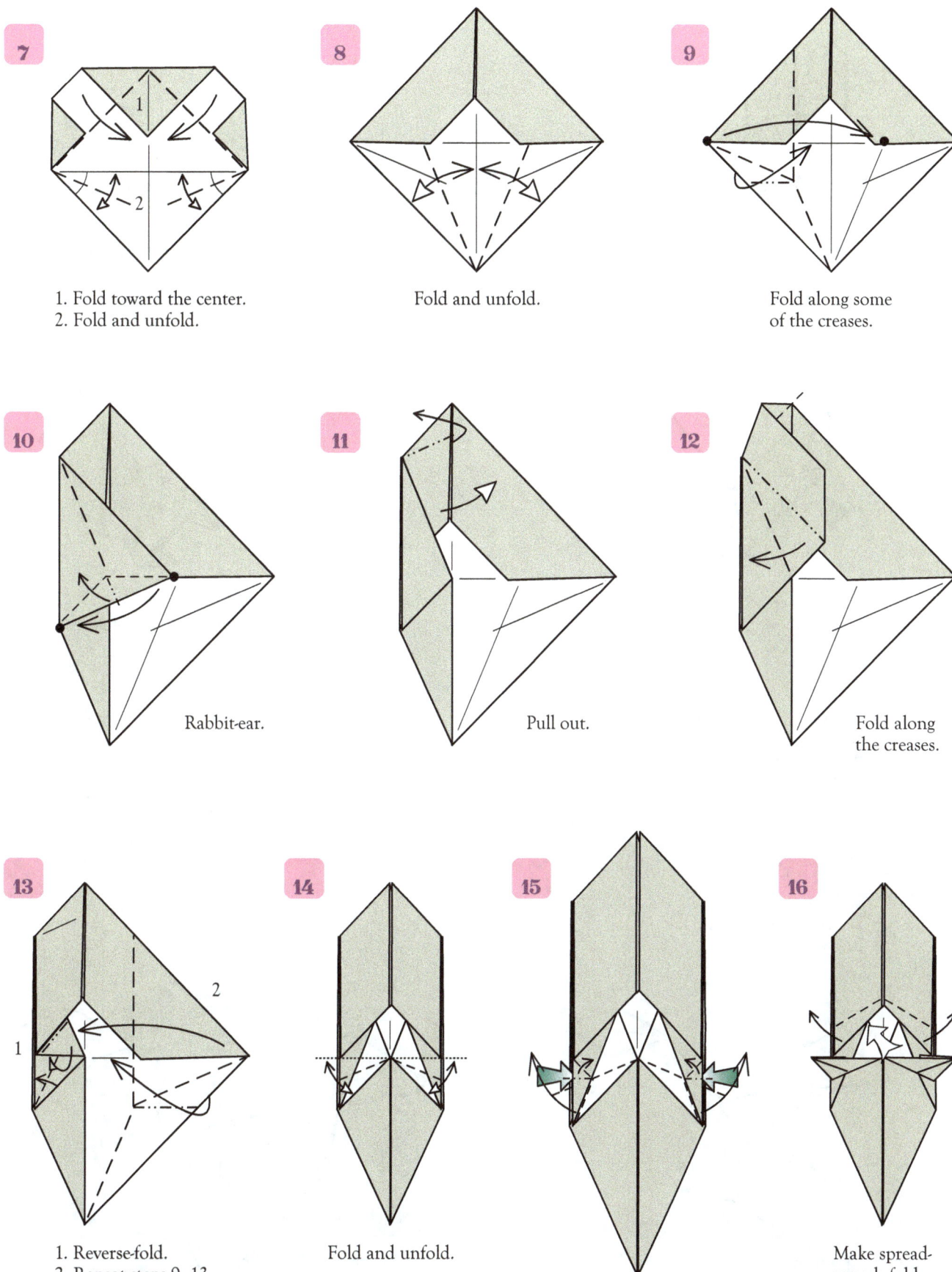

Squirrel 57

**17**

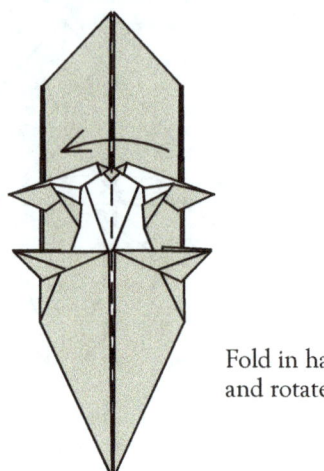

Fold in half and rotate.

**18**

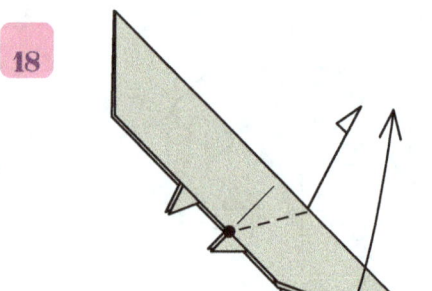

Outside-reverse-fold.

**19**

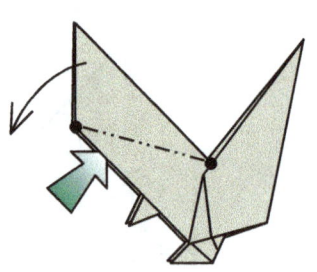

Reverse-fold.

**20**

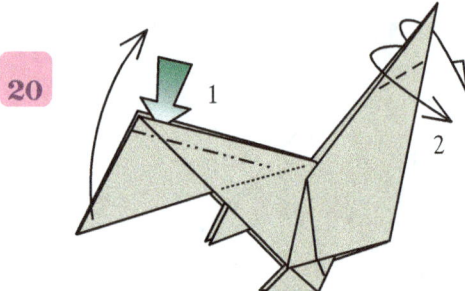

1. Reverse-fold.
2. Outside-reverse-fold.

**21**

1. Pull out.
2. Make a small squash fold. Repeat behind.

**22**

Crimp-fold.

**23**

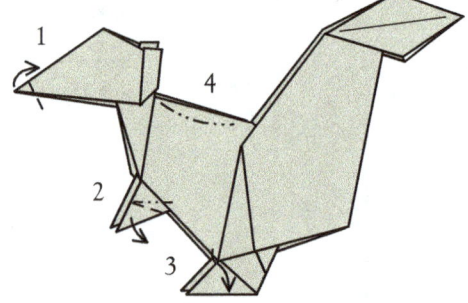

1. Outside-reverse-fold.
2. Pleat-fold, repeat behind.
3. Spread the legs, repeat behind.
4. Shape the back.

**24**

Squirrel

58  *Origami Symphony No. 5*

# Mouse

Mice are adventurous rodents that like to explore new places. They are excellent swimmers, jumpers, and can crawl through tiny spaces. They create intricate underground burrows with organized places for each activity including food storage and sleeping. This social animal lives in forests, greenlands, and manmade structures where they enjoy our food and shelter. They eat plenty of food each day, including seeds, vegetation, insects, and especially human garbage. They have excellent ears and can hear ultrasound. They communicate through ultrasound and even sing love songs which are too high for us to hear.

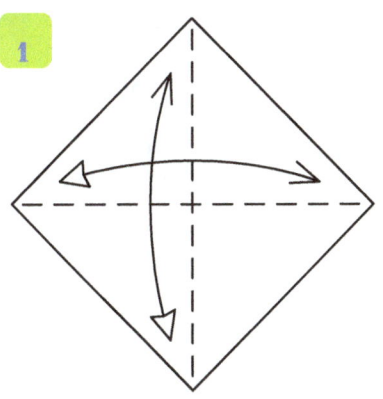

1. Fold and unfold.

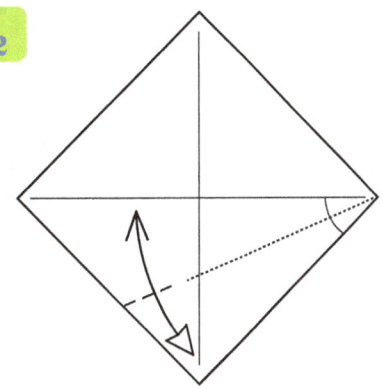

2. Fold and unfold on the edge.

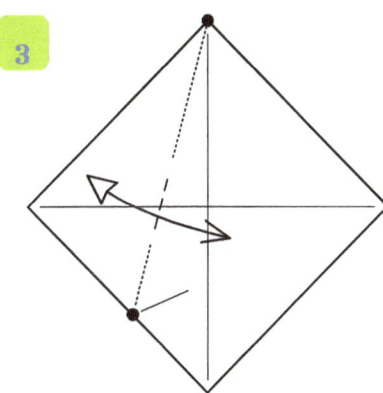

3. Fold and unfold on the diagonal.

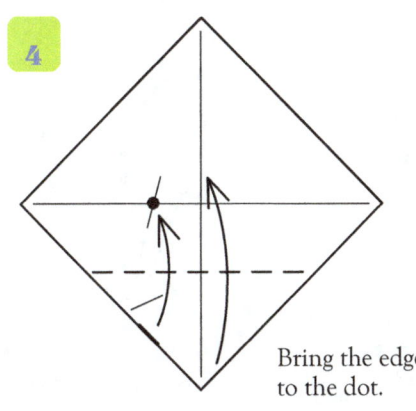

4. Bring the edge to the dot.

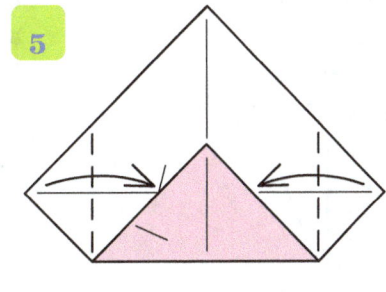

5.

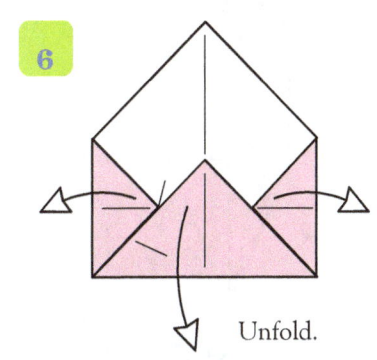

6. Unfold.

Mouse 59

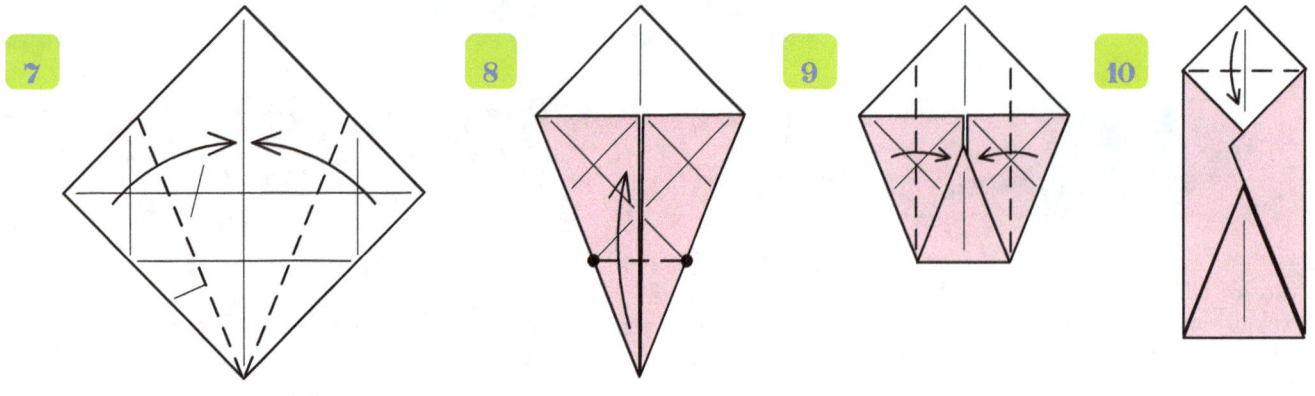

Fold to the center.

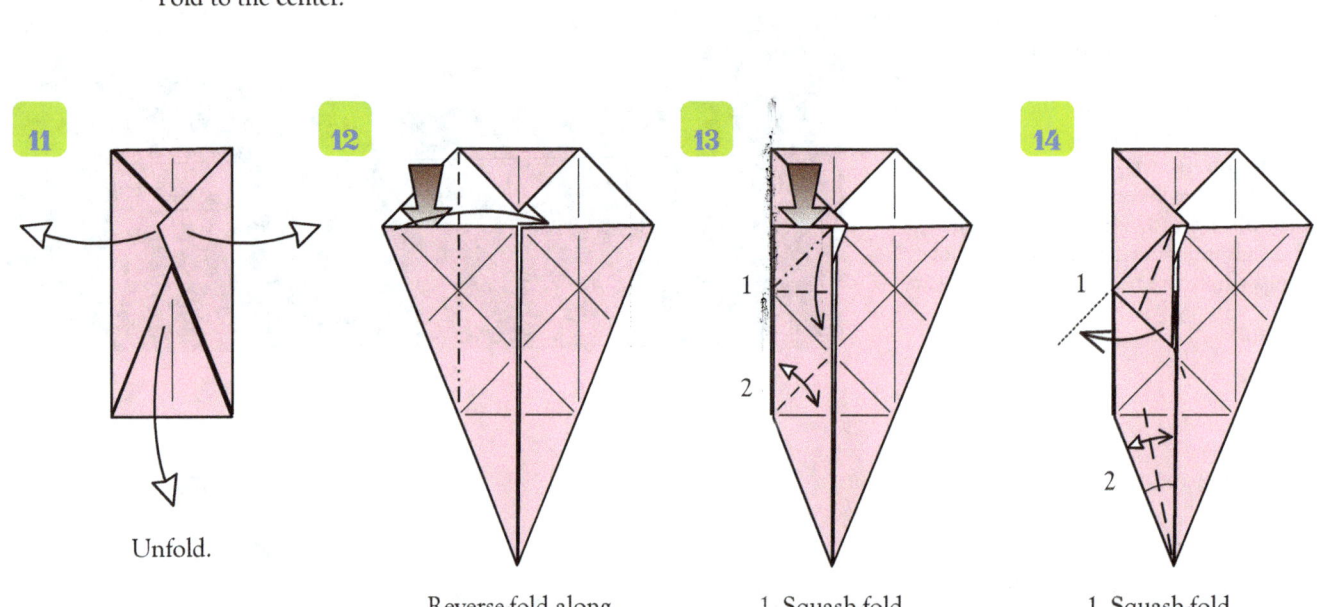

Unfold.

Reverse-fold along the creases.

1. Squash-fold.
2. Fold and unfold along the crease.

1. Squash-fold.
2. Fold and unfold.

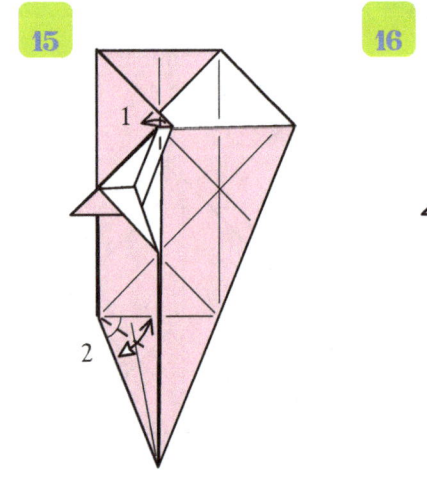
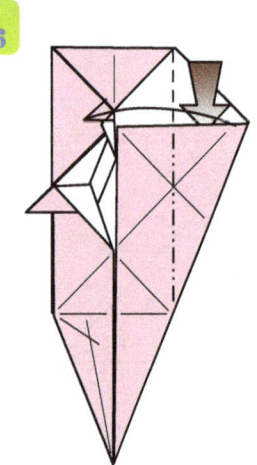
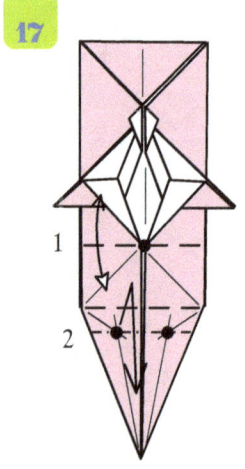

1. Valley-fold.
2. Fold and unfold.

Repeat steps 12–15 on the right.

1. Fold and unfold.
2. Pleat-fold.

Make squash folds.

**60** Origami Symphony No. 5

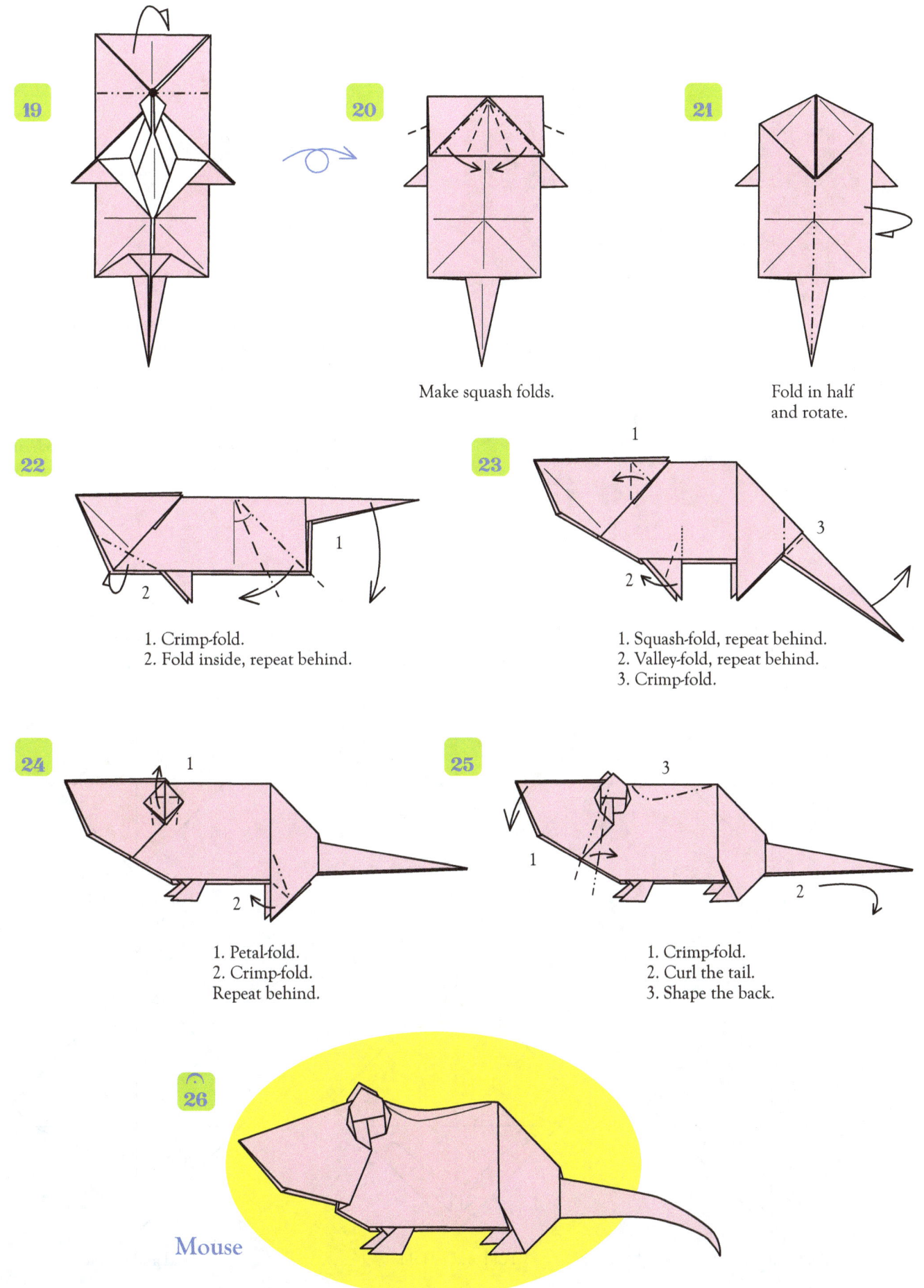

Mouse

# Rabbit

Rabbits are social animals found at the edges of forests, in grasslands, marshes and even deserts. They dig and create complex tunnels for protection and sleeping. They feed on weeds, grasses, leafy plants, and bark. They can see almost completely around themselves, except right in front. Their long ears allow them to hear extremely well and also help cool them down.

1. Fold and unfold.

2. Fold and unfold on the edge.

3. Fold and unfold on the edge.

4. Fold and unfold.

5. Fold and unfold.

6. Fold and unfold.

62  *Origami Symphony No. 5*

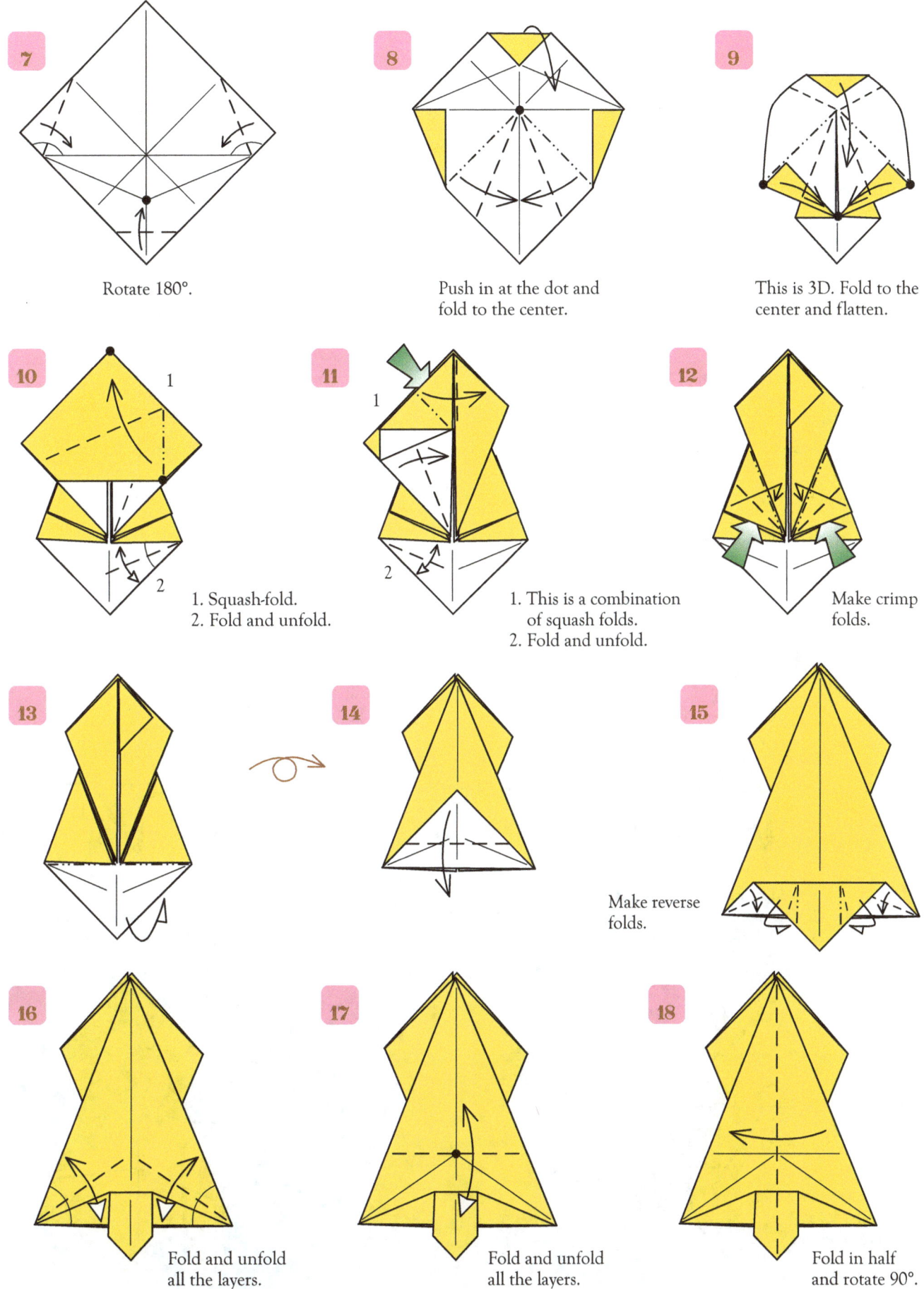

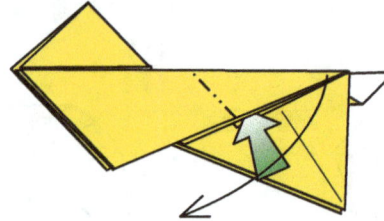

Place your finger into the second layer for this reverse fold. Repeat behind.

 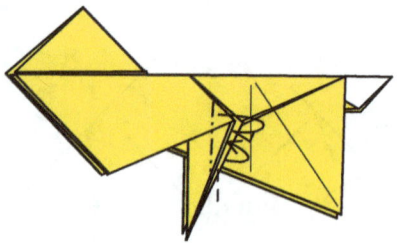

Fold inside on both sides of the leg. Repeat behind.

 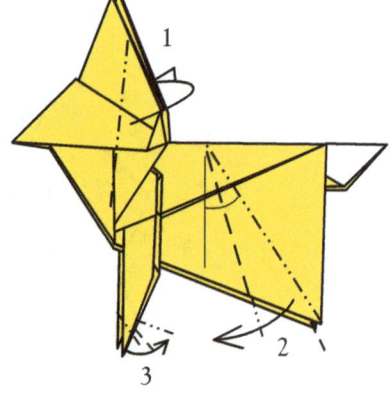

Outside-reverse-fold.

 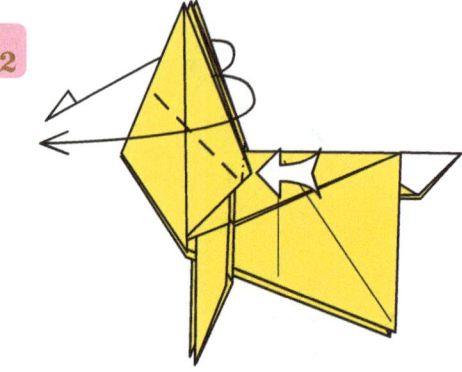

Outside-reverse-fold with a small spread-squash fold.

 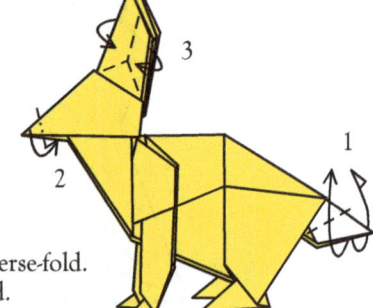

1. Fold inside, repeat behind.
2. Crimp-fold.
3. Squash-fold, repeat behind.

 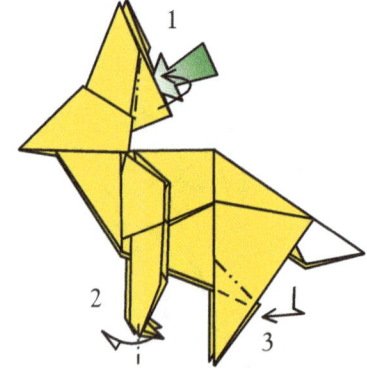

1. Reverse-fold.
2. Mountain-fold, repeat behind.
3. Crimp-fold, repeat behind.

1. Outside-reverse-fold.
2. Reverse-fold.
3. Shape the ears, repeat behind.

Rabbit

64   Origami Symphony No. 5

# Skunk

Skunks are cute but smelly nocturnal mammals. They live in dens such as holes in trees or will dig to make their own. They only travel short distances from their dens, in search of food. They feed on insects, rodents, snakes, berries, and mushrooms. Farmers like skunks because they act as pest controllers.

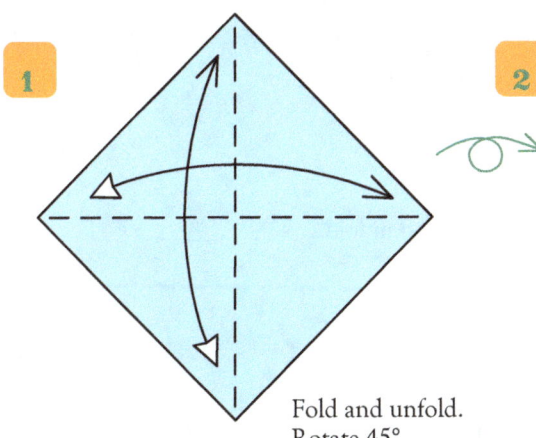

1. Fold and unfold. Rotate 45°.

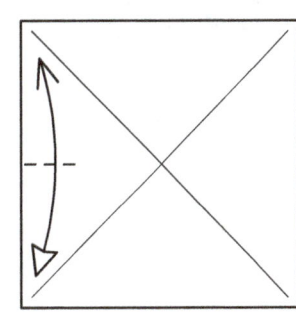

2. Fold and unfold on the left.

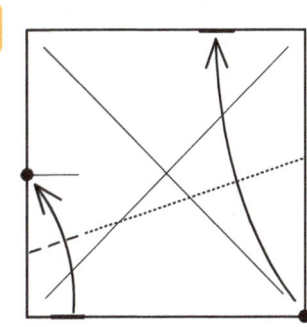

3. Bring the lower right corner to the top edge and the bottom edge to the left center. Crease on the left.

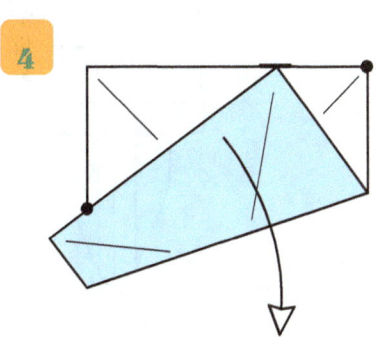

4. Unfold and rotate 45°.

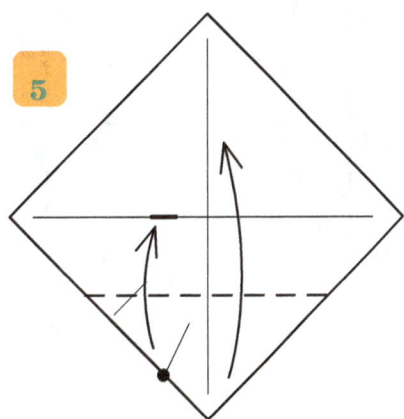

5. Bring the dot to the line.

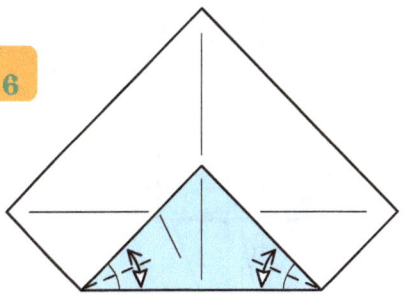

6. Fold and unfold both layers.

Skunk **65**

7
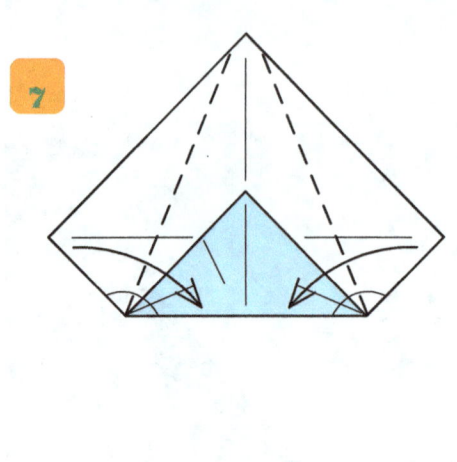

8
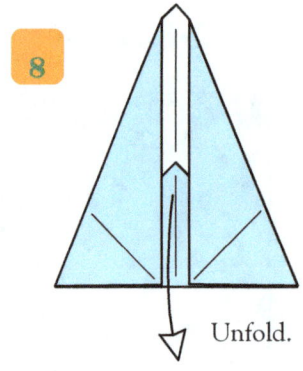
Unfold.

9
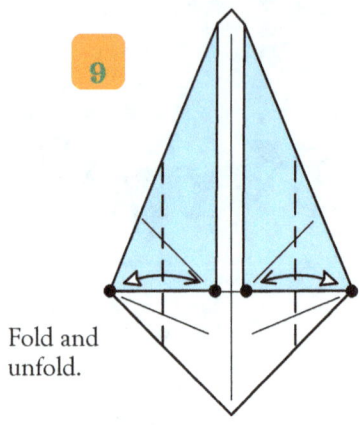
Fold and unfold.

10
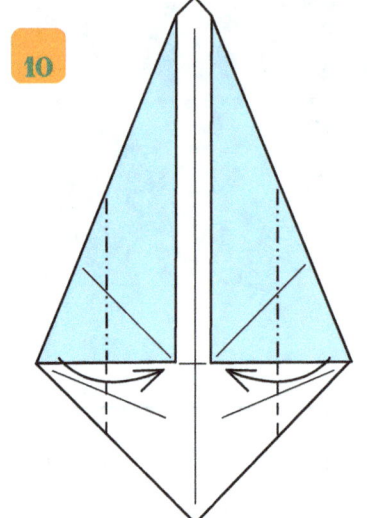
Fold along the creases for these reverse folds.

11
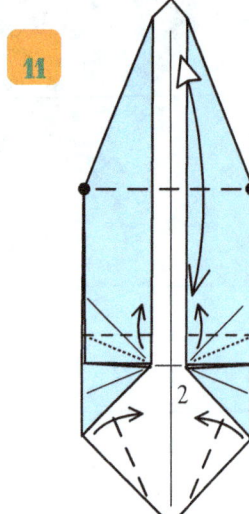
1. Fold and unfold.
2. Make squash folds. Fold along hidden creases shown as dotted lines.

12
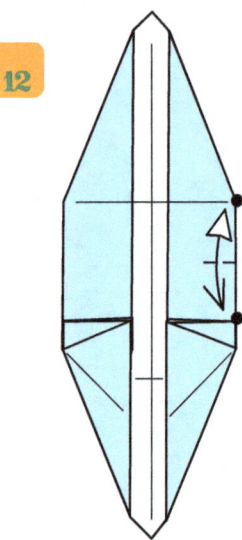
Fold and unfold.

13
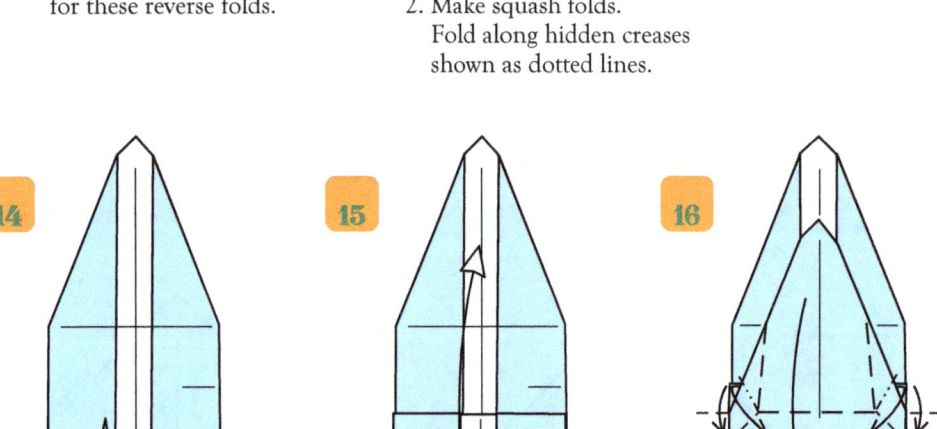

14

Mountain-fold along the crease for this pleat fold.

15
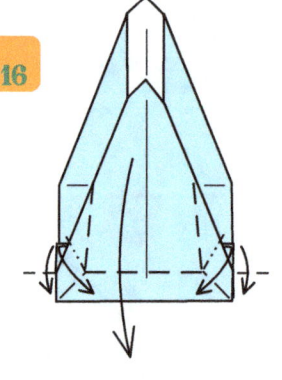
Unfold.

16

Fold some layers toward the center while folding the tail down.

17
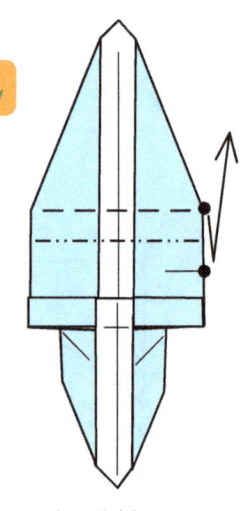
Pleat-fold so the dots meet.

**66** Origami Symphony No. 5

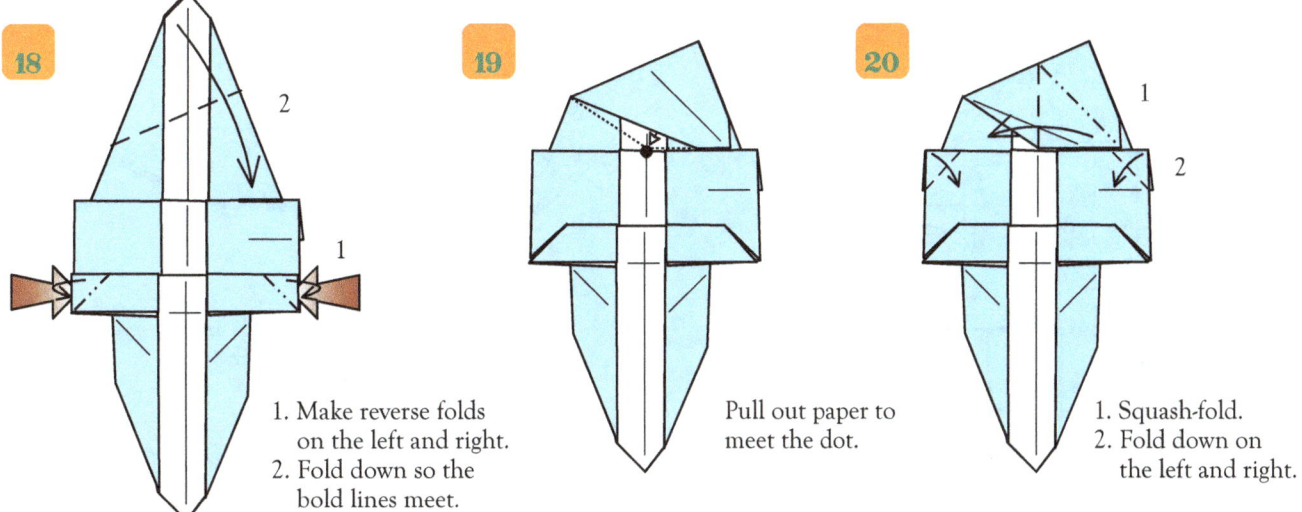

18.
1. Make reverse folds on the left and right.
2. Fold down so the bold lines meet.

19. Pull out paper to meet the dot.

20.
1. Squash-fold.
2. Fold down on the left and right.

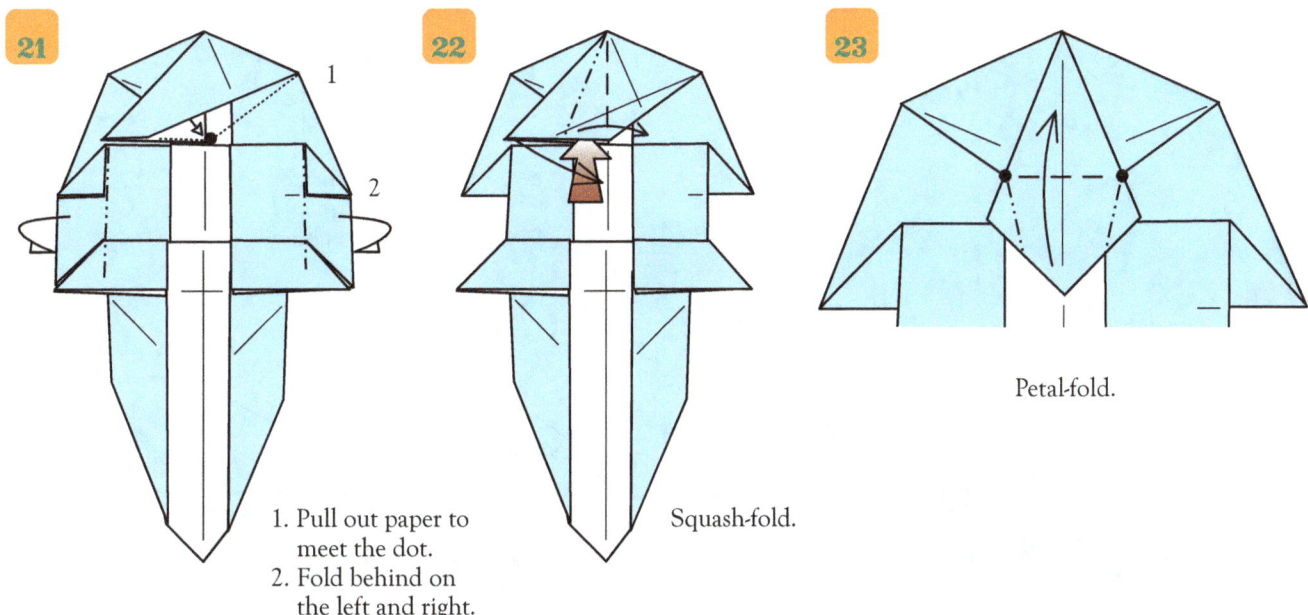

21.
1. Pull out paper to meet the dot.
2. Fold behind on the left and right.

22. Squash-fold.

23. Petal-fold.

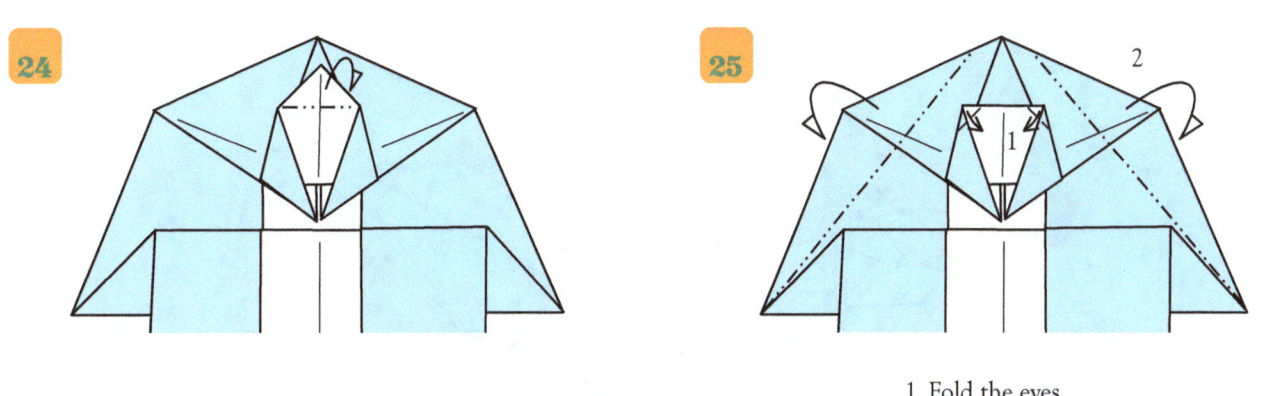

25.
1. Fold the eyes.
2. Fold behind on the left and right.

Skunk **67**

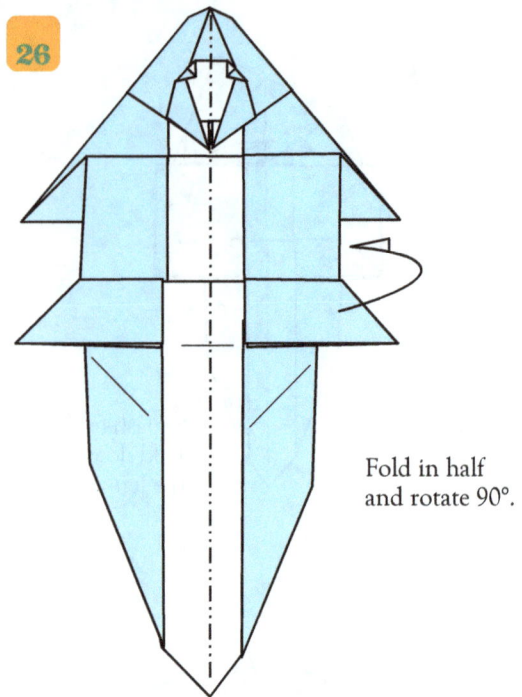

Fold in half and rotate 90°.

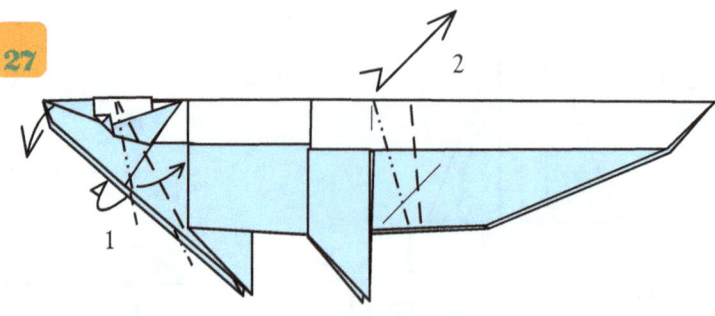

1. Crimp-fold. The folds are under the head detail.
2. Crimp-fold.

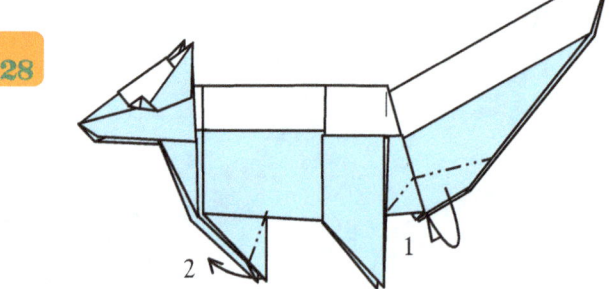

1. Fold inside.
2. Reverse-fold. Repeat behind.

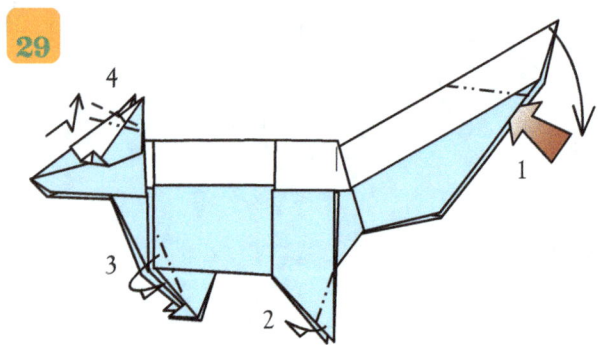

1. Reverse-fold.
2. Mountain-fold, repeat behind.
3. Fold inside, repeat behind.
4. Crimp-fold.

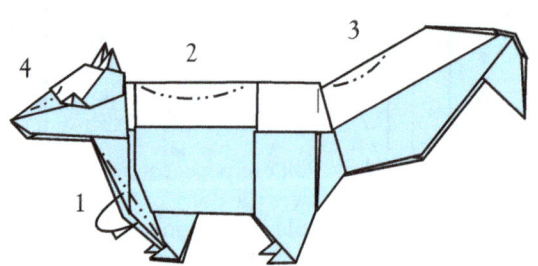

1. Fold inside, repeat behind.
2, 3, and 4. Shape the back, tail, and face.

Skunk

# Third Movement

## Minuet of Catalan Solids with a Trio of Sunken Quadruplet Solids

 Venturing into outer space, we circle four of the thirteen Catalan Solids, some which are quite spherical. These challenging worlds are the duals of the Archimedean Solids (from Origami Symphony No. 2). For each shape, all the faces are congruent but not regular polygons, arranged with spherical symmetry. While highly complex, three of them are captured in under 30 steps. These unusual subjects illuminate the limitless worlds of origami.

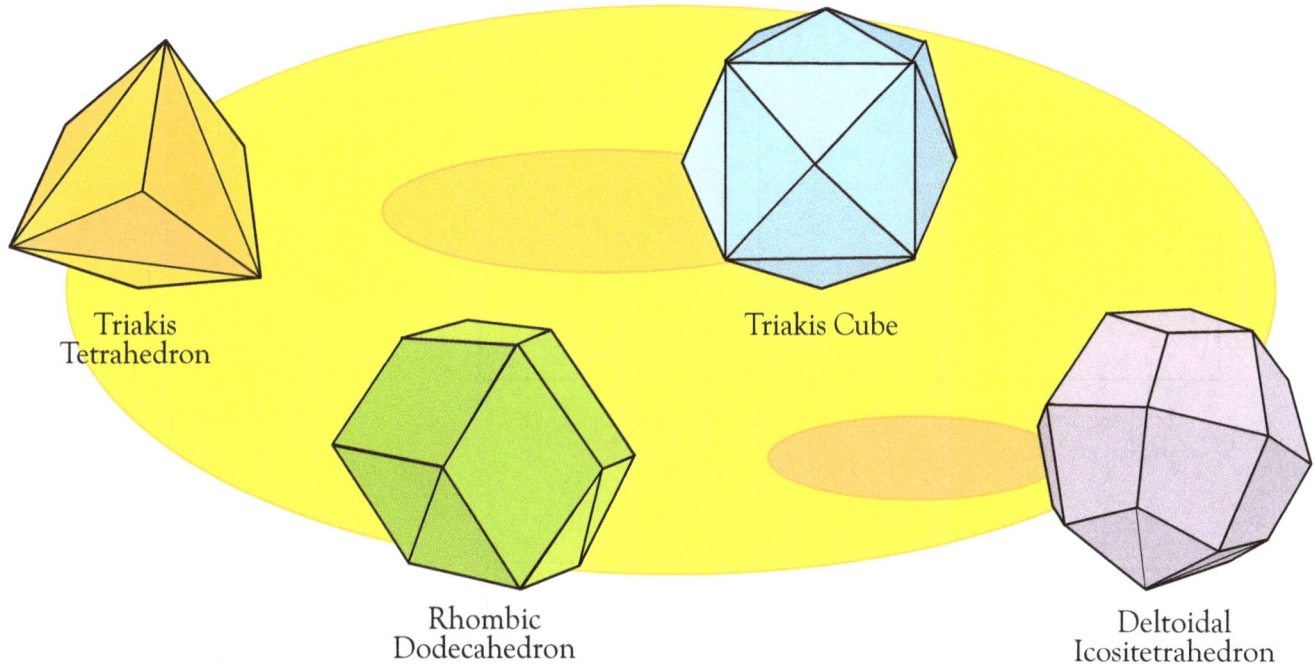

Triakis Tetrahedron

Triakis Cube

Rhombic Dodecahedron

Deltoidal Icositetrahedron

## Triakis Tetrahedron

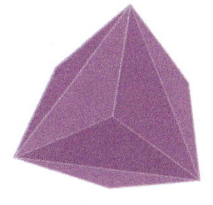

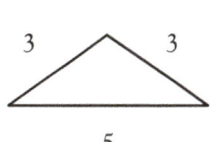

The Triakis Tetrahedron is a Catalan Solid composed of twelve triangular faces. The sides of each triangular face are proportional 3, 3, and 5. The crease pattern shows odd symmetry, which is the same when rotated 180°.

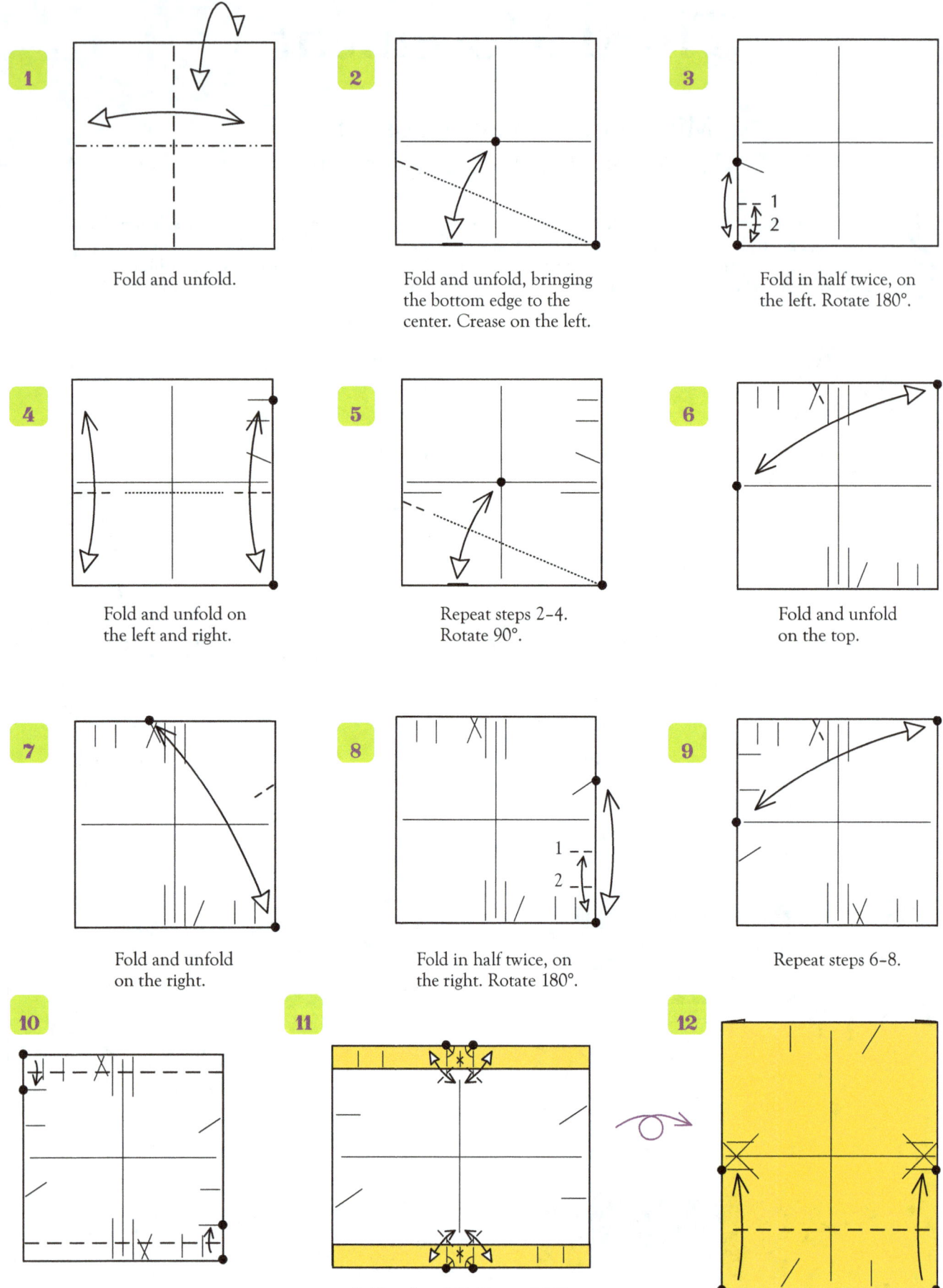

70 Origami Symphony No. 5

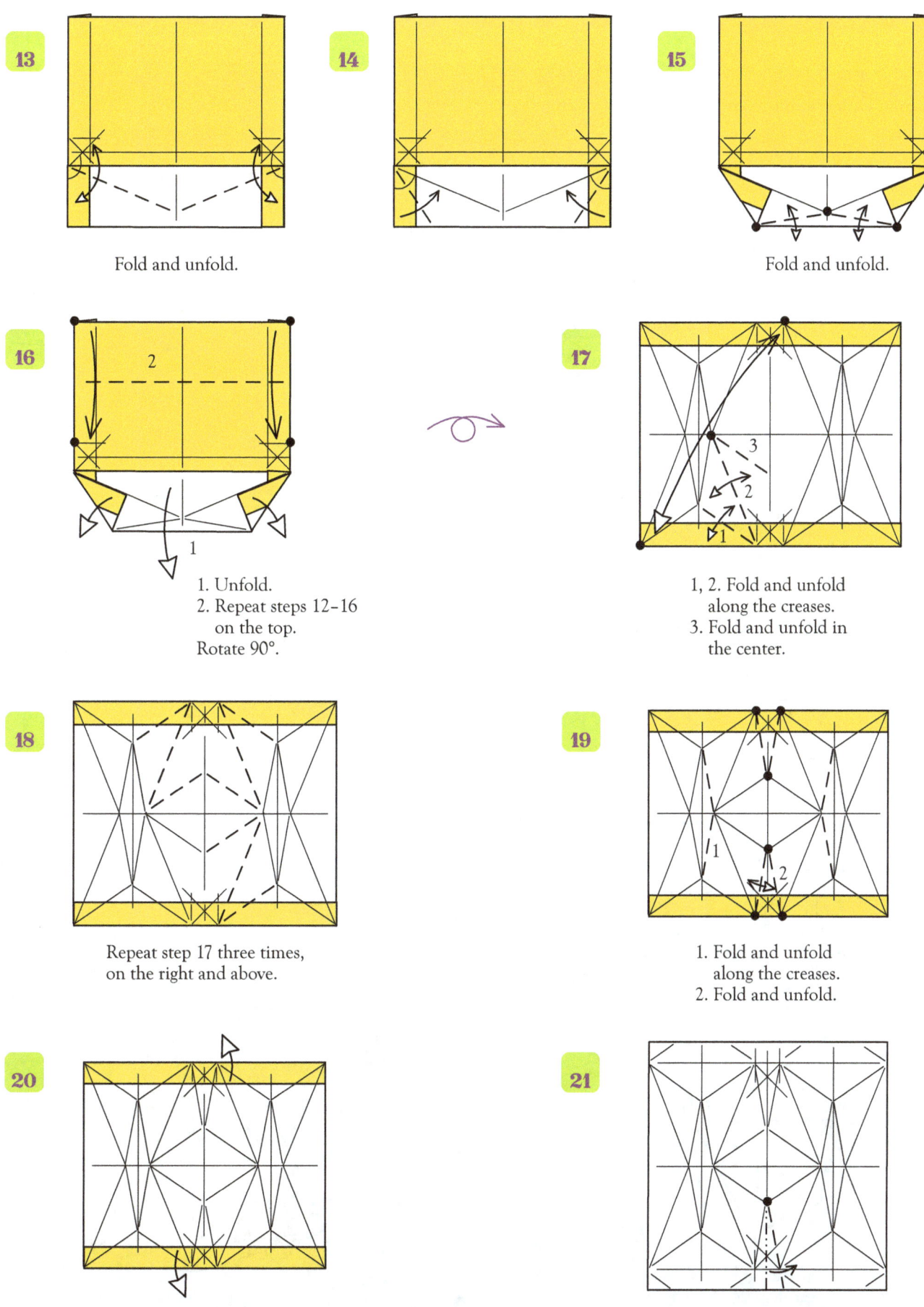

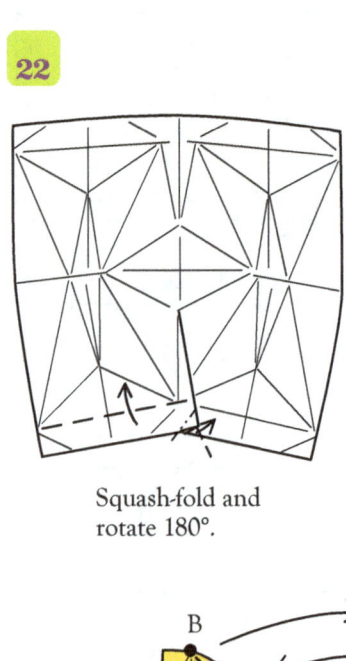

Squash-fold and rotate 180°.

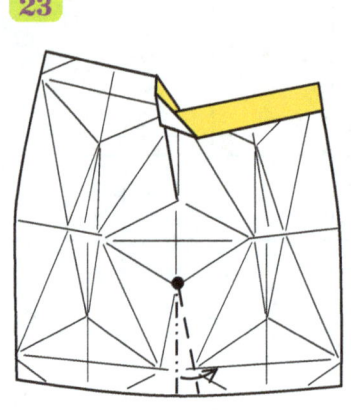

Repeat steps 21–22. Rotate 90°.

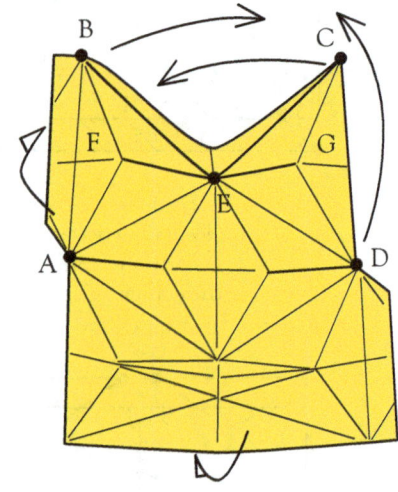

The center dots will meet. Puff out at all the dots. The dark region will be hidden. Curve the left and right sides toward the back.

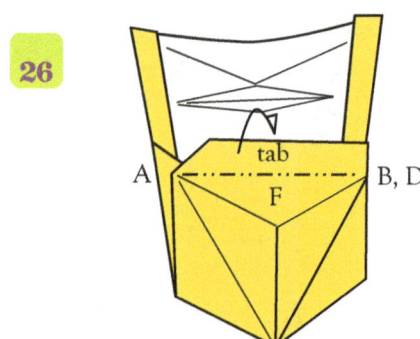

This is a 3D step. Do these together and follow the letters into the next step:
1. Puff out at E.
2. Point B will meet D and F will cover G.
3. C will meet A and tuck into a small pocket at A.

Wrap the tab around the inner layers.

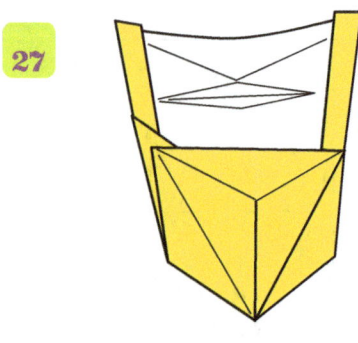

Turn over and repeat steps 24–26.

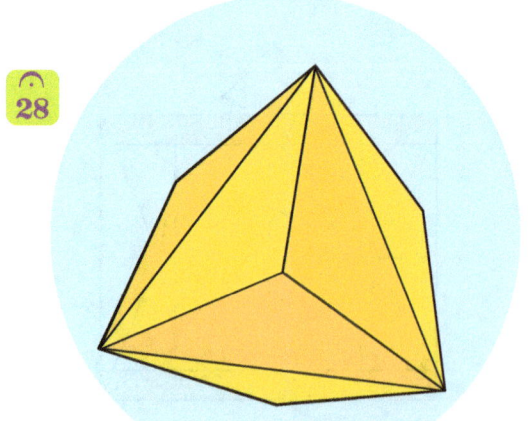

**Triakis Tetrahedron**

72  Origami Symphony No. 5

# Rhombic Dodecahedron

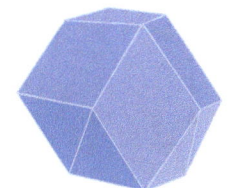
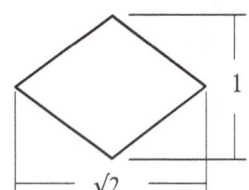
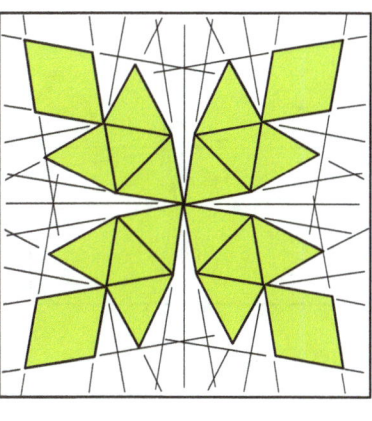

The Rhombic Dodecahedron is composed of twelve sides, each with diagonals proportional to 1 and $\sqrt{2}$. This model uses square symmetry to optimize the efficiency of its size and number of steps. The model closes with a twist lock.

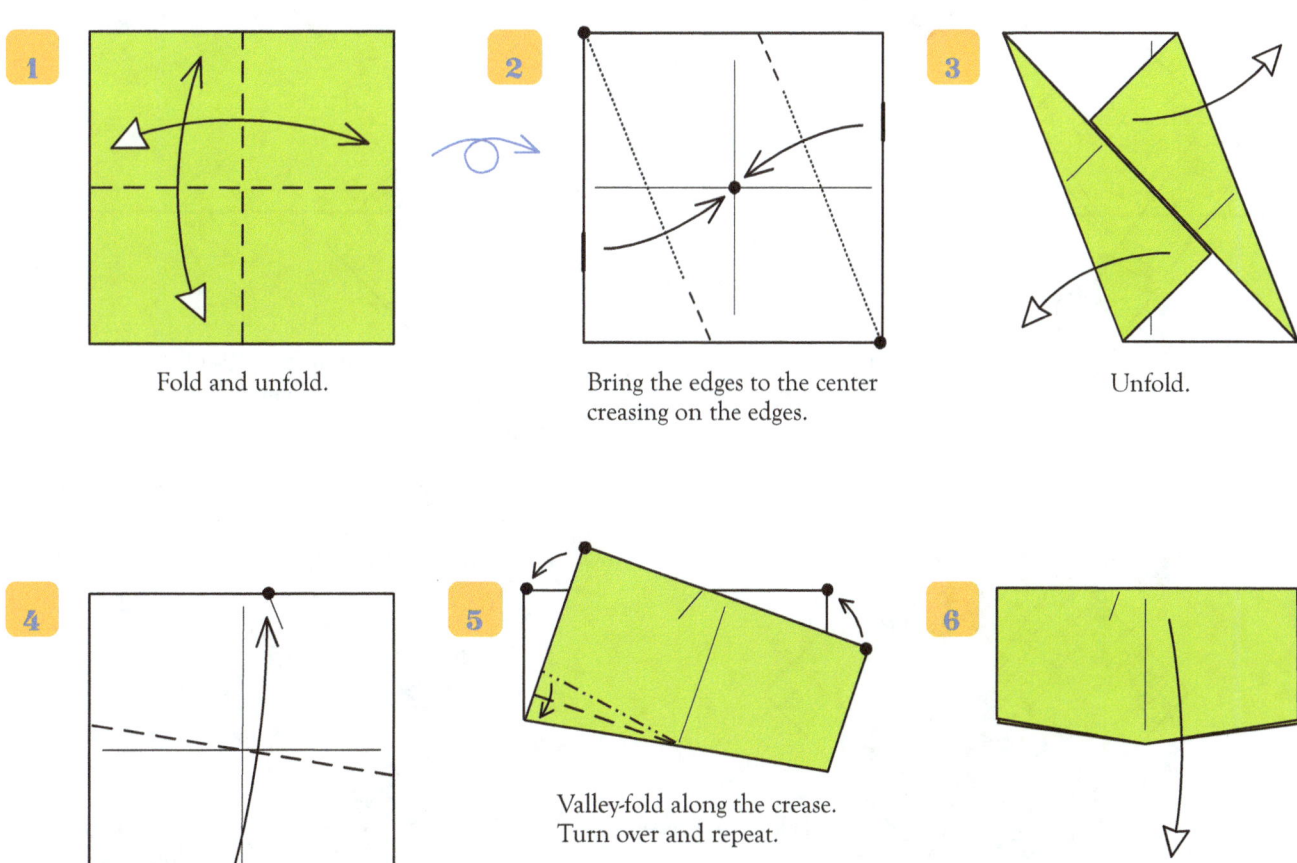

1. Fold and unfold.
2. Bring the edges to the center creasing on the edges.
3. Unfold.
4. 
5. Valley-fold along the crease. Turn over and repeat.
6. Unfold and rotate 90°.

*Rhombic Dodecahedron* 73

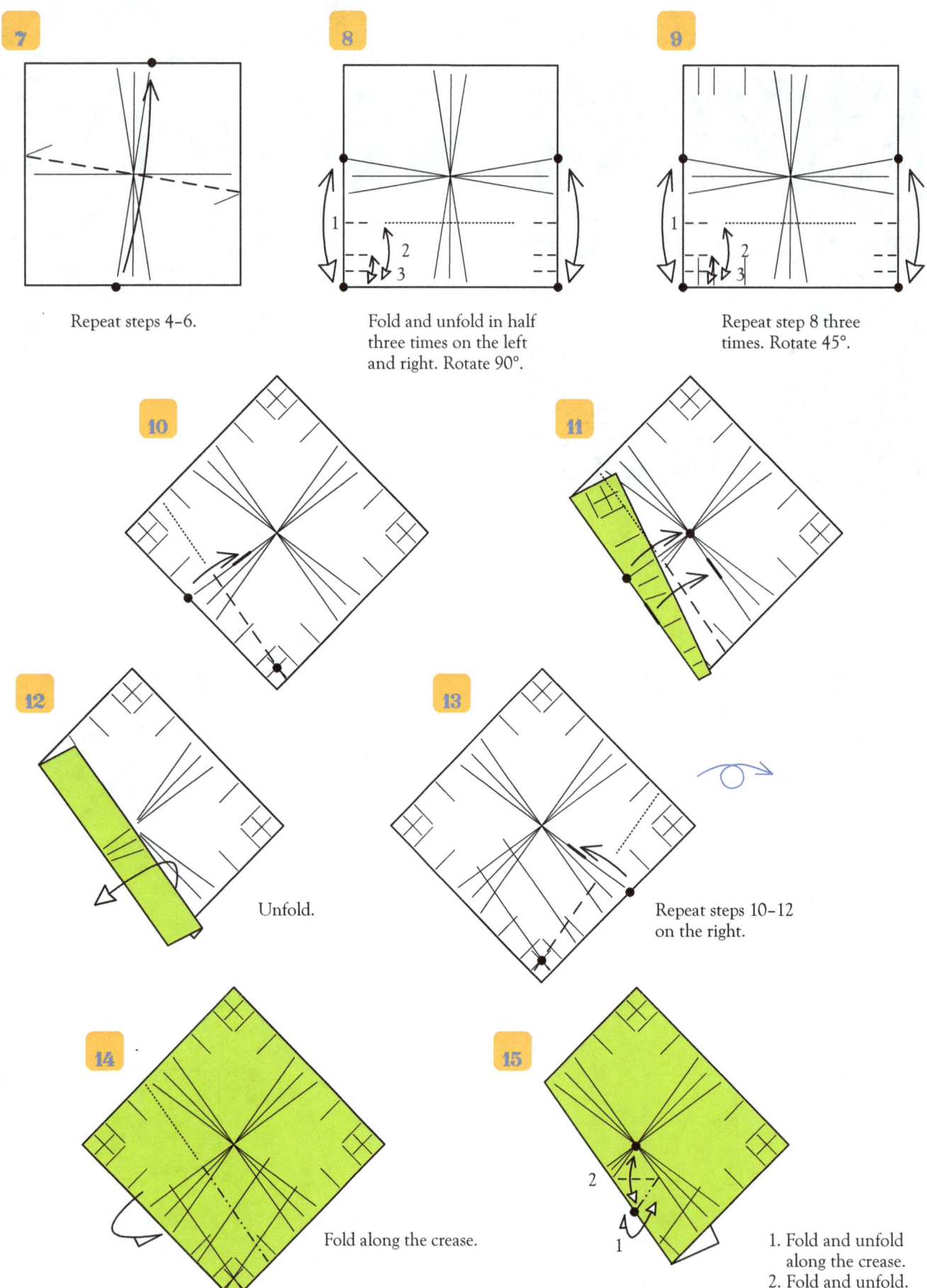

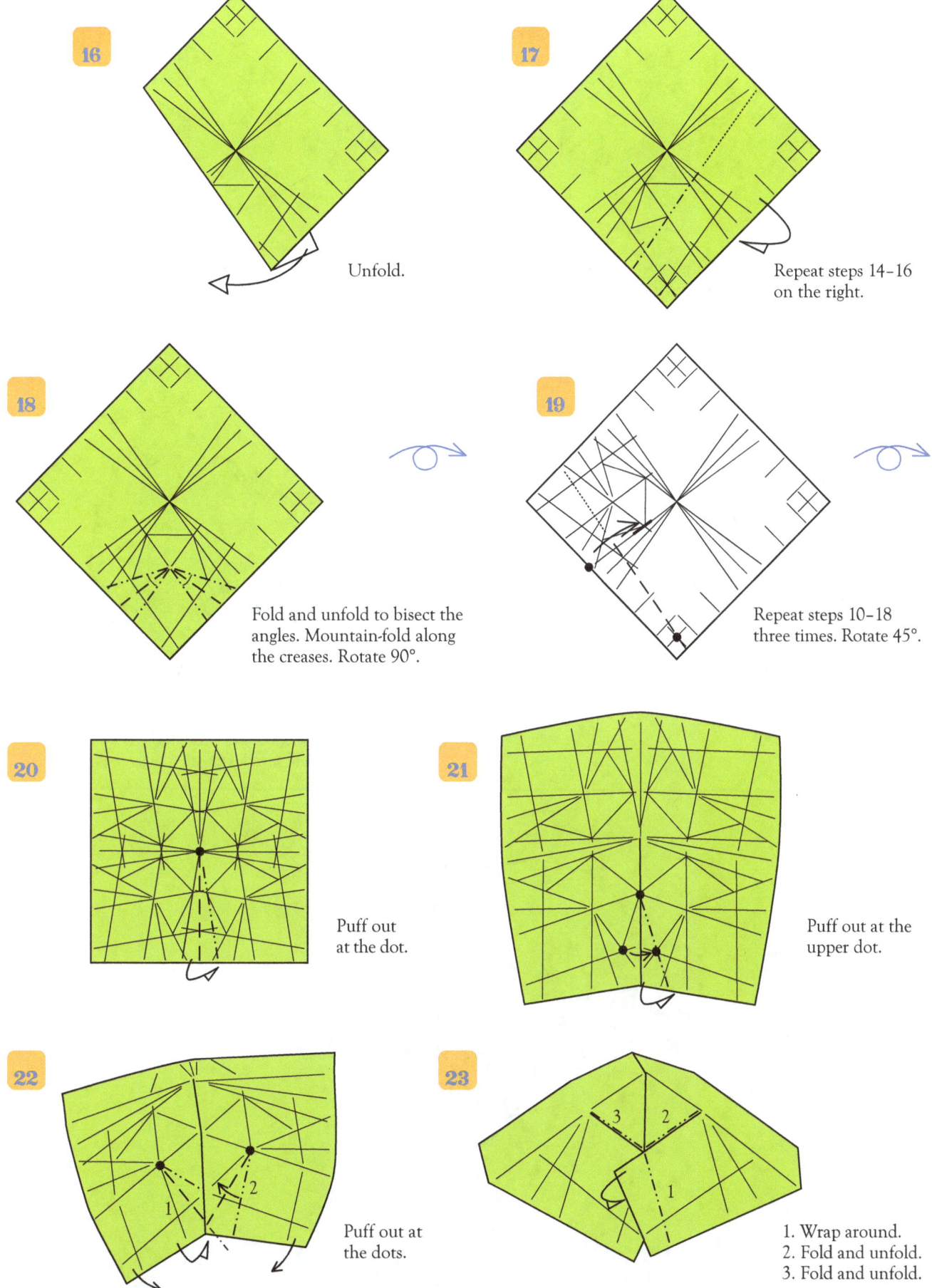

Rhombic Dodecahedron

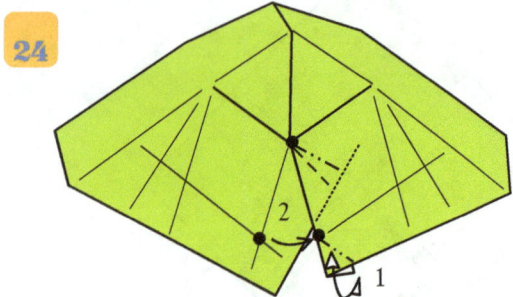

1. Fold and unfold.
2. Puff out at the upper dot, fold on a hidden layer, so the bottom dots meet.

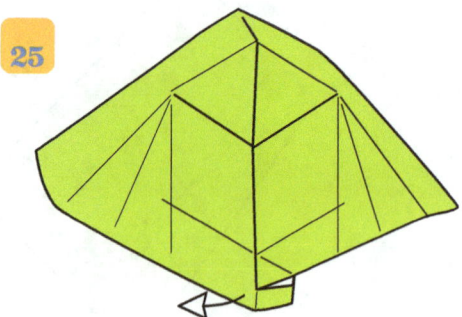

Unfold to step 24. Rotate 90.

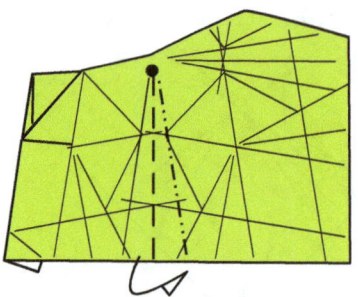

Repeat steps 20-25 three times. Rotate the top to the bottom.

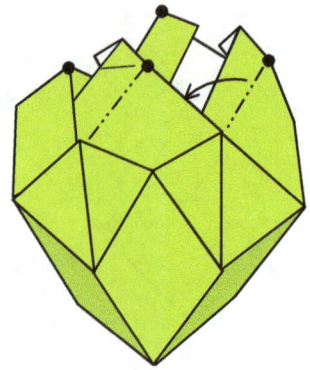

Tuck the tabs inside. At the top, the dots will meet and the tabs will interlock with a twist lock.

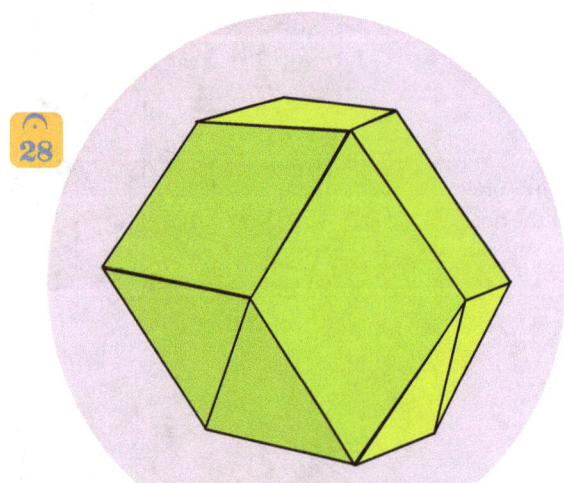

Rhombic Dodecahedron

# Triakis Cube

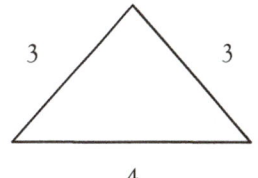

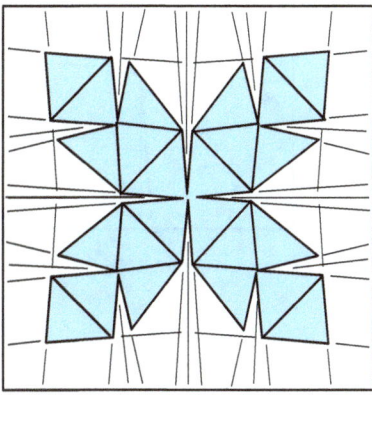

This 24-sided polyhedron is the dual to the truncated octahedron. It can also be called a Tetrahexahedron, Hexatetrahedron, Tetrakis Cube, or Kiscube. It resembles a cube where each side extends outward. The sides of each triangle are proportional to 3, 3, and 4. All the vertices are on the surface of a sphere. The layout shows square symmetry. Folding unusually thin angles are required for this design.

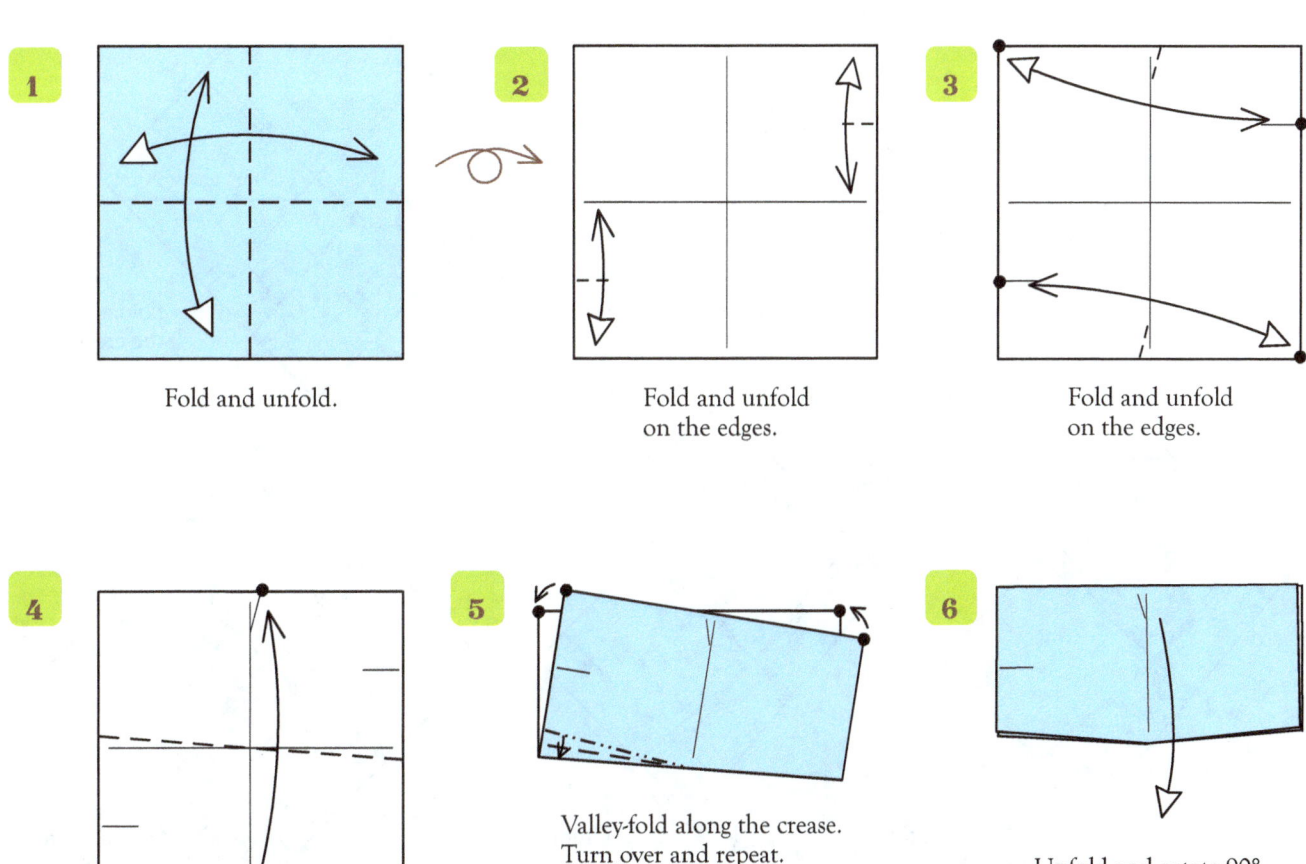

1. Fold and unfold.
2. Fold and unfold on the edges.
3. Fold and unfold on the edges.
4. 
5. Valley-fold along the crease. Turn over and repeat.
6. Unfold and rotate 90°.

Triakis Cube 77

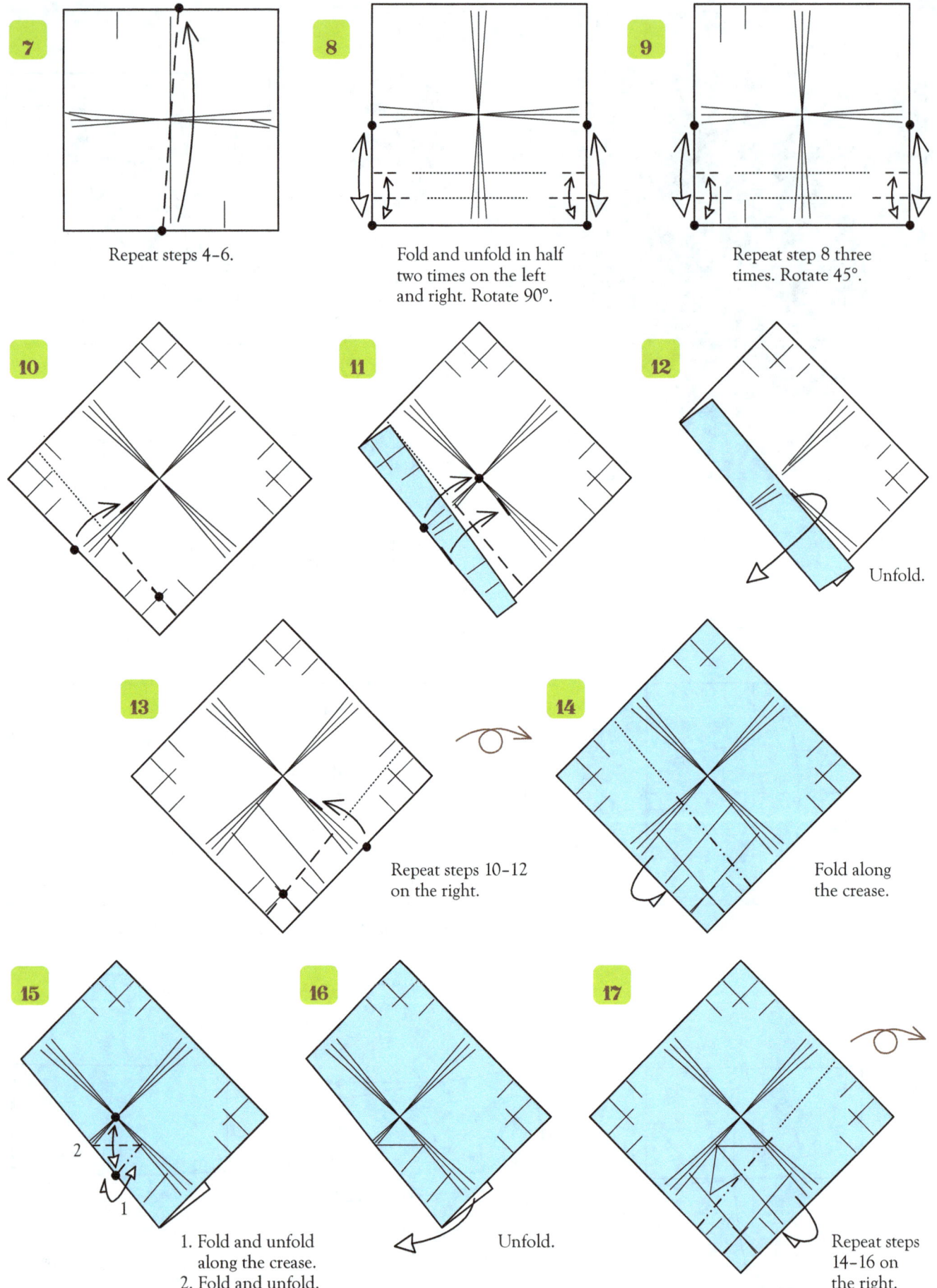

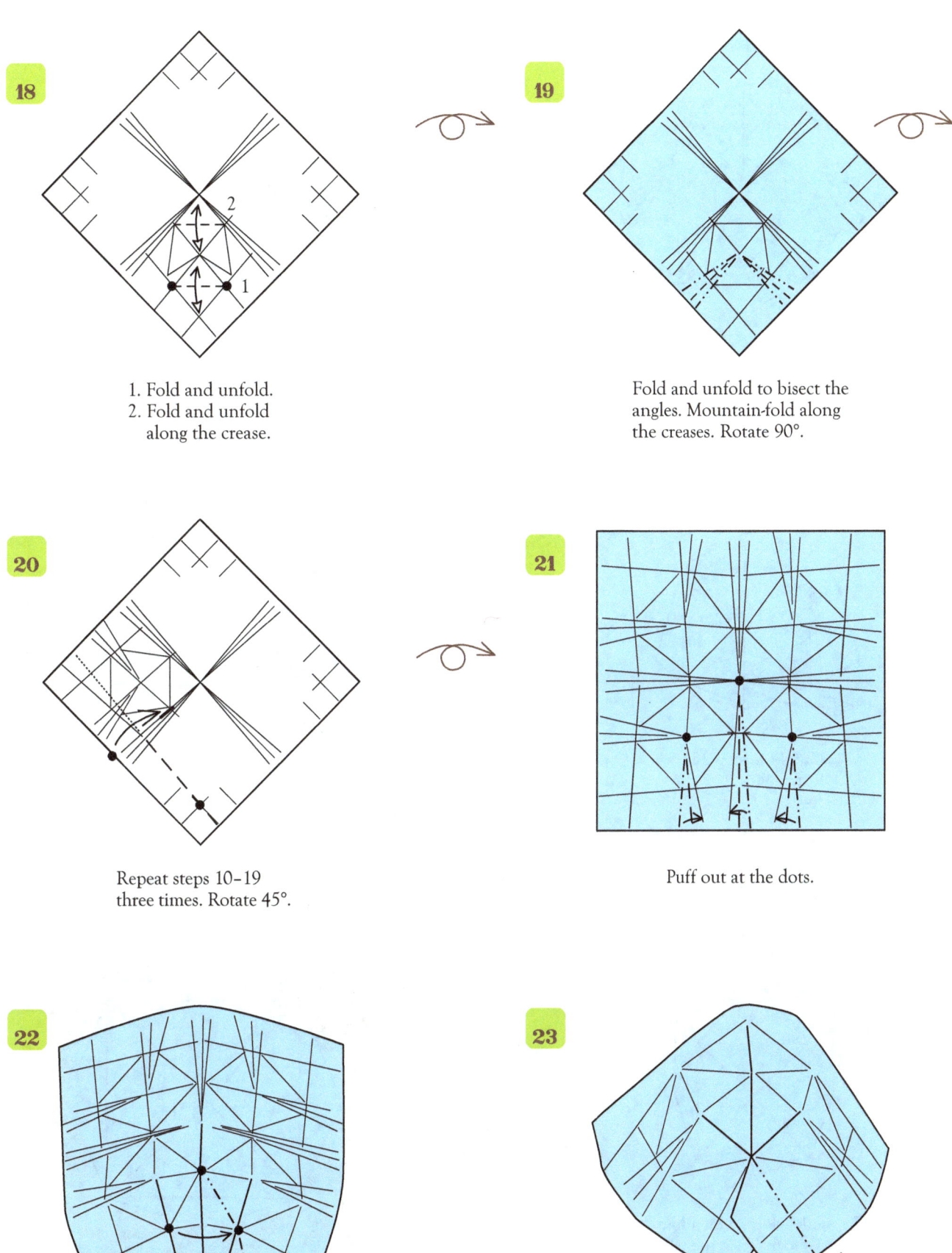

18
1. Fold and unfold.
2. Fold and unfold along the crease.

19
Fold and unfold to bisect the angles. Mountain-fold along the creases. Rotate 90°.

20
Repeat steps 10–19 three times. Rotate 45°.

21
Puff out at the dots.

22
Puff out at the upper dot. The lower dots will meet.

Triakis Cube

**24**

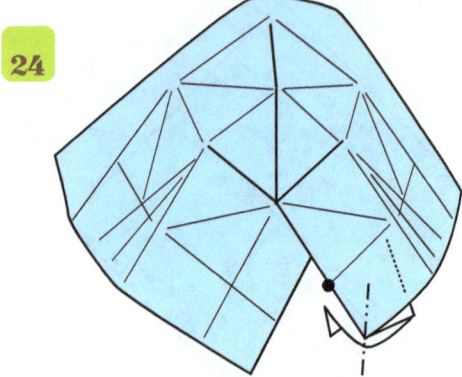

Bring the edge to the dot.

**25**

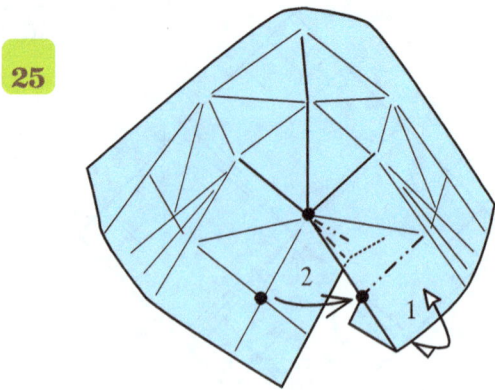

1. Fold and unfold.
2. Puff out at the upper dot, fold on a hidden layer, so the bottom dots meet.

**26**

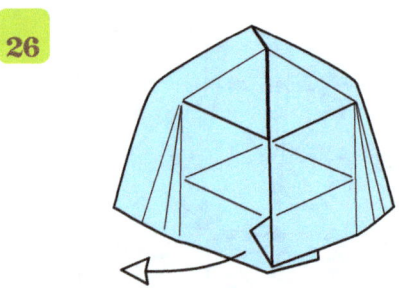

Unfold to step 25. Rotate 90.

**27**

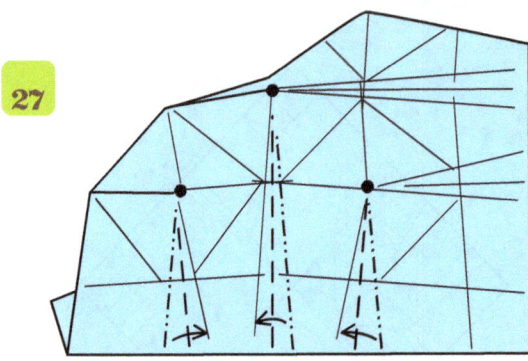

Repeat steps 21–26 three times. Rotate the top to the bottom.

**28**

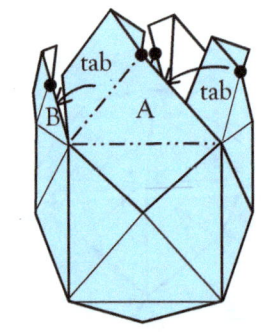

The model closes with a four-way twist lock. Tuck the tab on the left behind A, the next tab behind B and continue. The four dots will meet at the top.

**29**

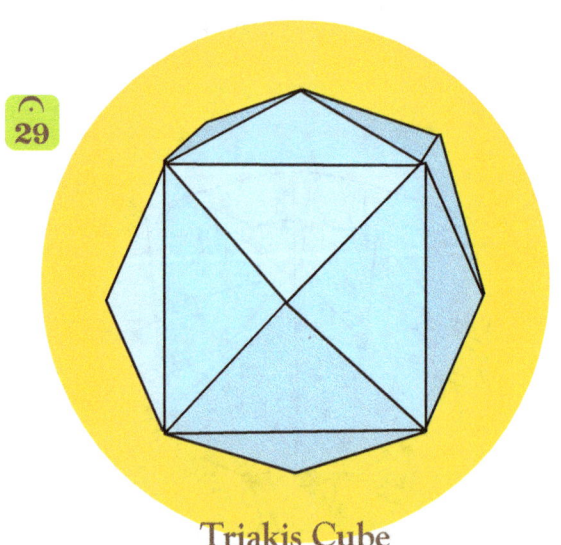

**Triakis Cube**

80 Origami Symphony No. 5

# Deltoidal Icositetrahedron

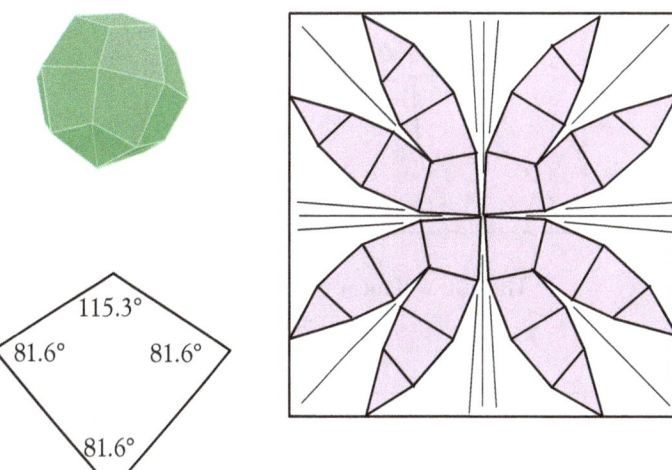

115.3°
81.6°  81.6°
81.6°

The Deltoidal Icositetrahedron is a Catalan solid composed of 24 kites. This is the dual of the small rhomicuboctahedron. The crease pattern shows square symmetry. This shape can also be called a Trapezoidal Icositetrahedron, Tetragonal Icosikaitetrahedron, or Strombic Icositetrahedron.

1. Fold and unfold.

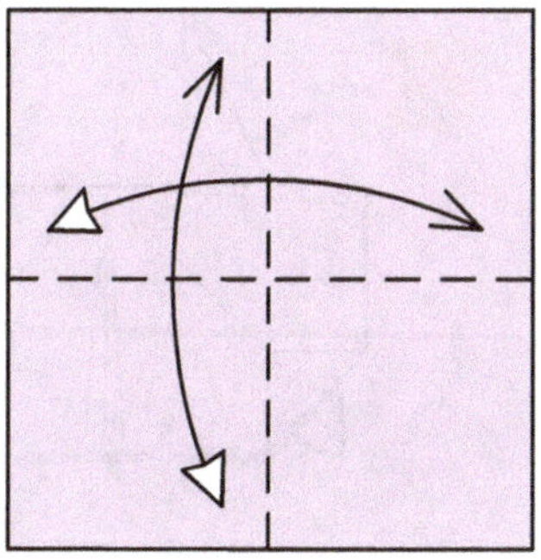

2. Fold and unfold.

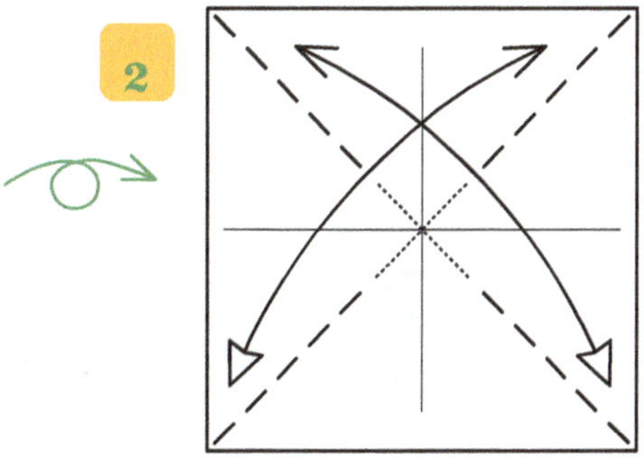

3. Fold and unfold on the right.

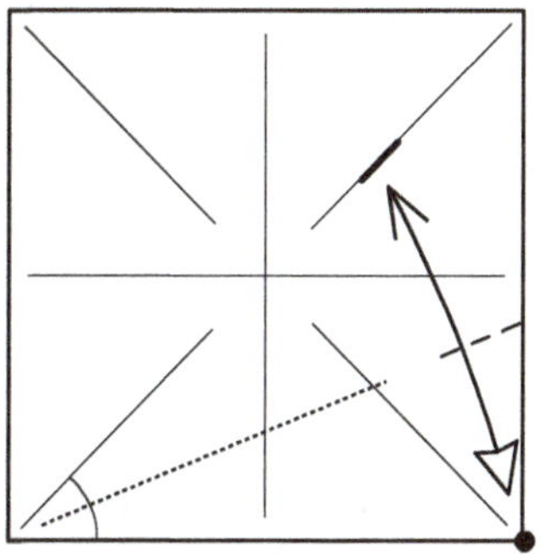

4. Fold and unfold in half three times on the right.

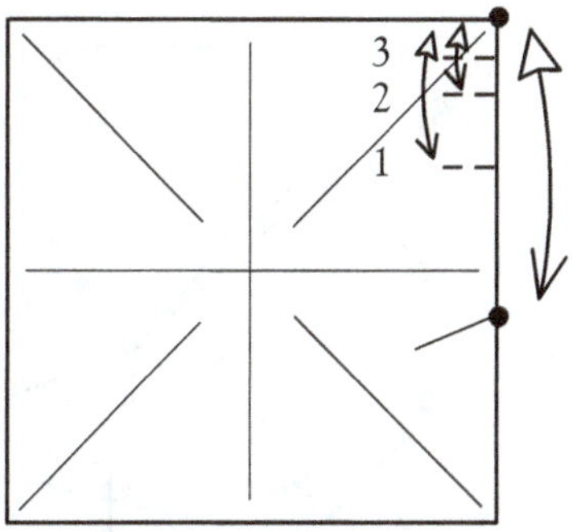

5. Fold and unfold on the right. Rotate 180°.

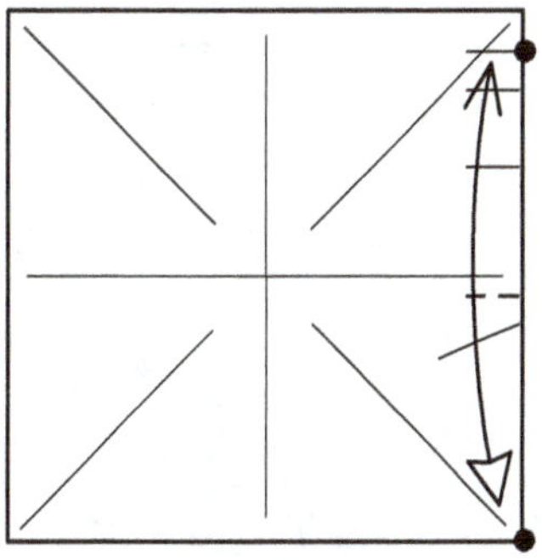

6. Repeat steps 3–5. Rotate 90°.

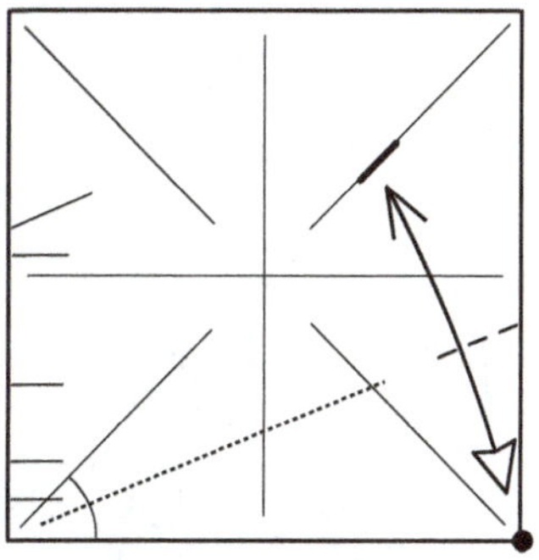

Deltoidal Icositetrahedron 81

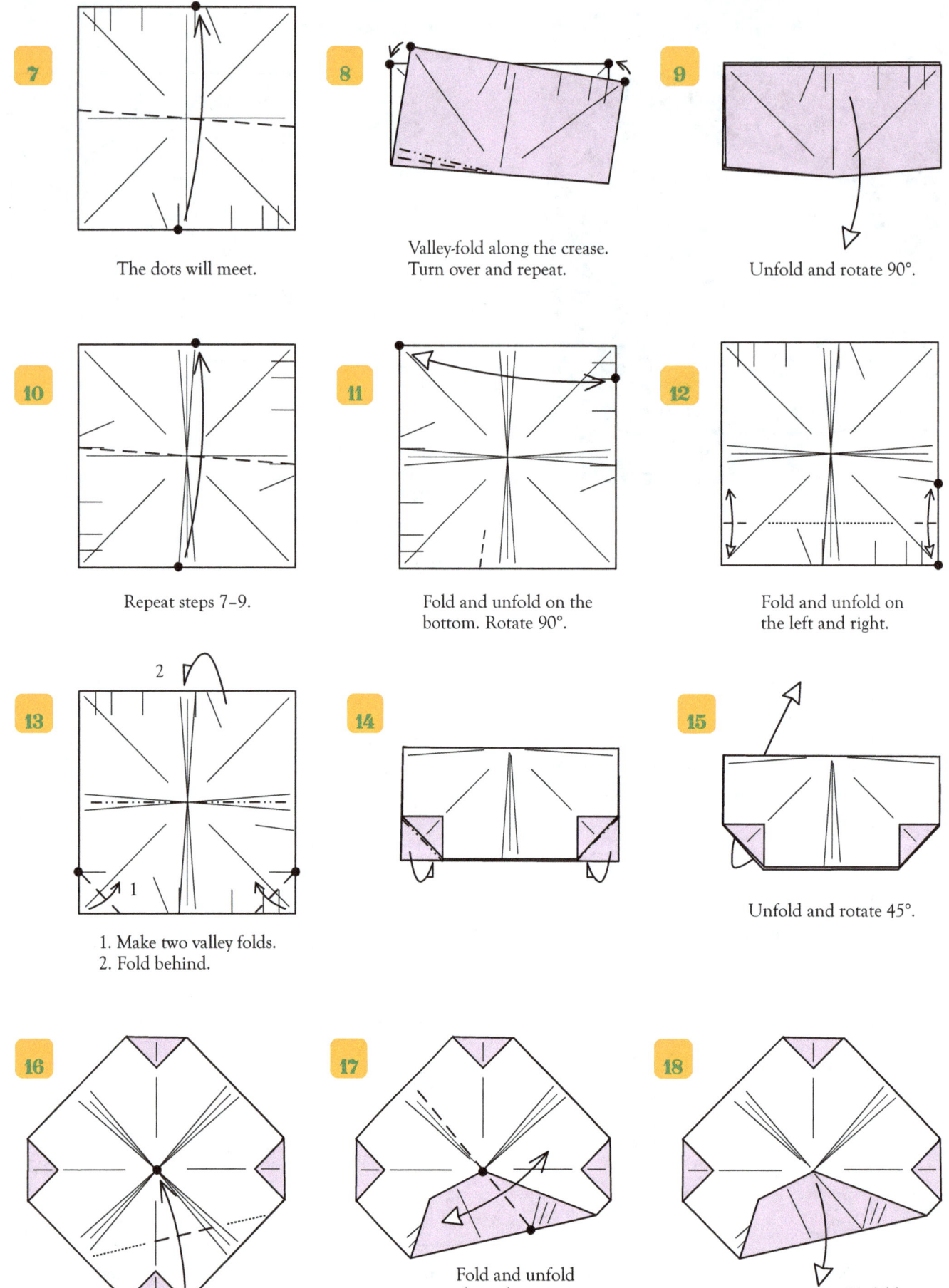

82 Origami Symphony No. 5

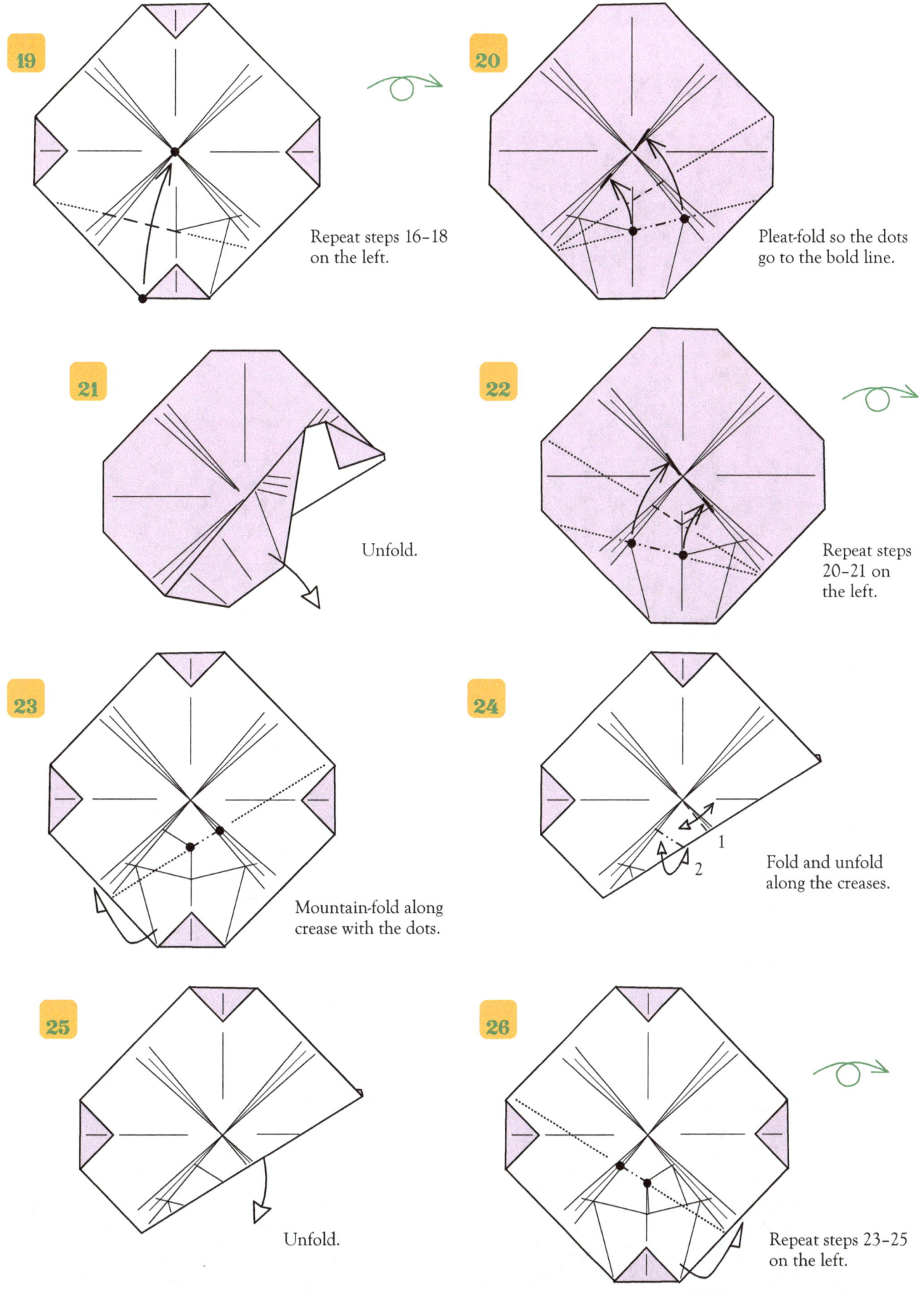

Deltoidal Icositetrahedron

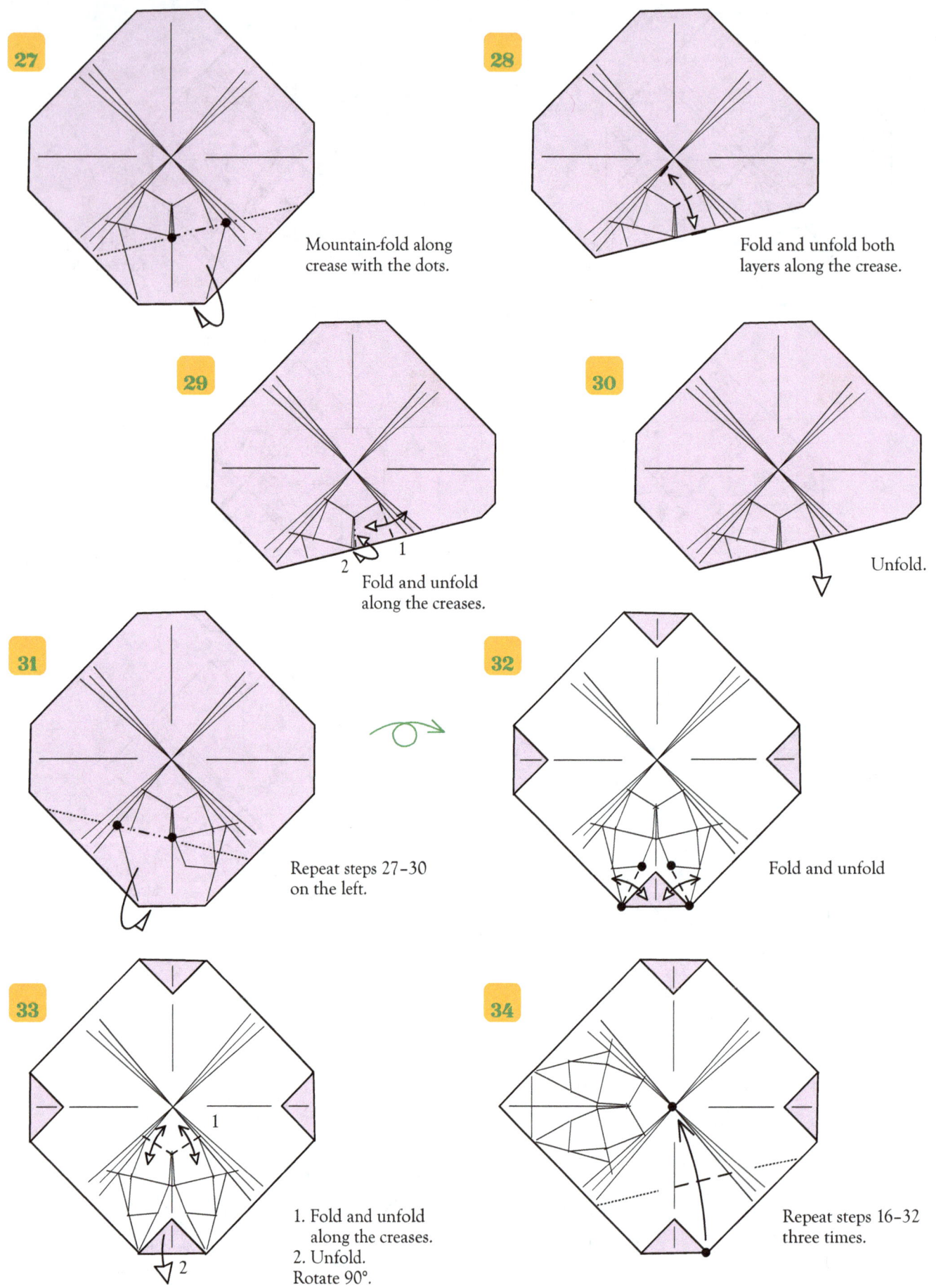

84 Origami Symphony No. 5

35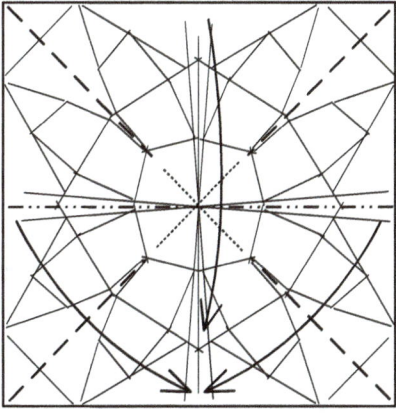
Fold along the creases to make a waterbomb base.

36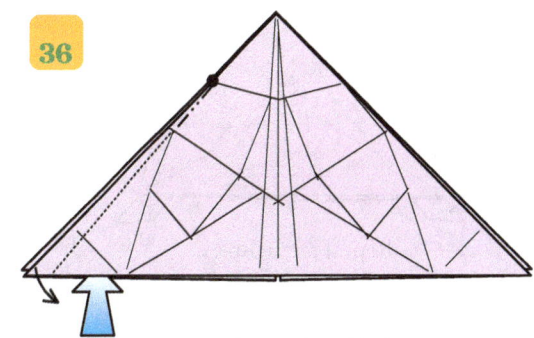
Reverse-fold. Only fold along the crease, there is not need to crease all the way.

37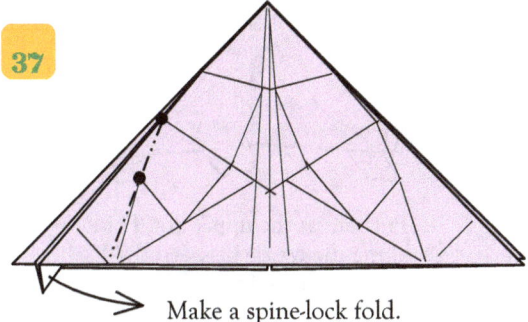
Make a spine-lock fold.

38
View of the inside.

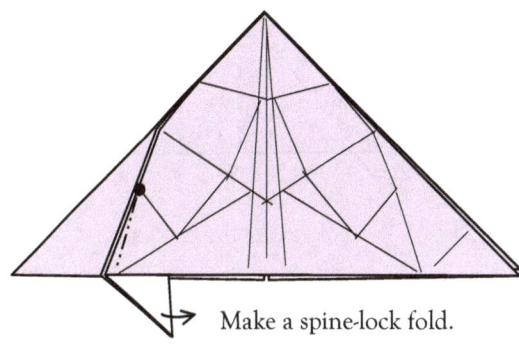
Make a spine-lock fold.

39
View of the inside.

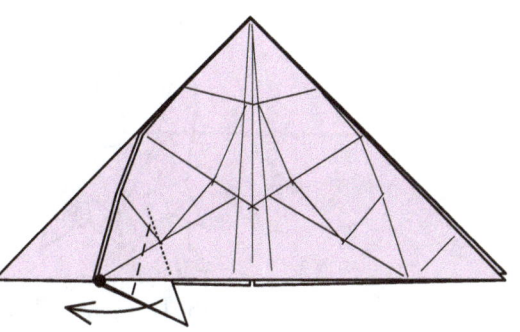
Bring the edge to the dot.

40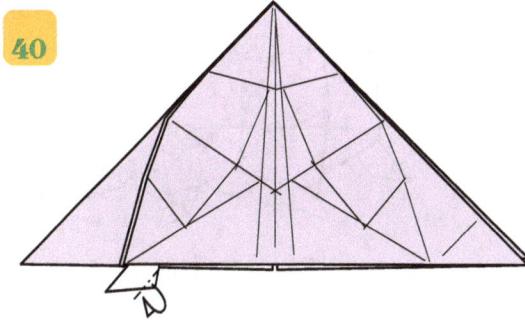

41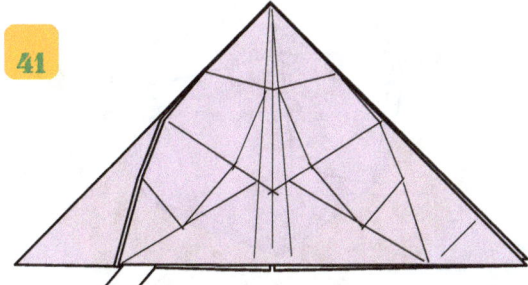
Turn over and repeat steps 36–40.

42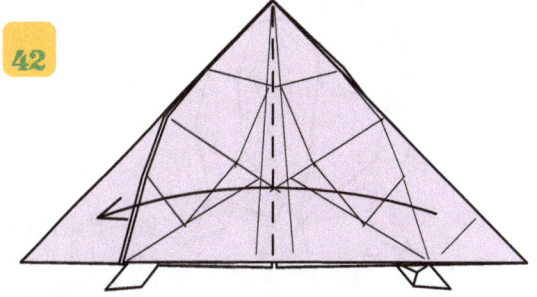
Repeat behind.

Deltoidal Icositetrahedron **85**

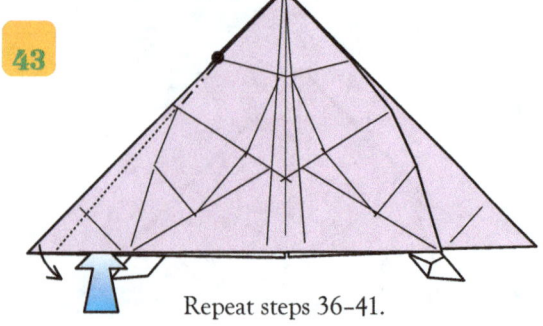

43

Repeat steps 36–41.

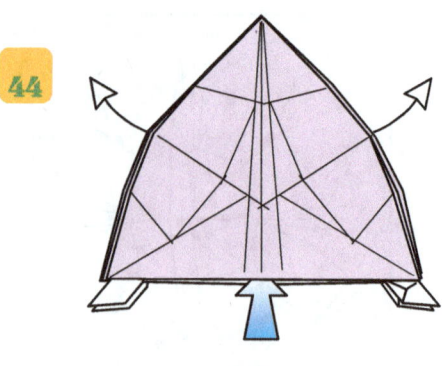

44

Puff out.

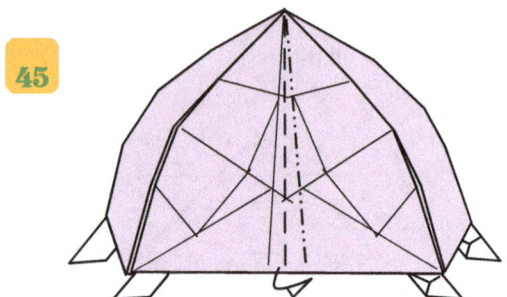

45

Fold along the creases.

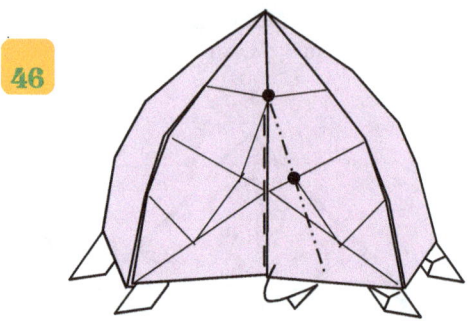

46

Puff out at the upper dot. Fold along the crease between the dots for this spine-lock fold.

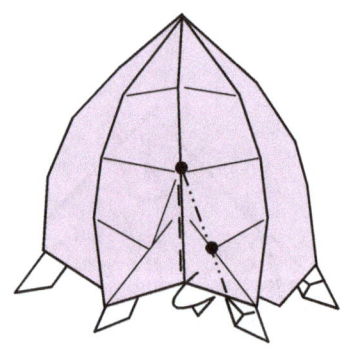

47

Fold along the crease between the dots for this spine-lock fold.

48

Fold along the crease for the last spine-lock fold.

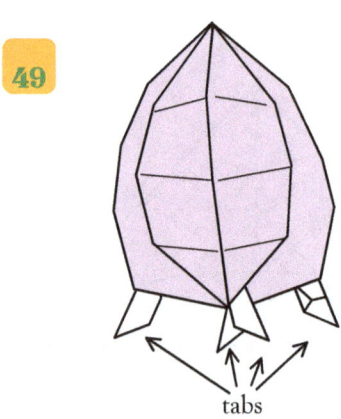

49

tabs

Repeat steps 45–48 three times. The white tabs will be hidden inside and close the model with a four-way twist lock.

50

**Deltoidal Icositetrahedron**

86 *Origami Symphony No. 5*

# Trio of Sunken Quadruplet Solids

These Sunken Quadruplet Solids each have four sunken sides meeting at a common vertex. Found throughout the galaxy, these starry objects can spin away quickly. It will be easy to fold these challenging shapes slowly since time is relative in outer space. Fold carefully or they will become black holes.

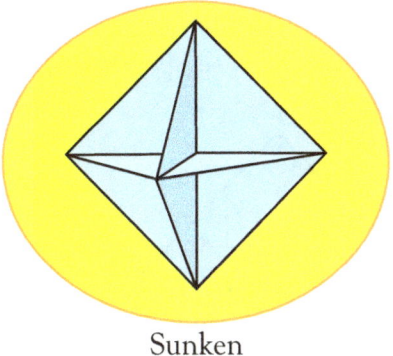
Sunken Octahedron

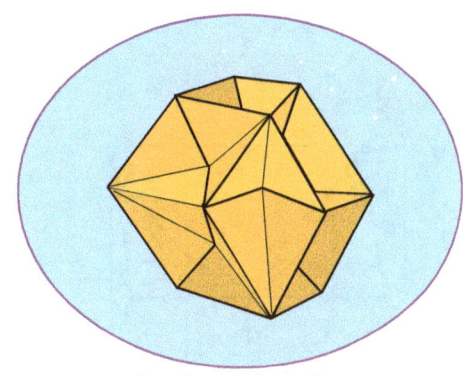
Sunken Rhombic Dodecahedron

Sunken Stellated Cube

## Sunken Octahedron

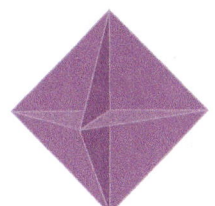

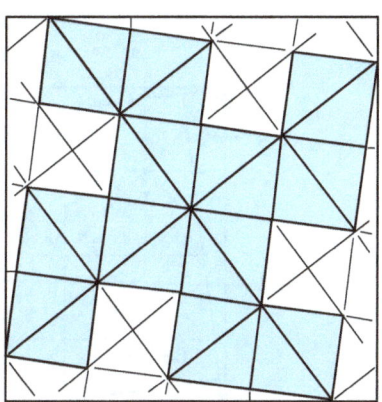

All the faces meet at the center, and this model can be viewed as three intersecting squares in three dimensions. Square symmetry is used.

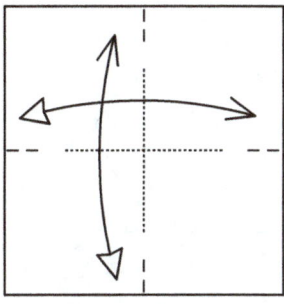

1. Fold and unfold on the edges.

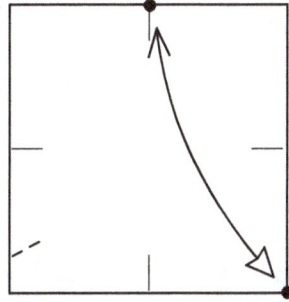

2. Fold and unfold on the left. Rotate 90°.

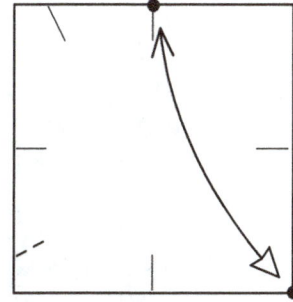

3. Repeat step 2 three times.

Sunken Octahedron **87**

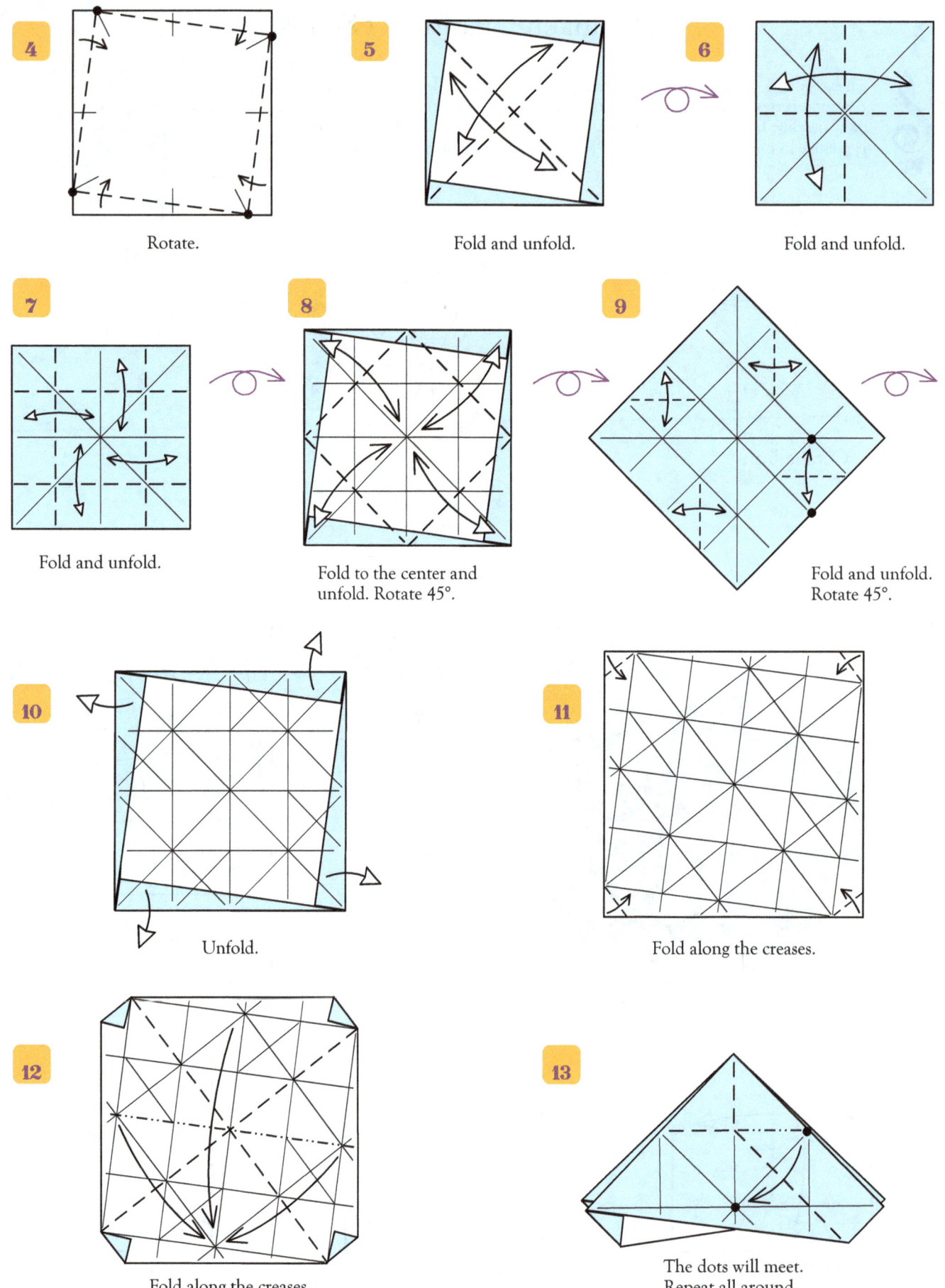

88 Origami Symphony No. 5

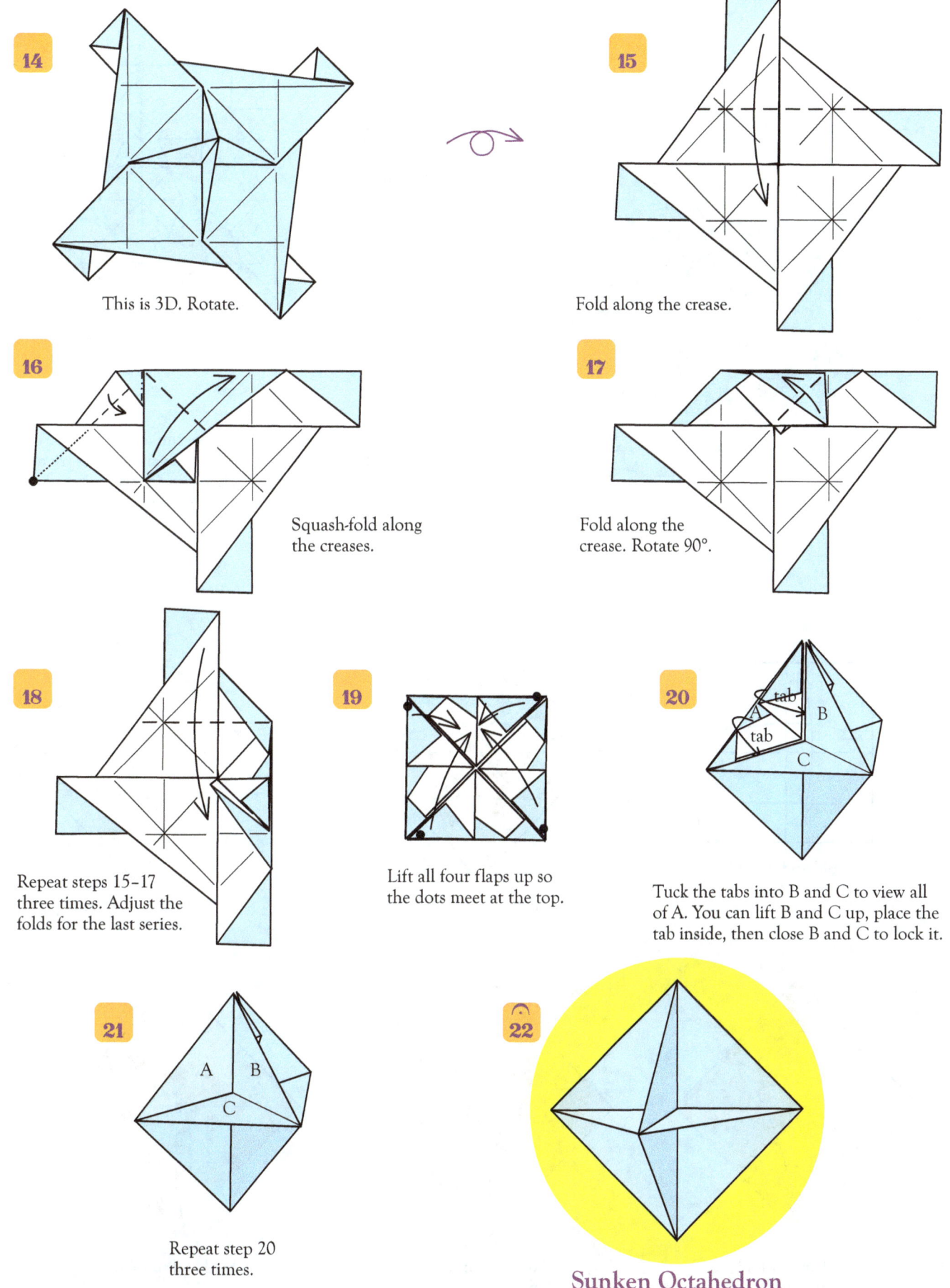

# Sunken Rhombic Dodecahedron

This model is composed of twelve sunken diamonds. Each sunken diamond has four faces, each an isosceles triangle with an apex angle of 45°. There are 48 triangular sides. The crease pattern shows square symmetry.

1. Fold and unfold. Rotate 45°.

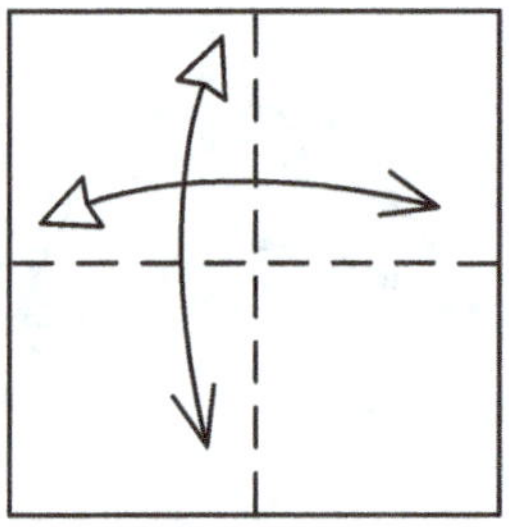

2. Fold and unfold.

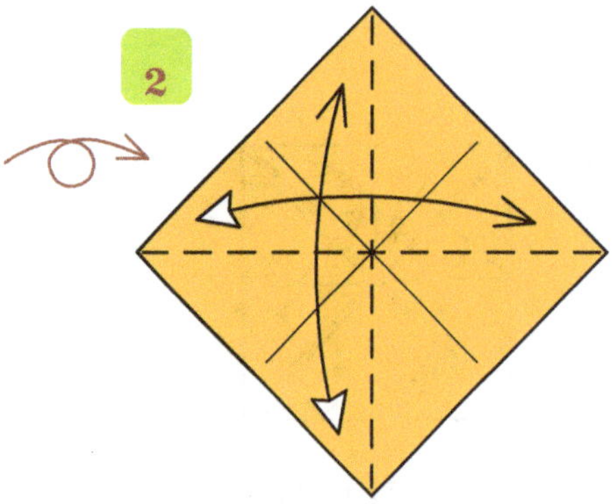

3. Fold and unfold on the edge.

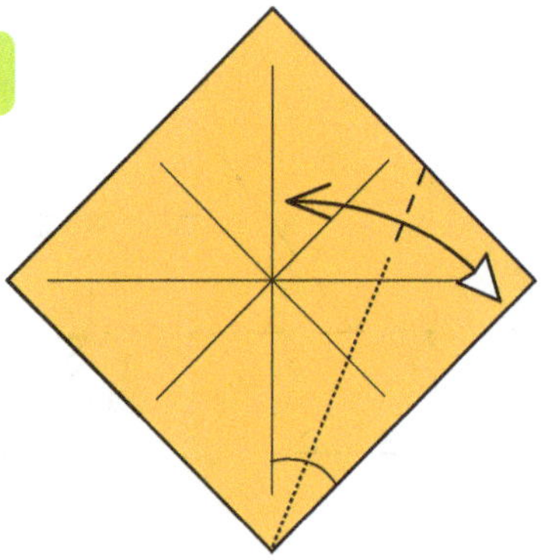

4. Fold and unfold on the edge.

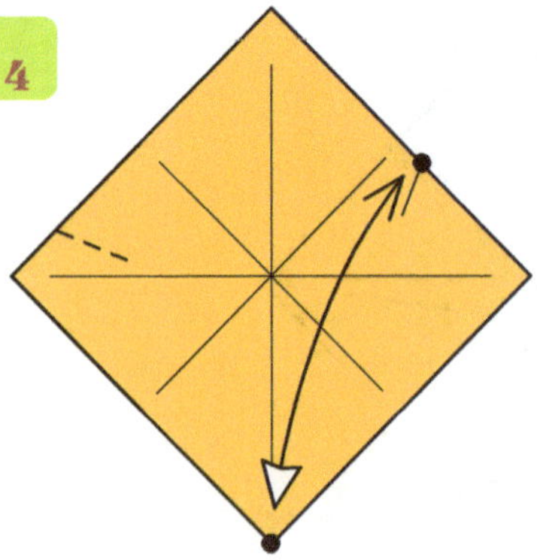

5. Fold and unfold on the diagonal.

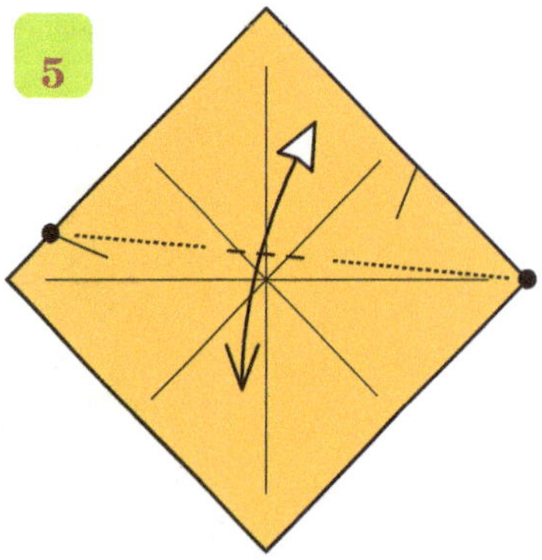

6. Fold and unfold.

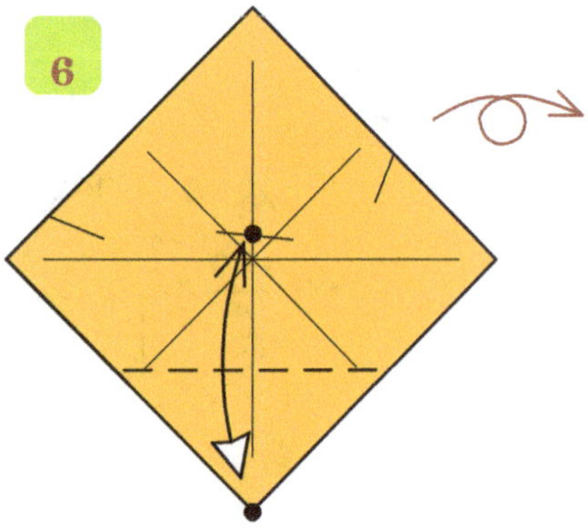

90 *Origami Symphony No. 5*

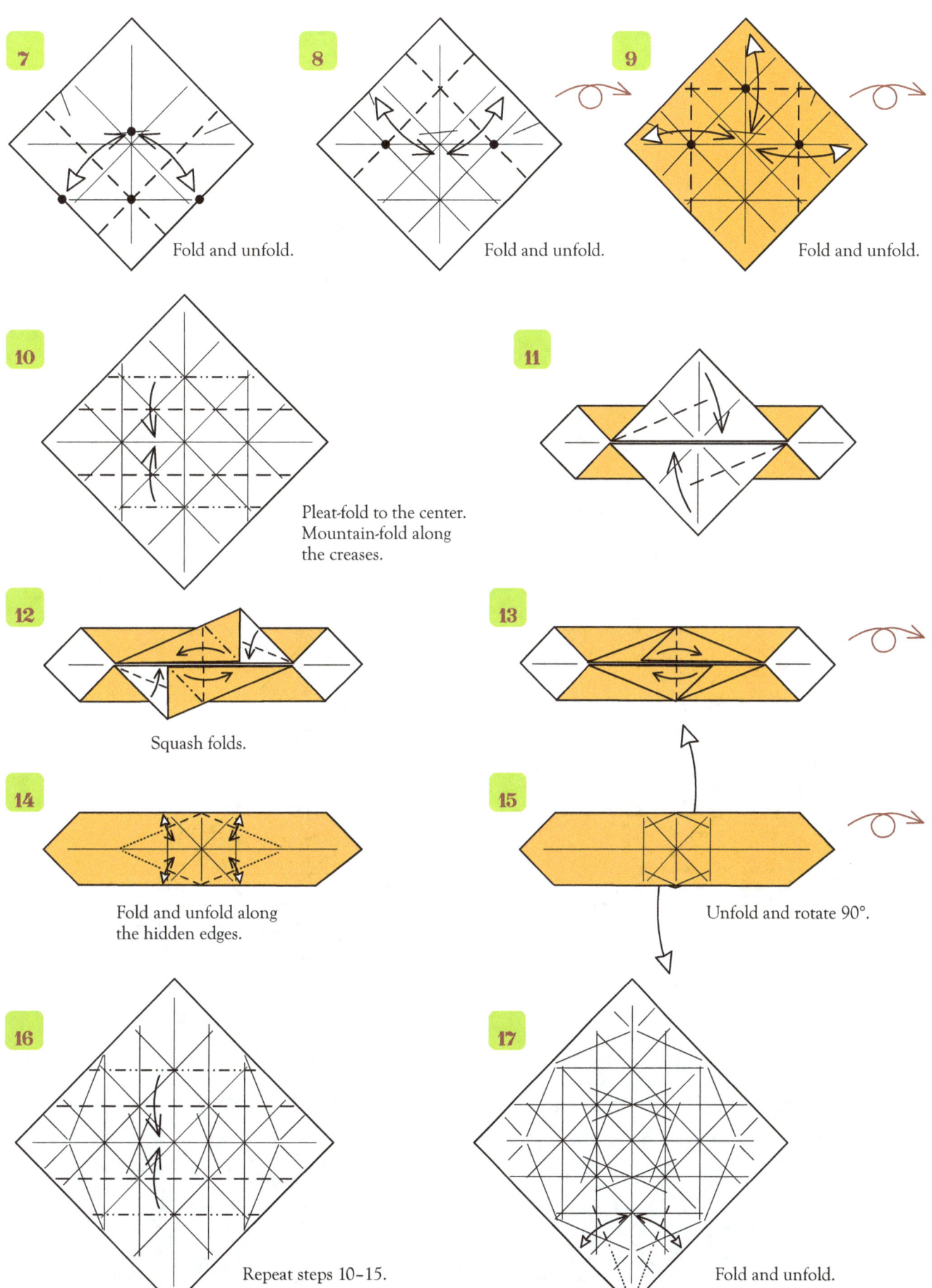

Sunken Rhombic Dodecahedron

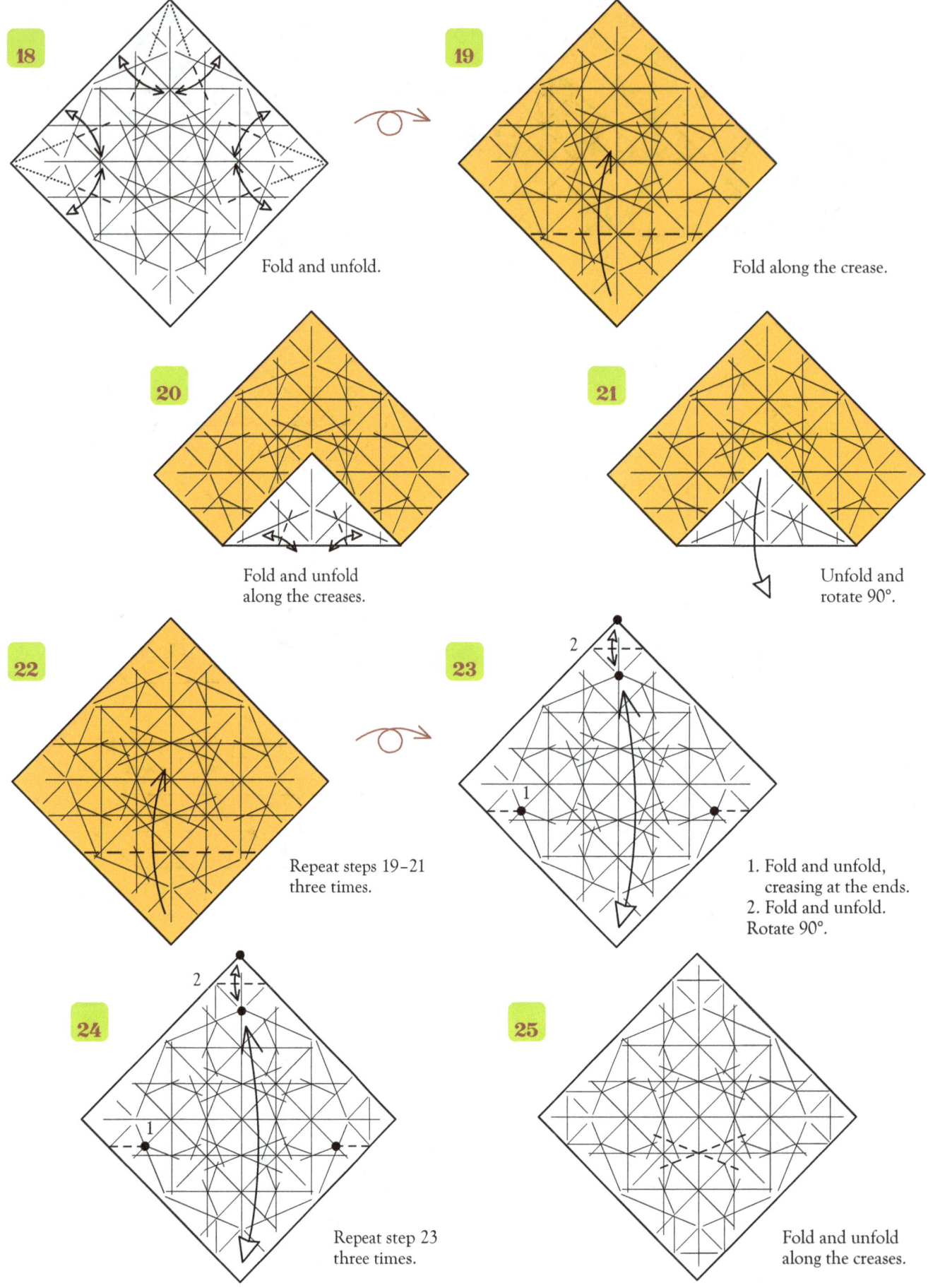

92  Origami Symphony No. 5

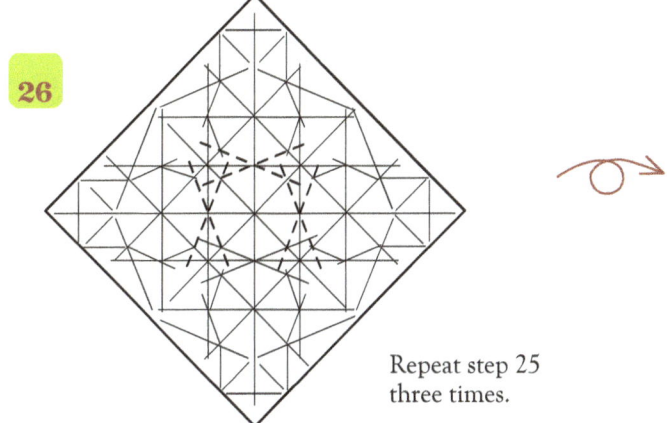

26

Repeat step 25 three times.

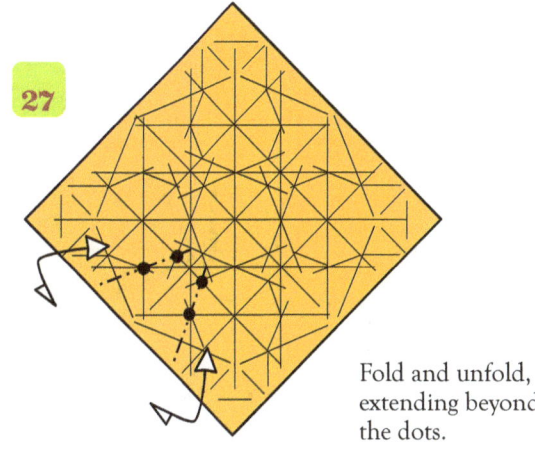

27

Fold and unfold, extending beyond the dots.

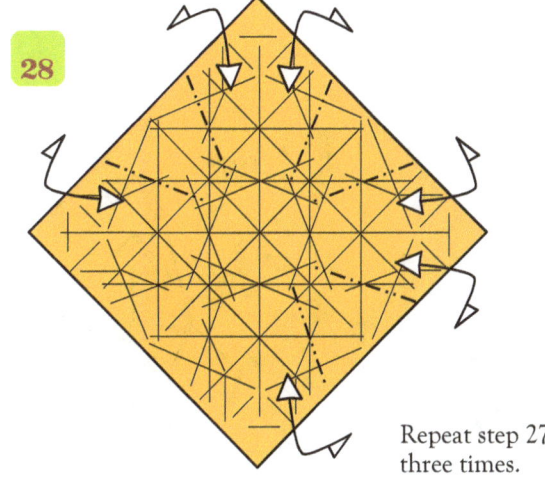

28

Repeat step 27 three times.

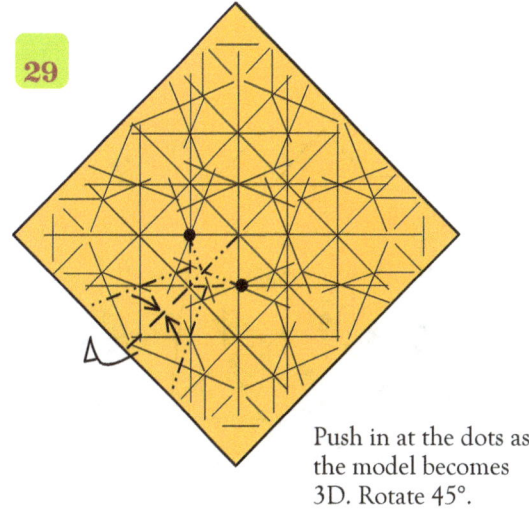

29

Push in at the dots as the model becomes 3D. Rotate 45°.

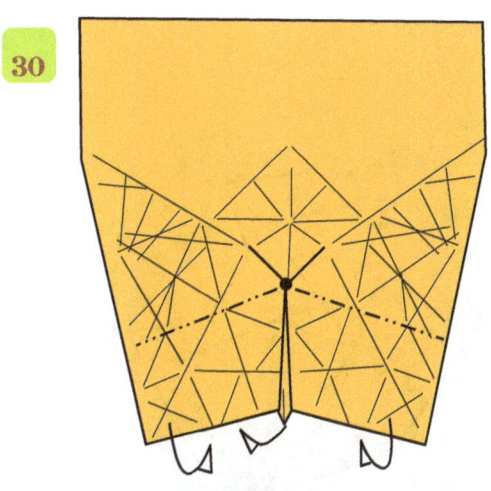

30

Puff out at the dot and fold the hidden layers to the left.

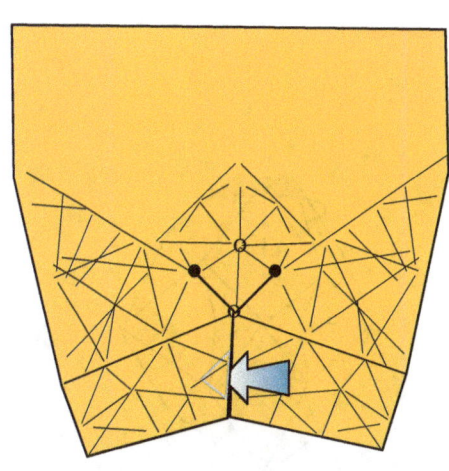

31

The o's are the mountain peaks and the dots are the lowest parts. Note the orientation of the layers. Repeat steps 29–30 three times.

*Sunken Rhombic Dodecahedron* **93**

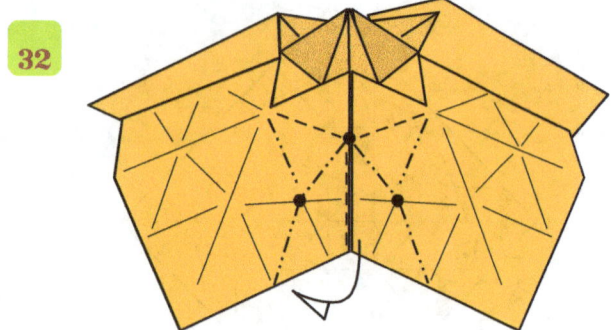

Bring the lower dots together and push in at the upper dot. Flatten inside.

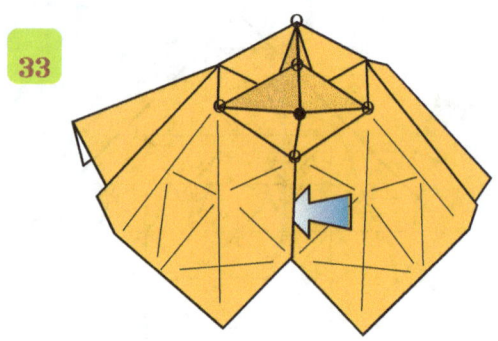

The o's are the mountain peaks and the dot is at the lowest point. Note the orientation of the layers. Repeat step 32 three times. Rotate the top to the bottom.

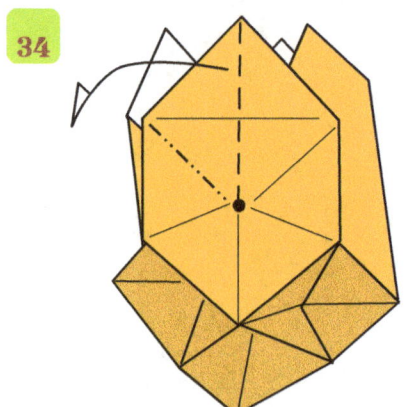

Push in at the dot.

Mountain-fold both layers together.

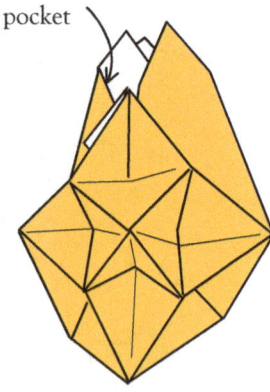

Repeat steps 34–35 three times. Note the pocket.

Tuck the white flap inside the pocket. Repeat three times.

**Sunken Rhombic Dodecahedron**

94 Origami Symphony No. 5

# Sunken Stellated Cube

Each face of a central cube is stellated to produce this star. All the sides are triangles, with angles 45°, 45°, and 90°. Square symmetry is used. The four corners of the square meet at the bottom to form a vertex and lock the star.

**1**

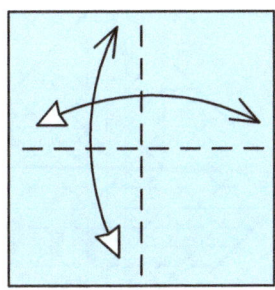

Fold and unfold.

**2**

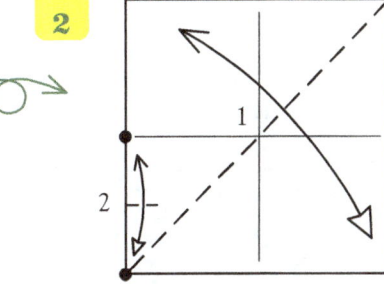

1. Fold and unfold.
2. Fold and unfold on the left.

**3**

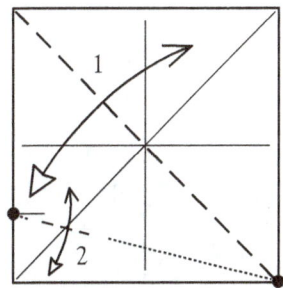

1. Fold and unfold.
2. Fold and unfold on the diagonal. Rotate 180°.

**4**

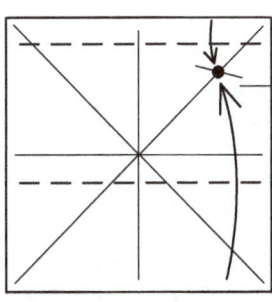

**5**

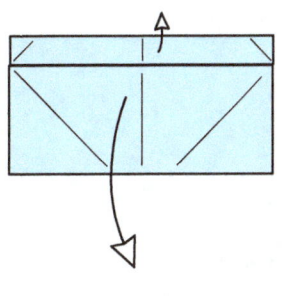

Unfold.

**6**

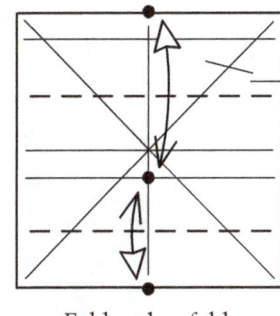

Fold and unfold.

*Sunken Stellated Cube* **95**

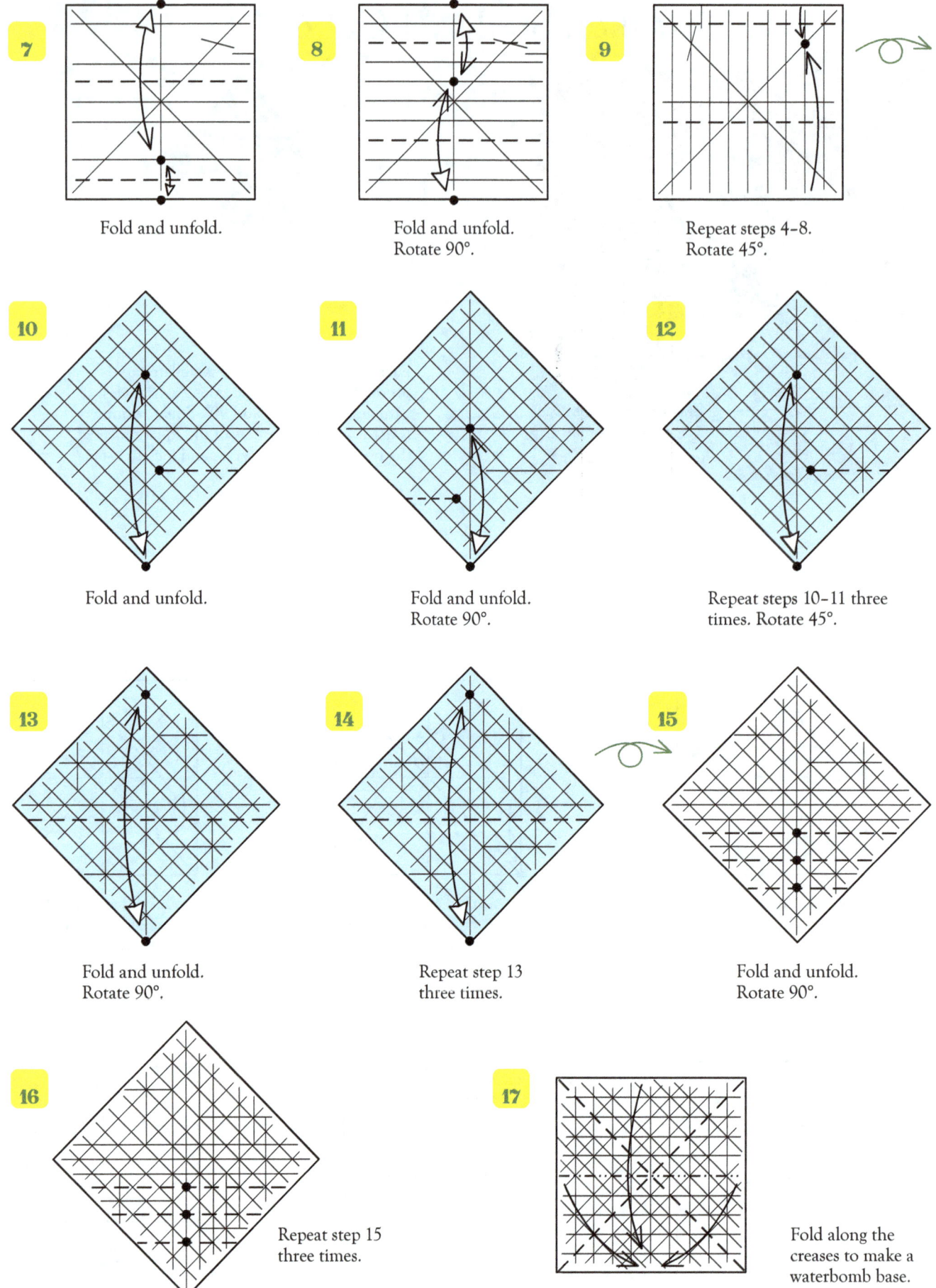

7. Fold and unfold.
8. Fold and unfold. Rotate 90°.
9. Repeat steps 4-8. Rotate 45°.
10. Fold and unfold.
11. Fold and unfold. Rotate 90°.
12. Repeat steps 10-11 three times. Rotate 45°.
13. Fold and unfold. Rotate 90°.
14. Repeat step 13 three times.
15. Fold and unfold. Rotate 90°.
16. Repeat step 15 three times.
17. Fold along the creases to make a waterbomb base.

96 *Origami Symphony No. 5*

18

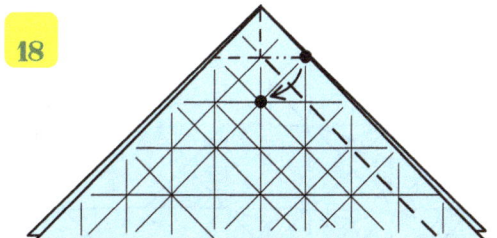

The dots will meet as the model opens. Repeat all around to form a 3D X in the center.

19

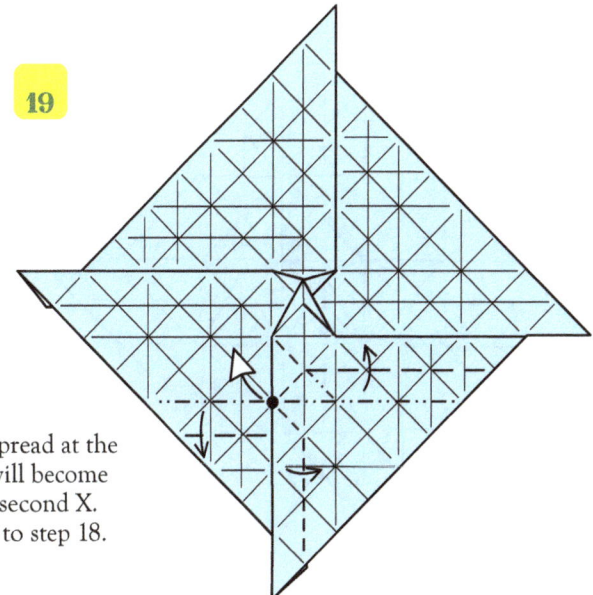

Puff out and spread at the dot. The dot will become the top of the second X. This is similar to step 18.

20

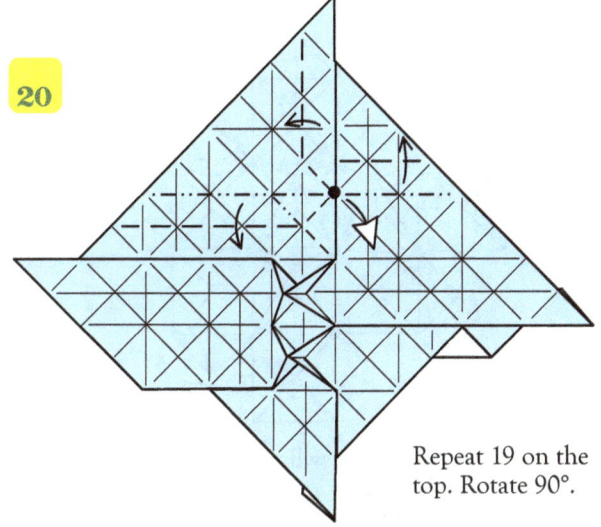

Repeat 19 on the top. Rotate 90°.

21

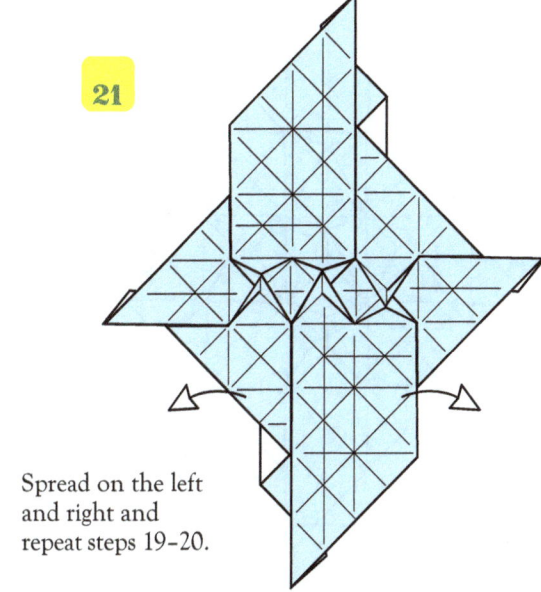

Spread on the left and right and repeat steps 19–20.

22

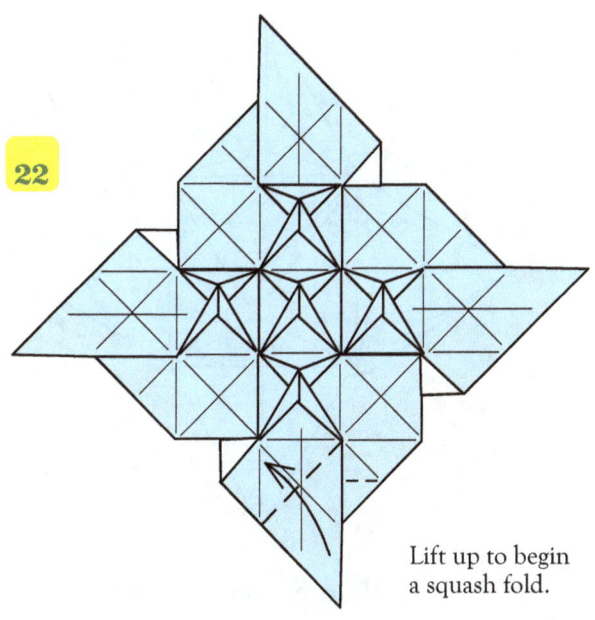

Lift up to begin a squash fold.

23

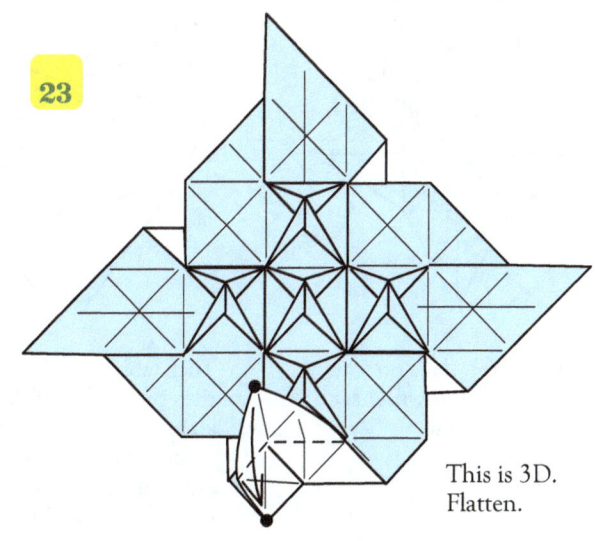

This is 3D. Flatten.

Sunken Stellated Cube **97**

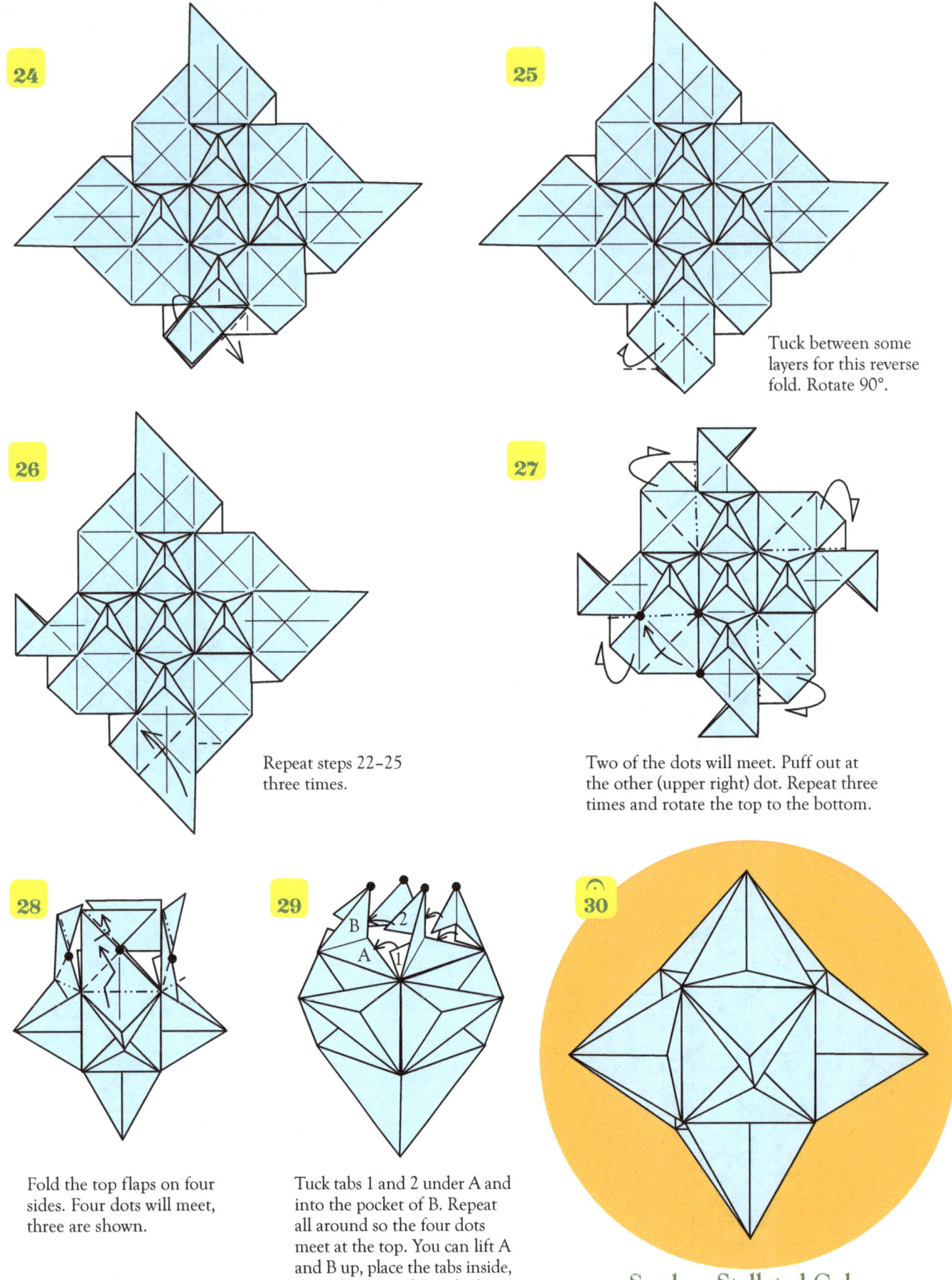

**25.** Tuck between some layers for this reverse fold. Rotate 90°.

**26.** Repeat steps 22–25 three times.

**27.** Two of the dots will meet. Puff out at the other (upper right) dot. Repeat three times and rotate the top to the bottom.

**28.** Fold the top flaps on four sides. Four dots will meet, three are shown.

**29.** Tuck tabs 1 and 2 under A and into the pocket of B. Repeat all around so the four dots meet at the top. You can lift A and B up, place the tabs inside, then close A and B to lock it.

**Sunken Stellated Cube**

Origami Symphony No. 5

# Fourth Movement

## March of the Horns & Antlers

𝄢 Let's journey into mountains, snow covered regions, savannas, and even deserts to find horns and antlers. Horns, found on sheep and antelopes, are made of bone covered by a keratin sheath. Horns grow continuously throughout their lives. Antlers, found mainly on male deer, are branched structures made of bone. Every year the antlers are shed and regrown. Be nimble and be prepared as we encounter these magnificent creatures.

## Musk Ox

Closely related to goats and sheep, the Musk Ox is a social animal that lives in herds. Their strong hooves and multiple layers of fur protect them in their natural habitat in the frozen Arctic tundra. They feed on roots, mosses, seeds, grass, and willows. During the summer, their diet includes the seasonal wild flowers. These massive mammals have a height of four to five feet. When threatened by predators (wolves and bears) they form circles around the young, with their heads facing outward.

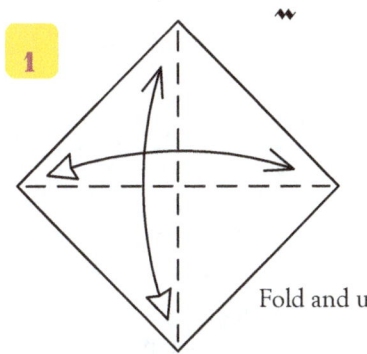

**1.** Fold and unfold.

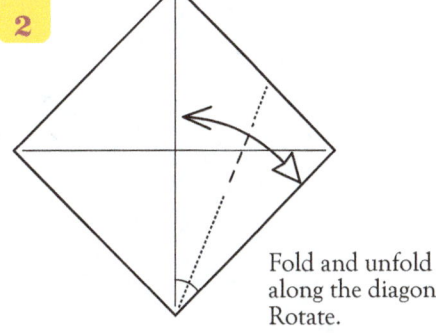

**2.** Fold and unfold along the diagonal. Rotate.

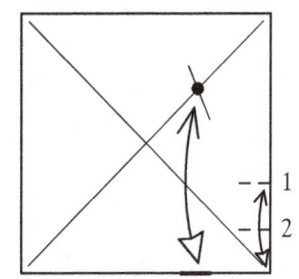

**3.**
1. Bring the bottom to the dot, fold and unfold on the right.
2. Fold and unfold on the right.

*Musk Ox*

**4**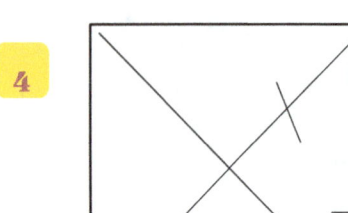

Fold and unfold on the right.

**5**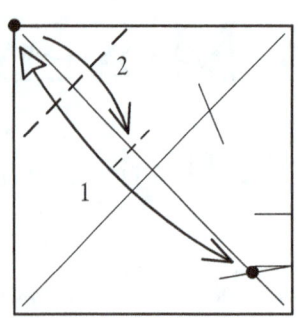

1. Fold and unfold in the center so the dots meet.
2. Fold to the new crease.
Rotate.

**6**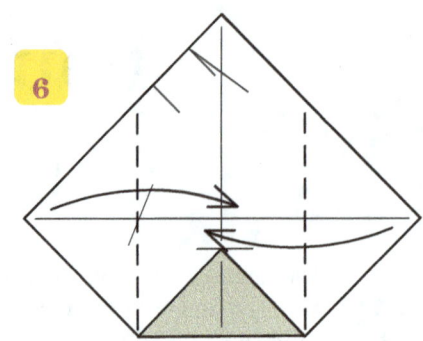

**7**

**8**

**9**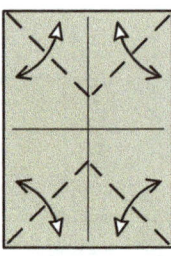

Fold and unfold.

**10**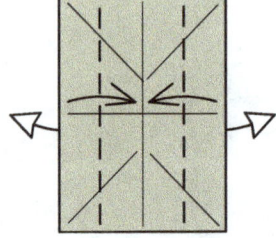

Fold to the center and swing out from behind.

**11**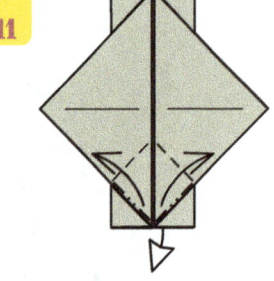

Petal-fold and swing out from behind. Rotate 90°.

**12**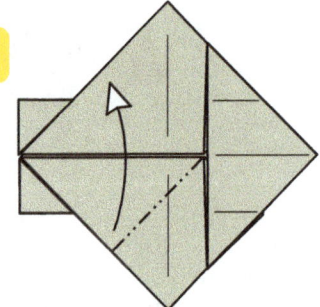

Pull out.

**13**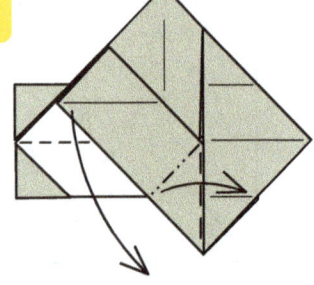

Squash-fold.

**14**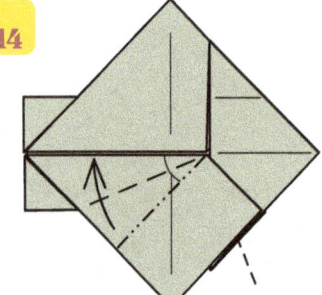

Squash-fold.

**15**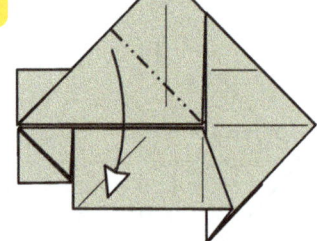

Repeat steps 12–14 on the top.

100 Origami Symphony No. 5

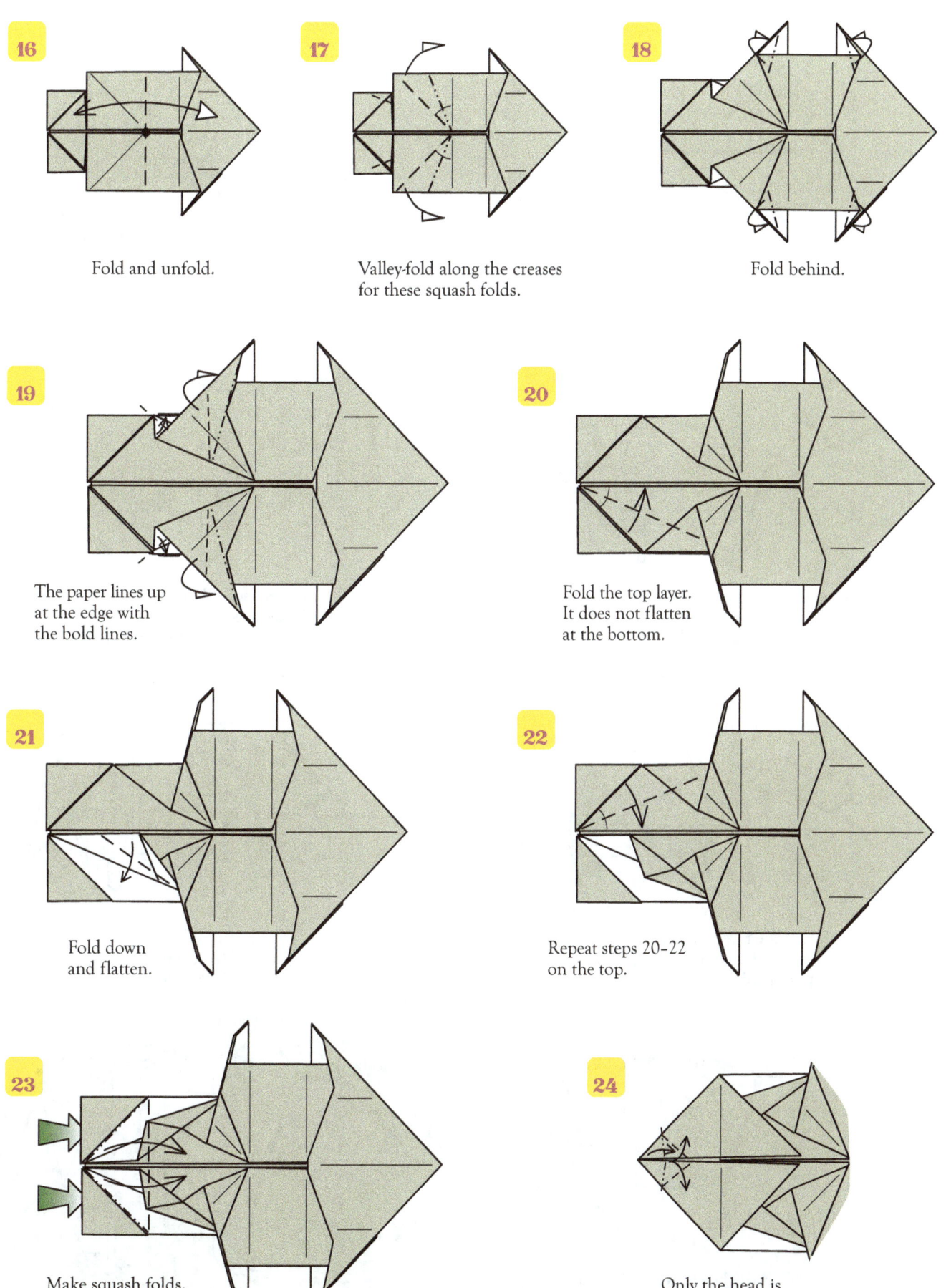

**25**

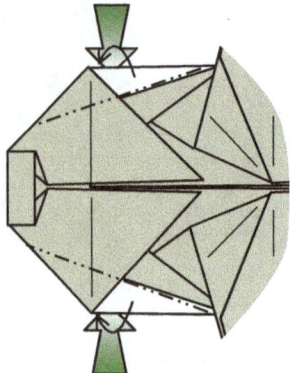

Make reverse folds.

**26**

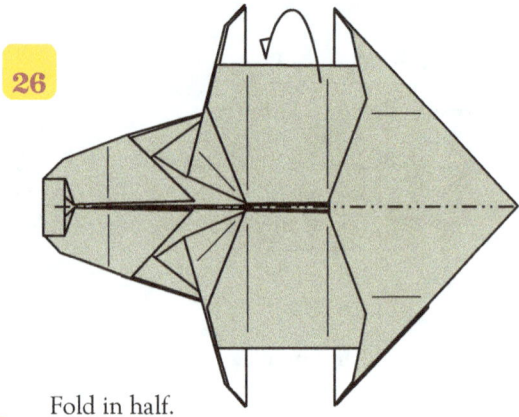

Fold in half.

**27**

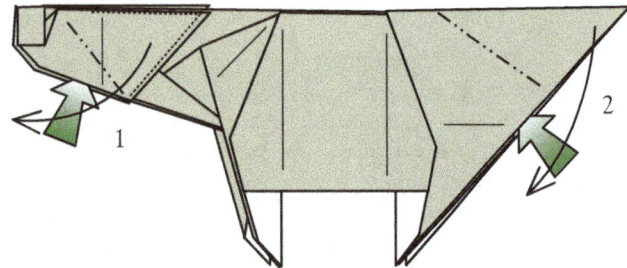

1. Reverse-fold the inner flap to form the beard.
2. Reverse-fold.

**28**

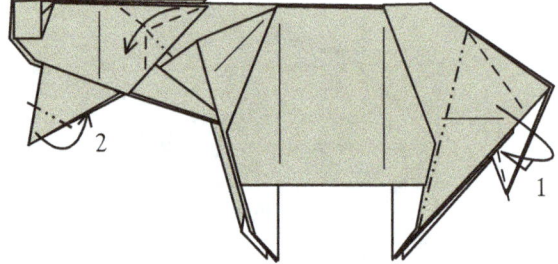

1. Reverse-fold, repeat behind.
2. Reverse-fold.
3. Rabbit-ear, repeat behind.

**29**

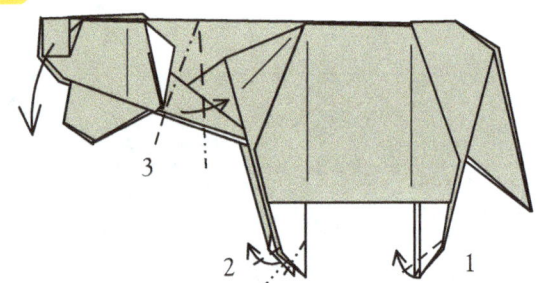

1. Outside-reverse-fold, repeat behind.
2. Squash-fold, repeat beinhd.
3. Crimp-fold.

**30**

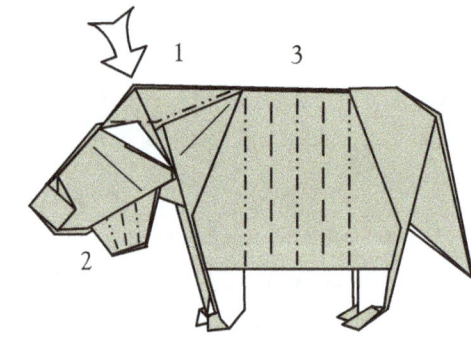

1. Sink.
2. Pleat-fold.
3. Pleat-fold.

**31**

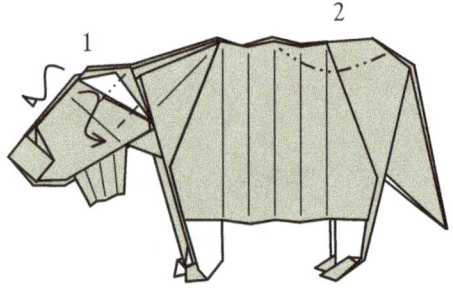

1. Curl the horns, repeat behind.
2. Shape the back.

**32**

Musk Ox

102　*Origami Symphony No. 5*

# Mountain Goat

Mountain Goats are members of the antelope family but are not goats. They live in the alpine and subalpine regions of North America. They are very agile walking around steep cliffs and ledges, and have hooves that are well adapted to these rocky ledges. As the largest mammals in these rocky areas they are protected from predators. Mountain Goats feed on grasses, shrubs, mosses, and other plants. All through their lives, the horns continue to grow. The rings on their horns reveal their ages, which is the number of rings minus one.

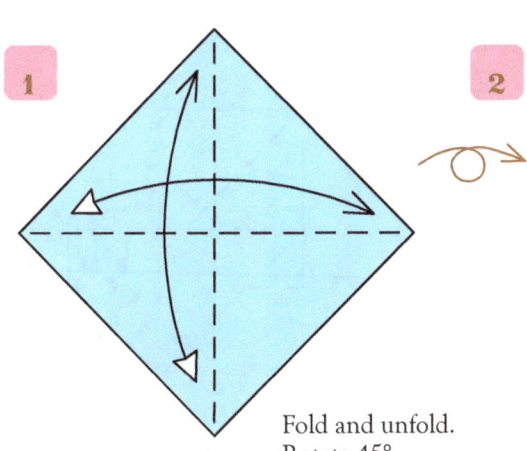

1. Fold and unfold. Rotate 45°.

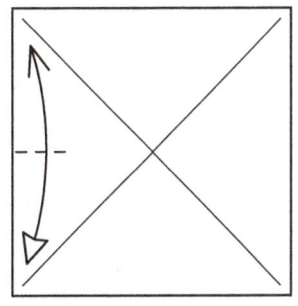

2. Fold and unfold on the left.

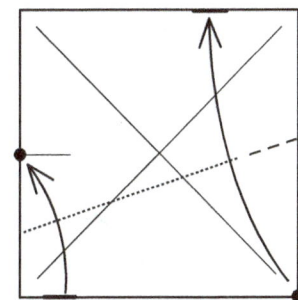

3. Bring the lower right corner to the top edge and the bottom edge to the left center. Crease on the right.

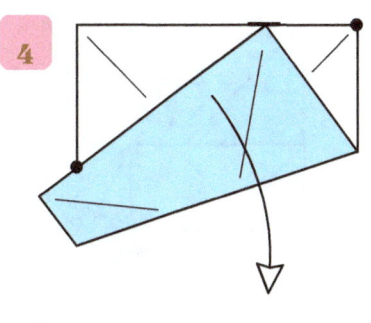

4. Unfold.

5.

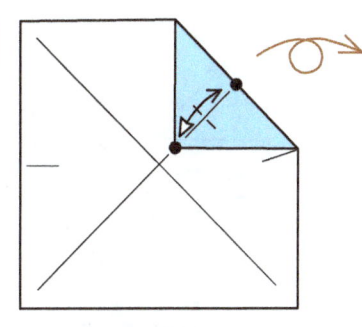

6. Fold and unfold. Rotate 45°.

Mountain Goat 103

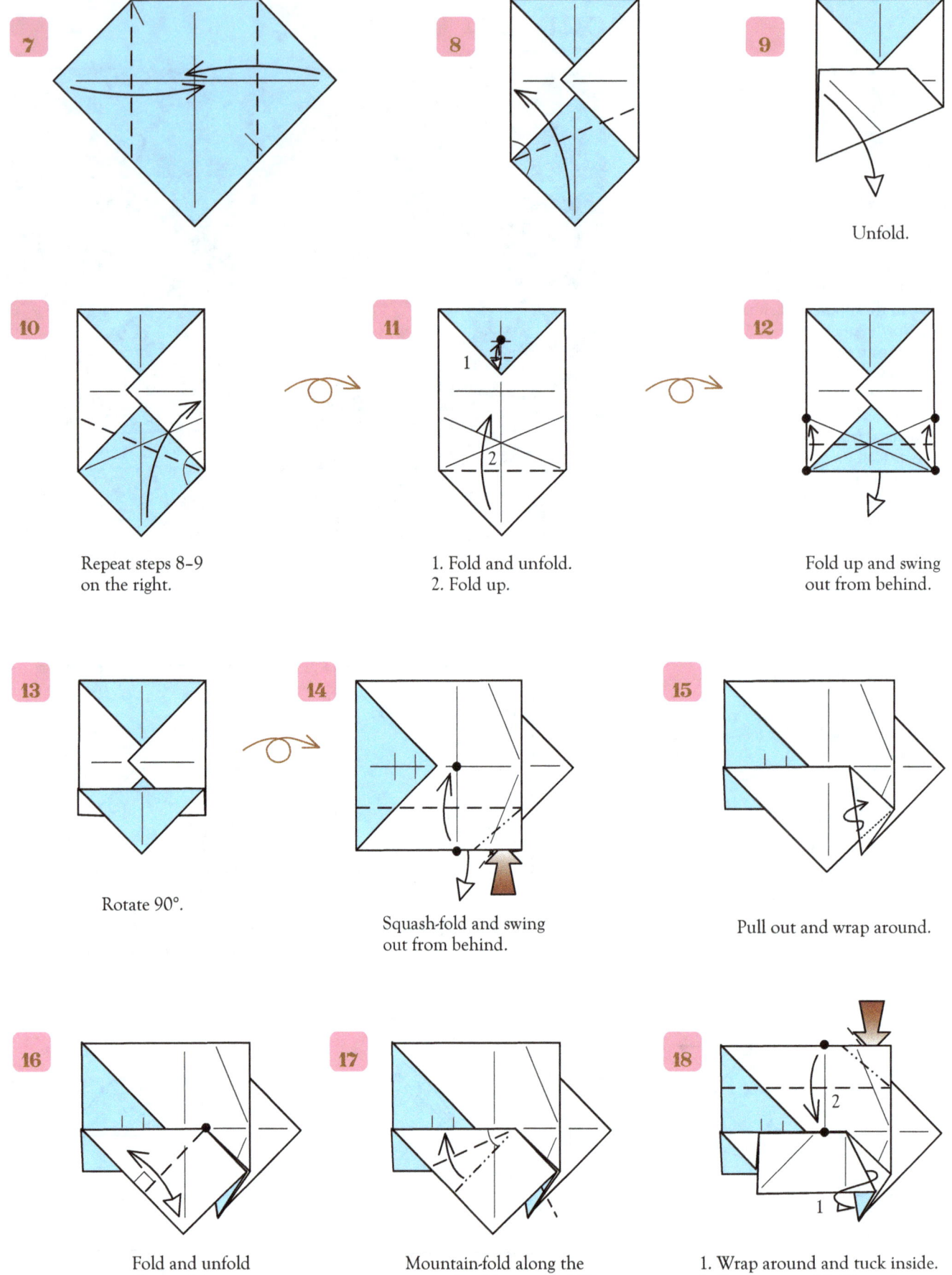

104 Origami Symphony No. 5

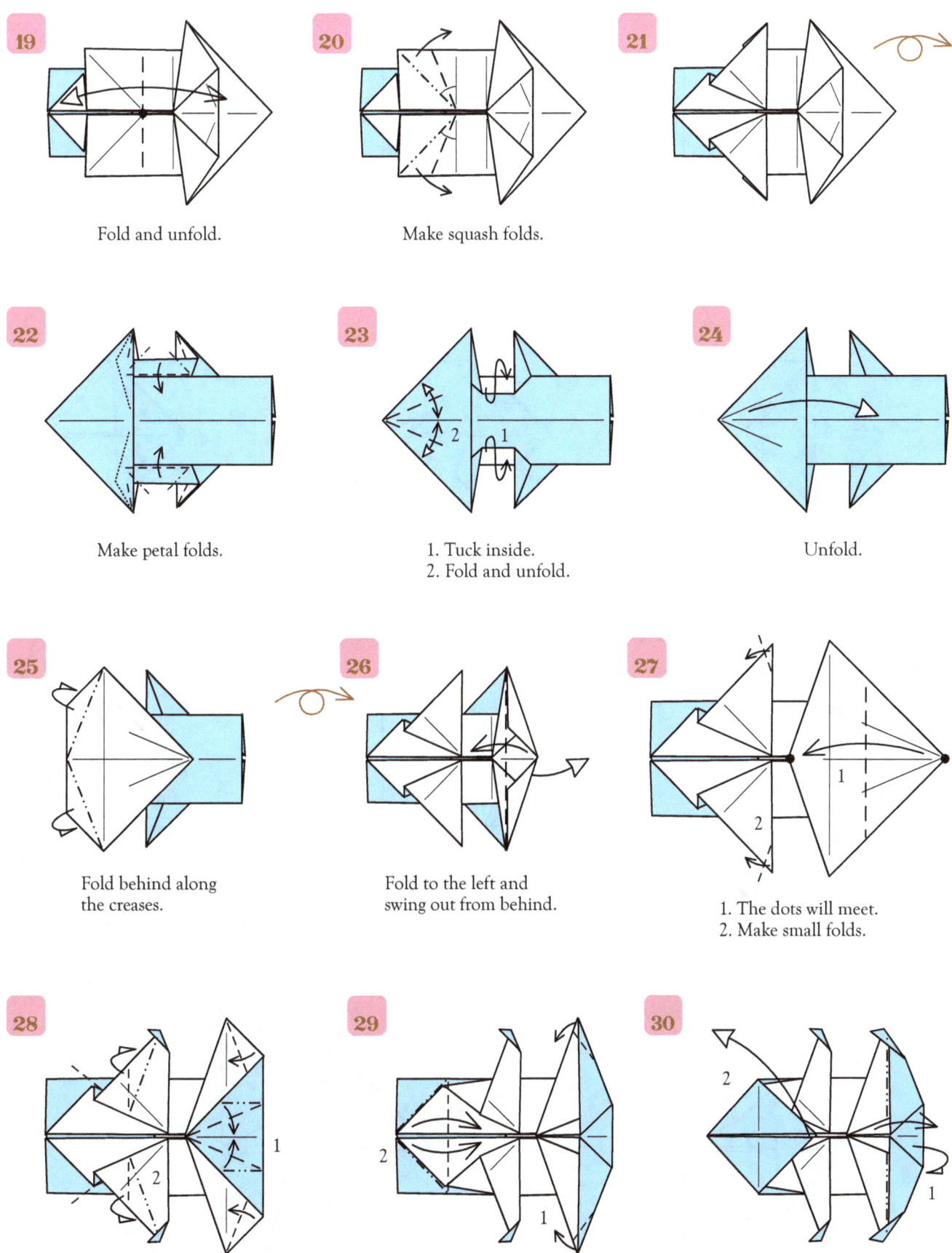

19. Fold and unfold.
20. Make squash folds.
21. 
22. Make petal folds.
23. 1. Tuck inside.
    2. Fold and unfold.
24. Unfold.
25. Fold behind along the creases.
26. Fold to the left and swing out from behind.
27. 1. The dots will meet.
    2. Make small folds.
28. 1. Make squash folds.
    2. Thin the legs.
29. 1. Make small folds.
    2. Make squash folds.
30. 1. Fold behind.
    2. Pull out the hidden corner.

*Mountain Goat*

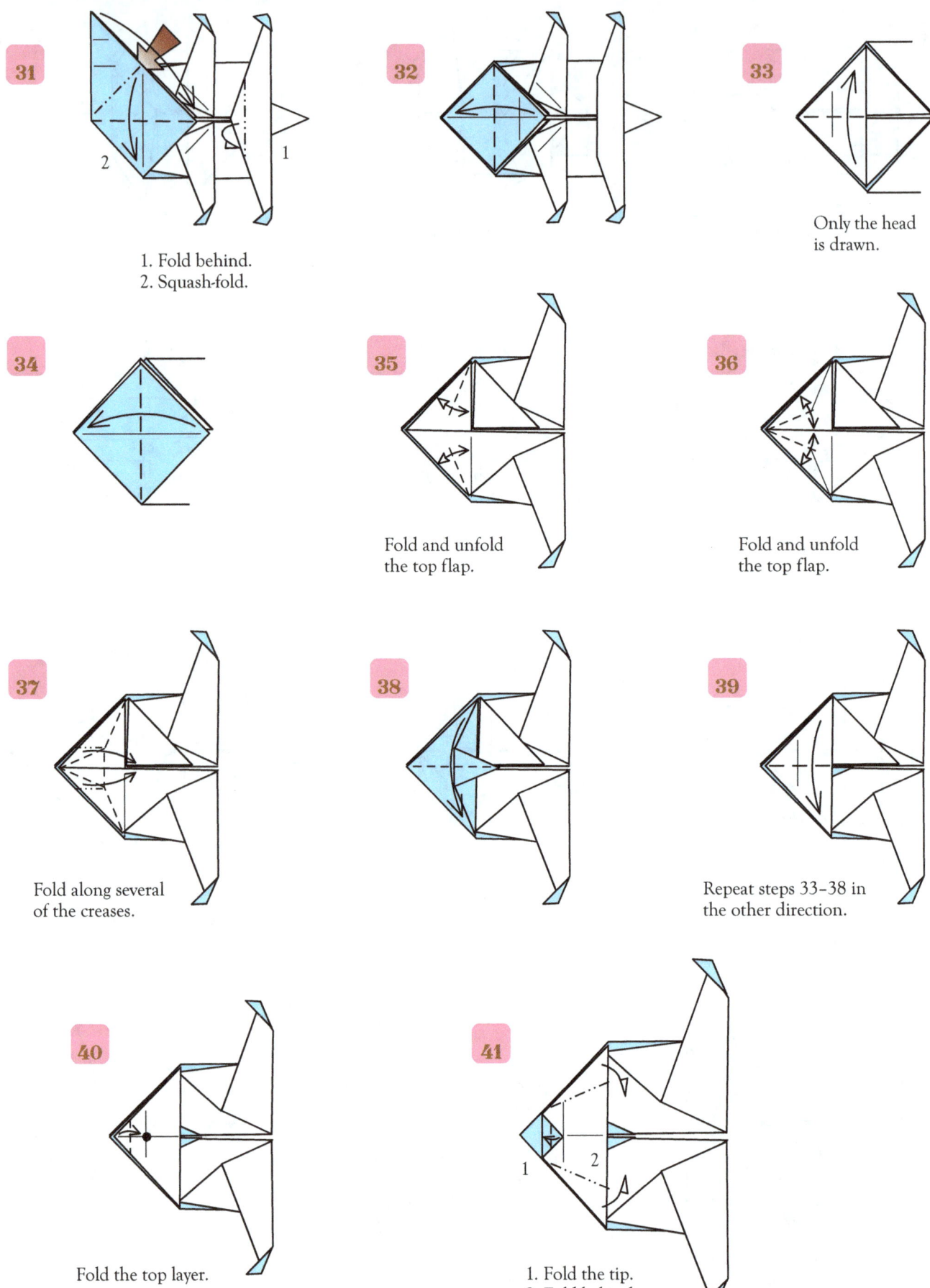

106 Origami Symphony No. 5

**42**

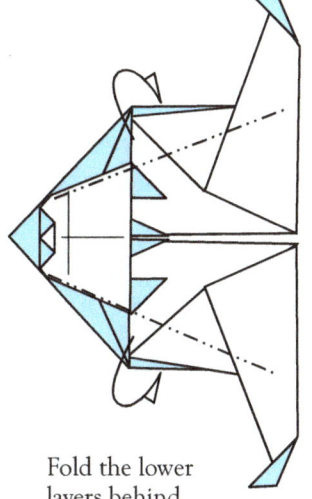

Fold the lower layers behind.

**43**

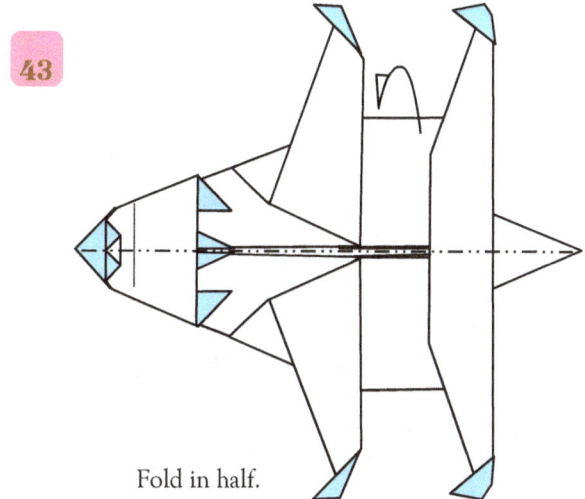

Fold in half.

**44**

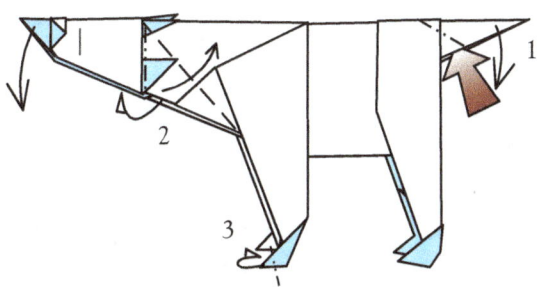

1. Reverse-fold.
2. Crimp-fold.
3. Fold behind, repeat behind.

**45**

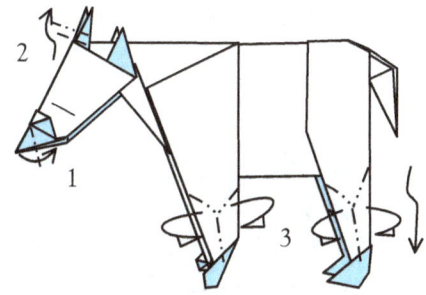

1. Reverse-fold.
2. Shape the horns, repeat behind.
3. Shape the legs, repeat behind.

**46**

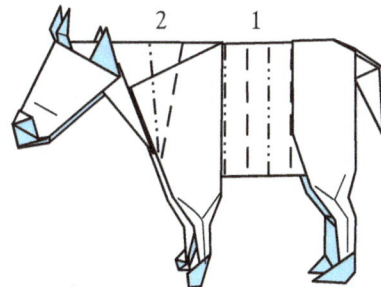

Make pleat folds.

**47**

Mountain Goat

Mountain Goat **107**

# Antelope

Found mostly in Africa and Asia, Antelopes are hoofed animals that look like deer. While all the males have horns, some females do not. Their horns continue to grow throughout their lives. Found in grasslands, woodlands, savannas, and other open spaces, they feed on grass, seeds, and other plants. They can hear and smell very well, which protects them from predators. When they detect the predators, they run quickly.

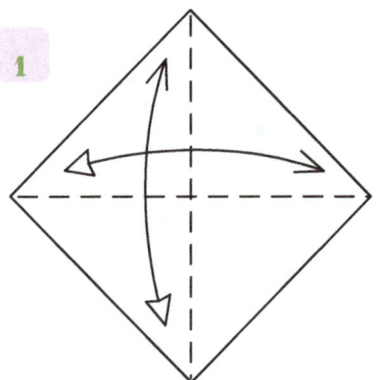

Fold and unfold.

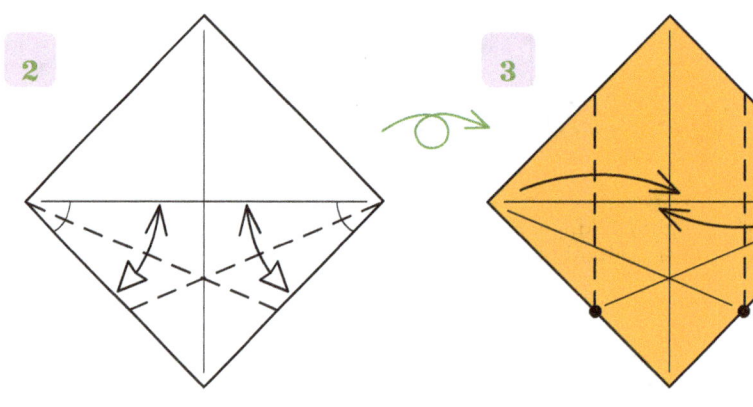

Fold and unfold.

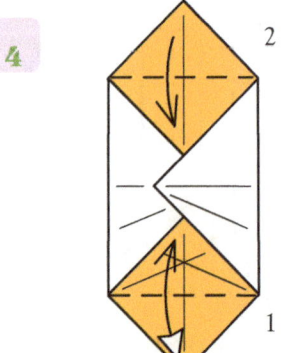

1. Fold and unfold.
2. Valley-fold.

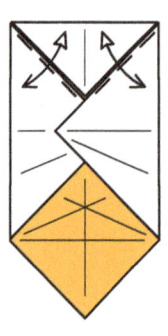

Fold and unfold

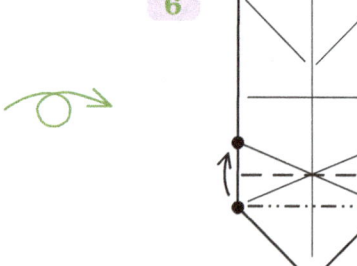

Pleat-fold.

108   Origami Symphony No. 5

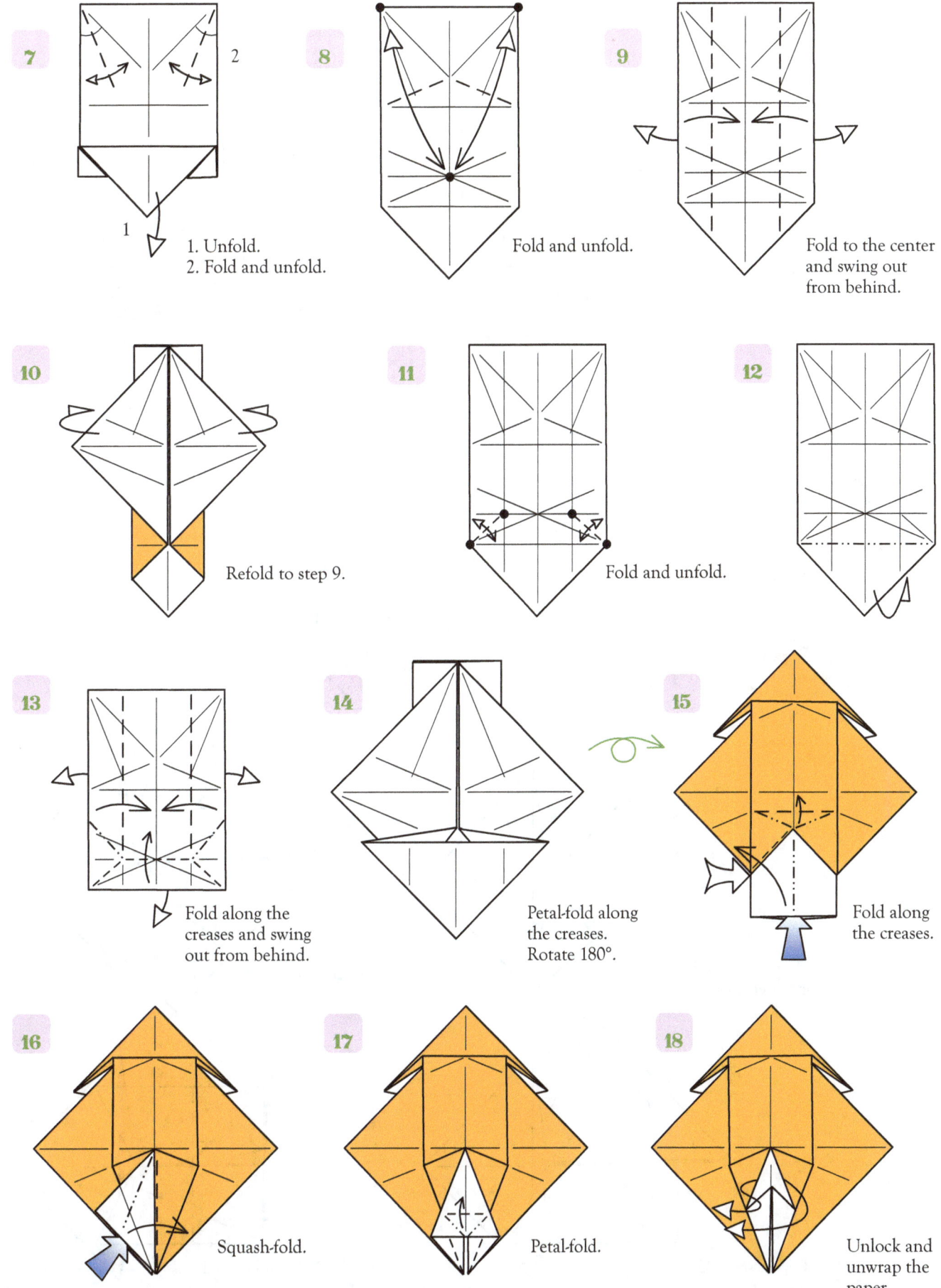

Antelope 109

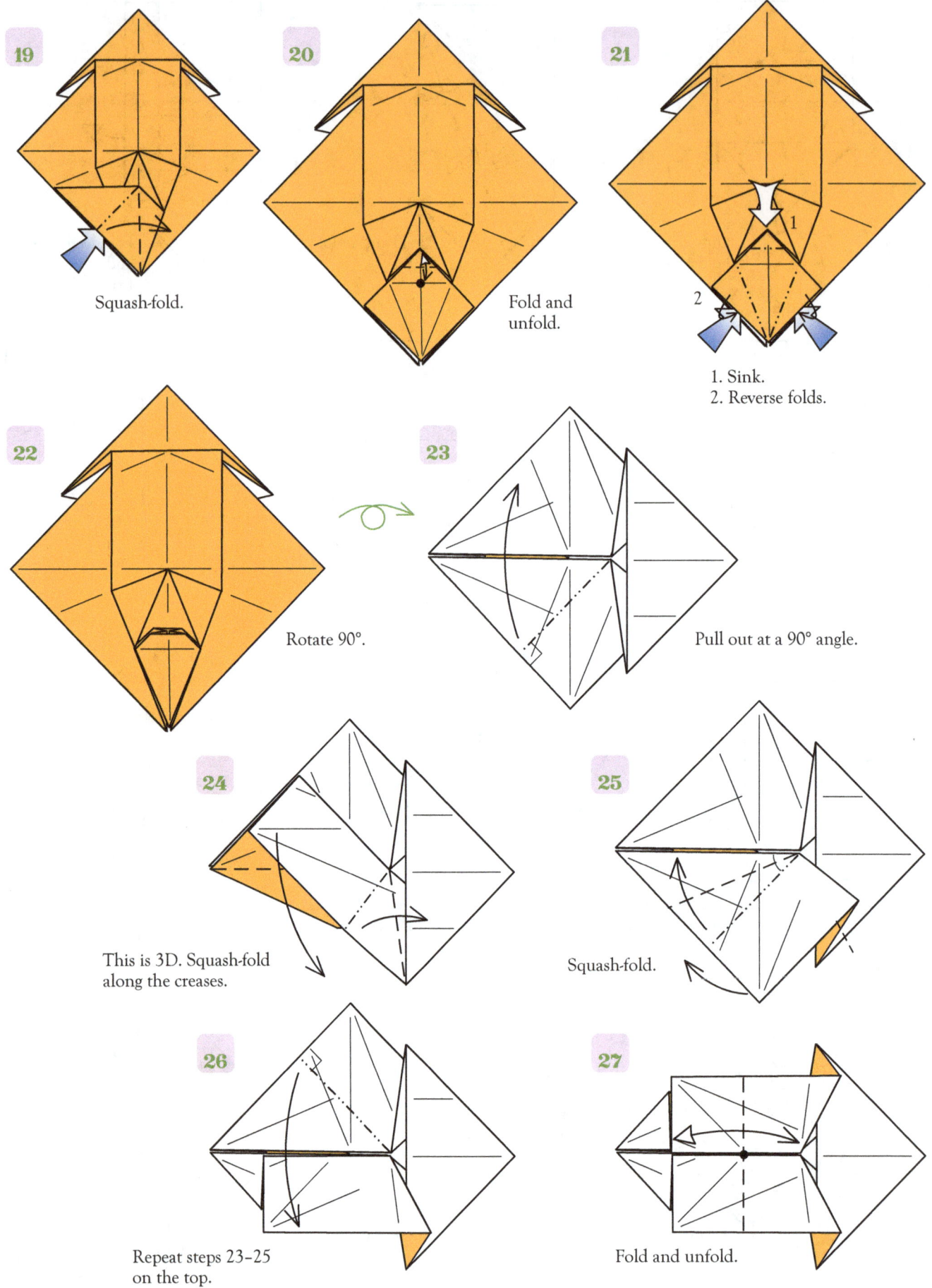

110  Origami Symphony No. 5

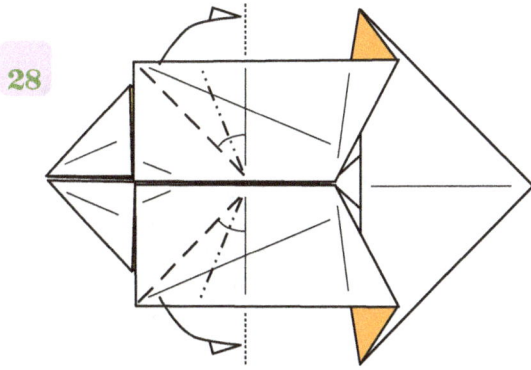

28
Make squash folds.

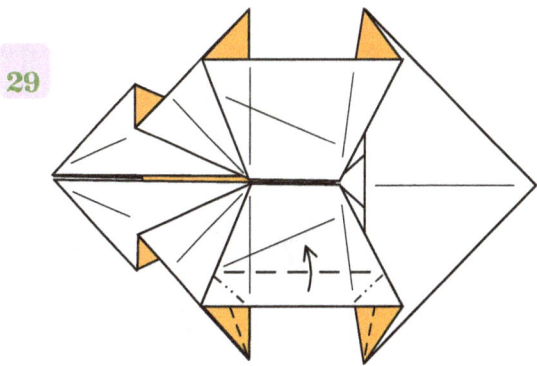

29
Petal-fold.

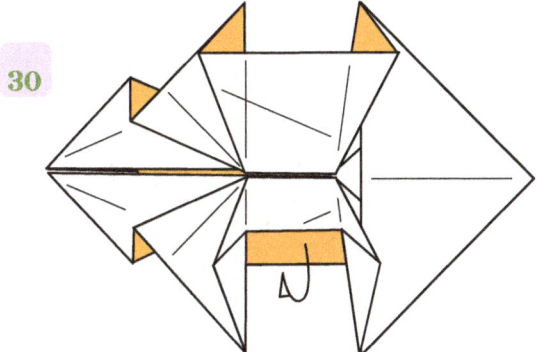

30
Wrap around.

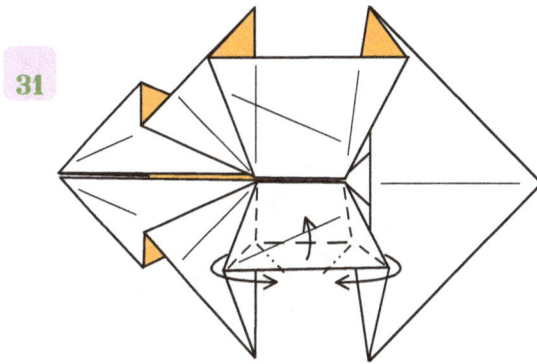

31
Lift up in the center while folding the flaps inward.

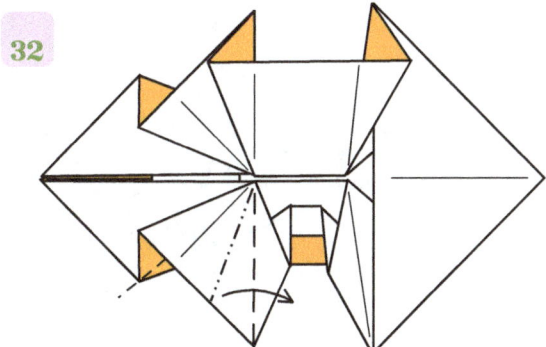

32
Squash-fold.

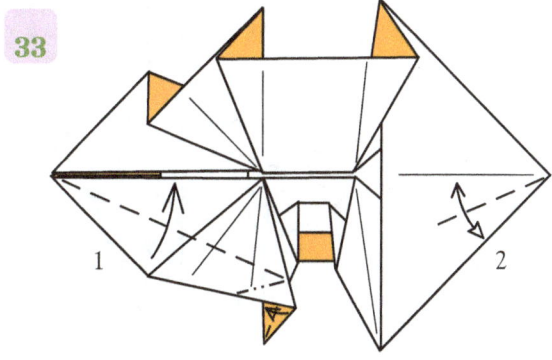

33
1. Squash-fold.
2. Fold and unfold.

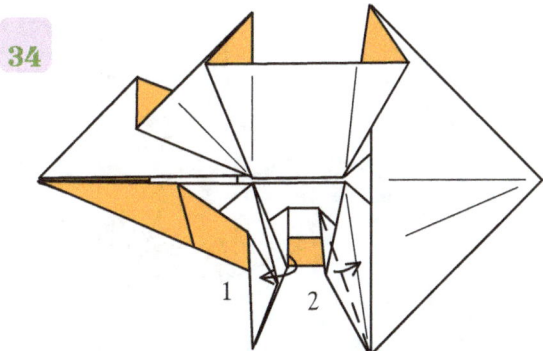

34
1. Wrap around.
2. Valley-fold.

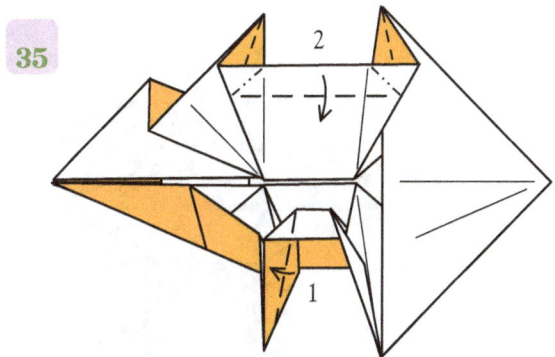

35
1. Valley-fold.
2. Repeat steps 29–35 on the top.

Antelope **111**

**36**

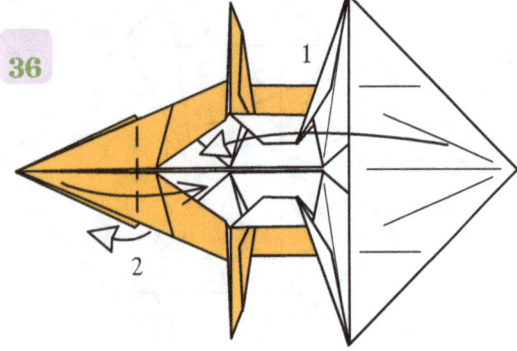

1. Unfold.
2. Fold to the right and swing out from behind.

**37**

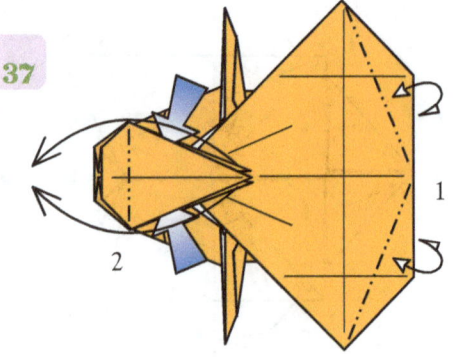

1. Fold and unfold.
2. Make reverse folds.

**38**

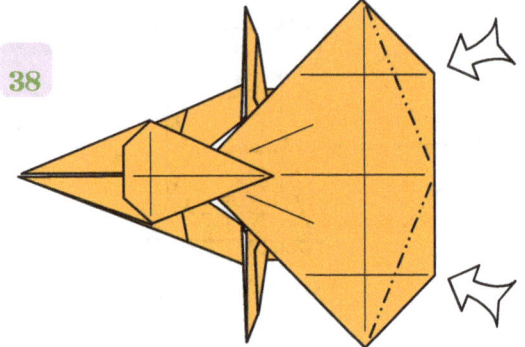

Sink.

**39**

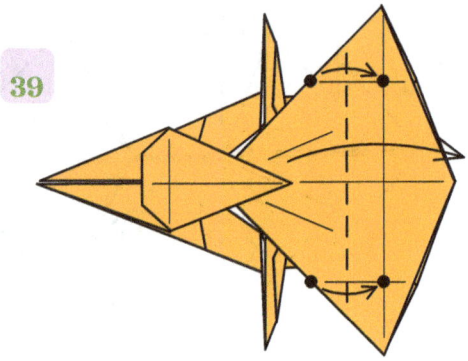

**40**

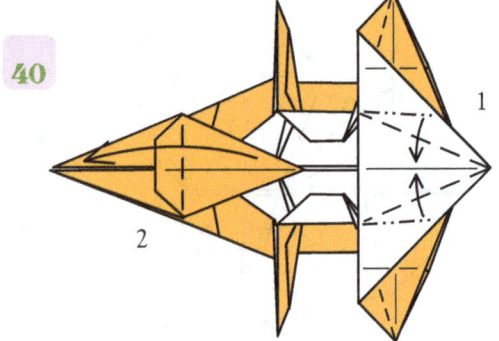

1. Make squash folds.
2. Valley-fold.

**41**

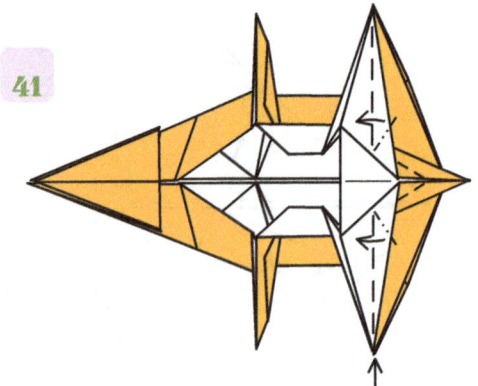

Make thin squash folds. Fold along a vertical line, shown by the arrow at the bottom.

**42**

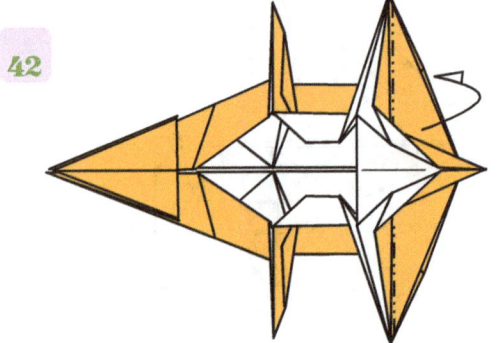

**43**

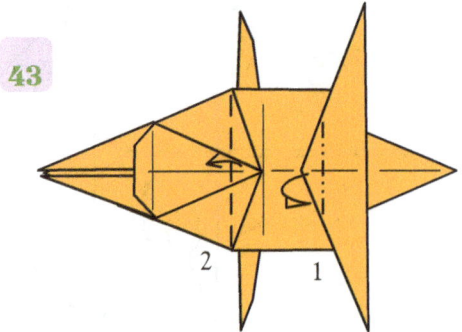

1. Mountain-fold.
2. Valley-fold.

112 Origami Symphony No. 5

**44**

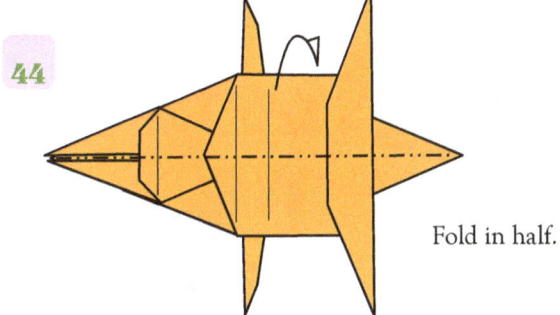

Fold in half.

**45**

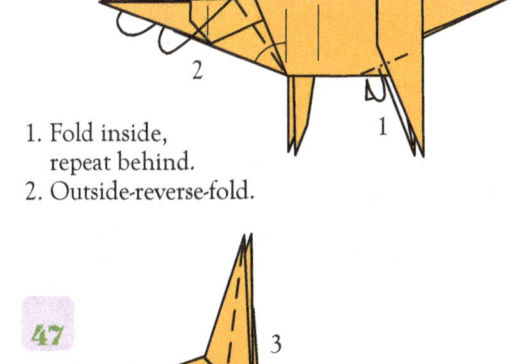

1. Fold inside, repeat behind.
2. Outside-reverse-fold.

**46**

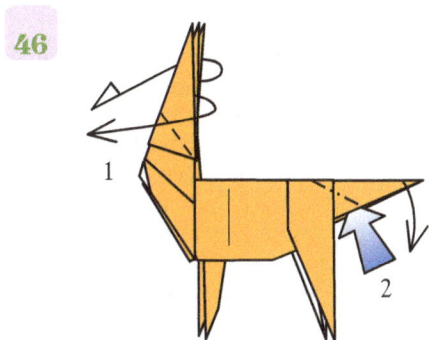

1. Outside-reverse-fold.
2. Reverse-fold.

**47**

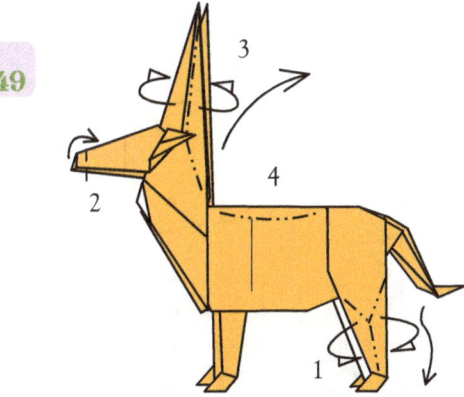

1. Reverse-fold.
2. Make squash folds, repeat behind.
3. Rabbit-ear, repeat behind.

**48**

1. Repeat behind.
2. Reverse-fold.
3. Thin the tail, repeat behind.

**49**

1. Shape the legs, repeat behind.
2. Outside-reverse-fold.
3. Shape the horns, repeat behind.
4. Shape the back

**50**

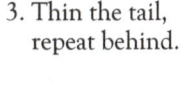

Antelope

Antelope 113

# Arabian Oryx

The Arabian Oryx is a desert antelope. It became extinct in the wild and was reintroduced to the Arabian Peninsula in 1980. Well adapted for the desert, its white fur reflects the sun, the wide feet help it stay on the desert sand, and it can survive without water for extended periods of time. The Oryx can smell rain from far away. Leading a nomadic life, herds wander around in search of rain and more grass, roots, and other vegetation they feed upon.

1.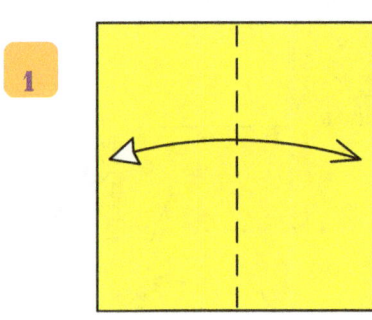

Fold and unfold.

2.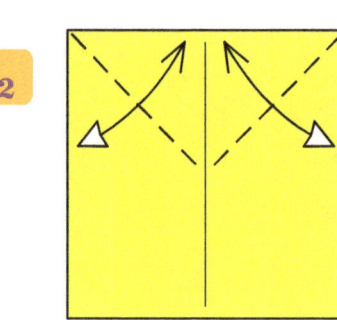

Fold and unfold.

3.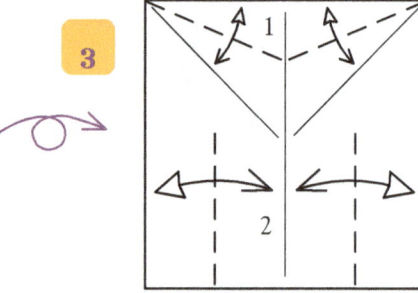

1. Fold and unfold.
2. Fold and unfold.

4.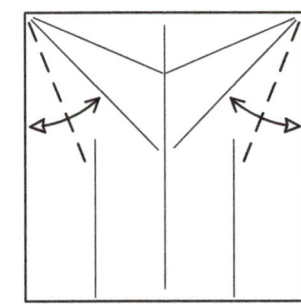

Fold and unfold.
Rotate 90°.

5.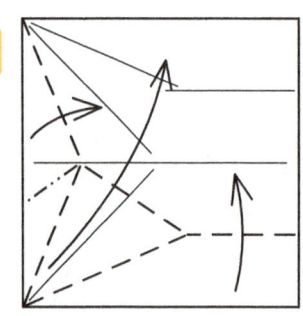

Fold along several of the creases.

6.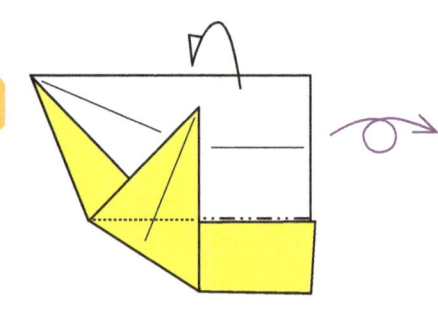

114   Origami Symphony No. 5

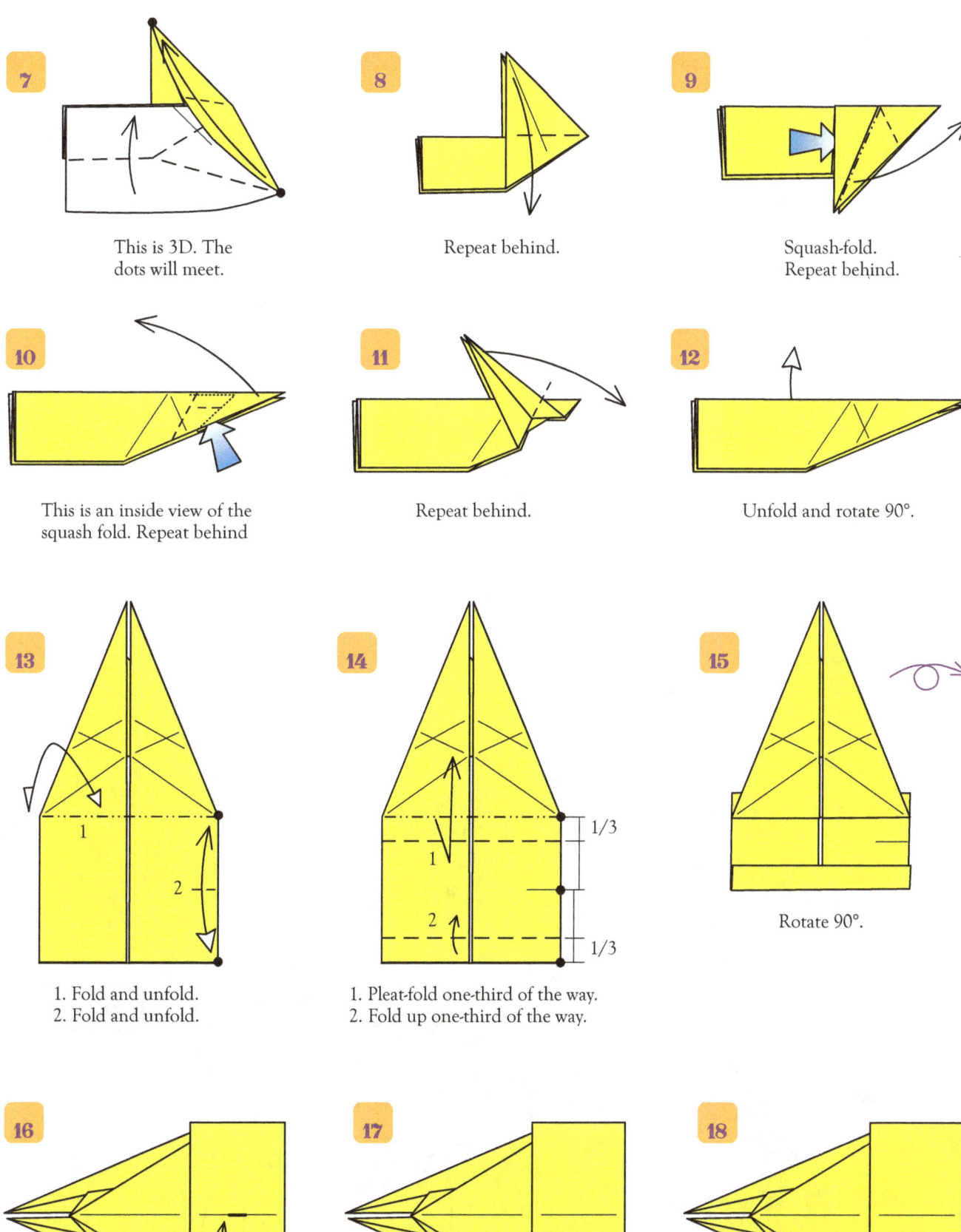

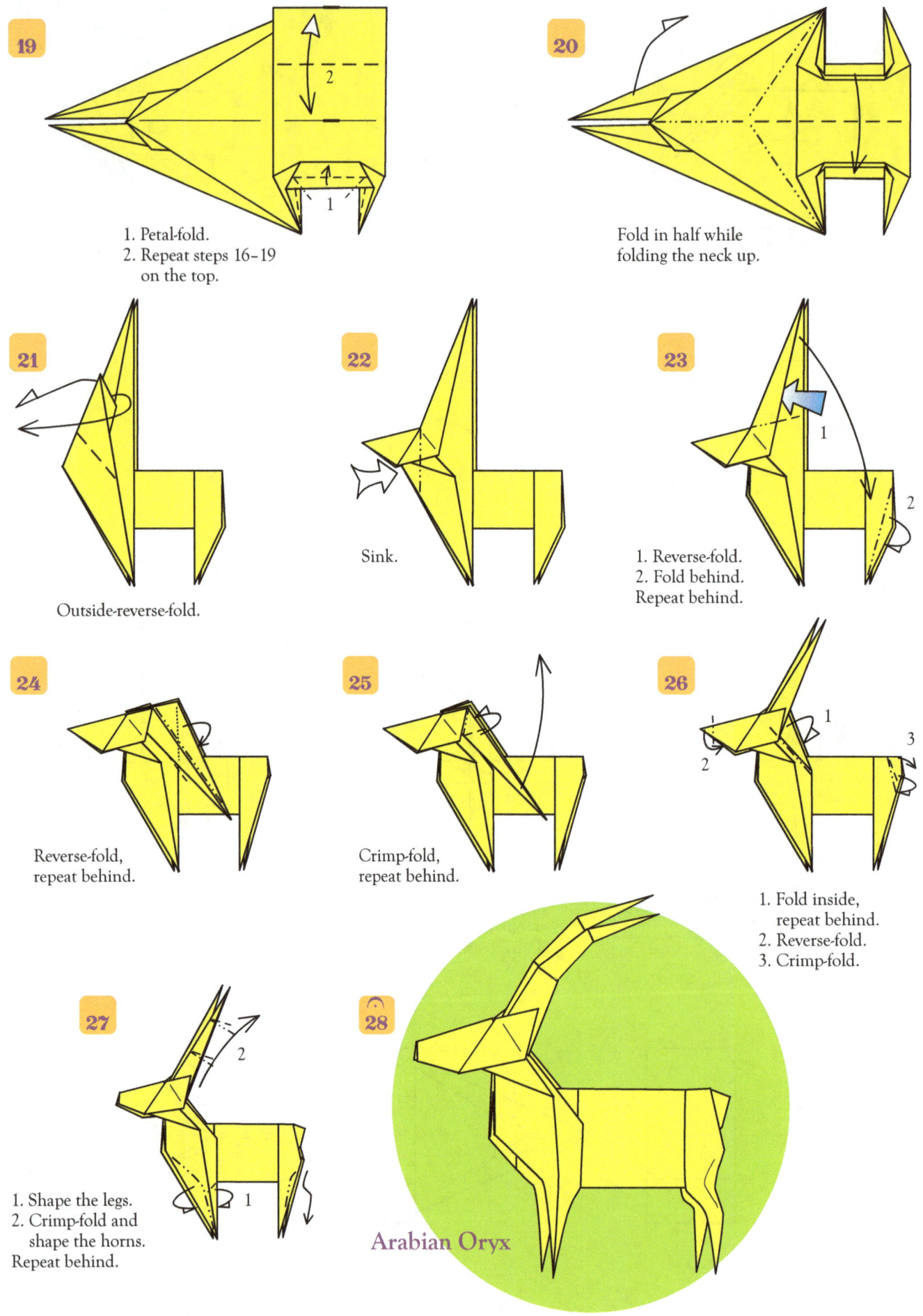

# Bighorn Sheep

Bighorn Sheep live in mountain slopes, alpine meadows, and deserts of North America. They are adapted for climbing in steep rocky mountain regions. Unlike most sheep, they can jump over 30 feet from ledge to ledge. They live in herds and feed on seeds, grass, and plants. Named for their massive horns, a pair of horns can weigh 30 pounds.

Begin with step 23 of the Arabian Oryx (page 114).

**1**

1. Reverse-fold.
2. Fold behind.
Repeat behind.
Continue with steps 24–27 for the head of the Oryx.

**2**

1. Crimp-fold.
2. Make a small squash fold, repeat behind.

**3**

1. Curl the horns with inside and outside reverse folds.
2. Shape the hind legs.
3. Shape the front legs and hooves.
Repeat behind.

**4**

Bighorn Sheep

Bighorn Sheep 117

# White-tailed Deer

The White-tailed Deer is found in great abundance throughout North America. It is the smallest deer in North America. It feeds on grass, mushroom, twigs, bark, and other plants. Every winter, they shed and regrow their antlers.

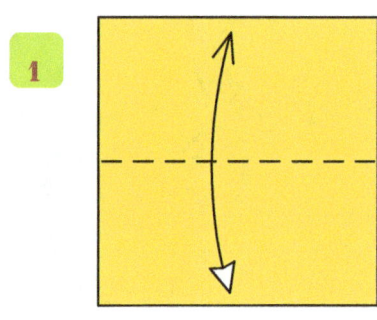

1

Fold and unfold.

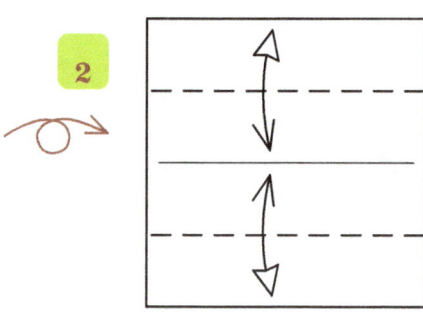

2

Fold and unfold.

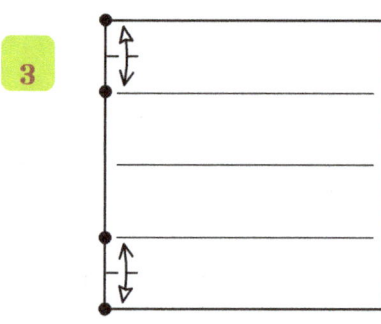

3

Fold and unfold on the left. Rotate 90°.

4

Fold in half.

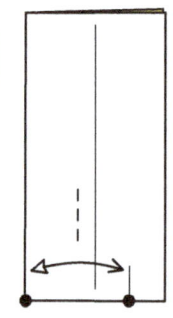

5

Fold and unfold.

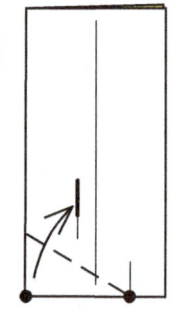

6

Bring the corner to the line.

7

118 Origami Symphony No. 5

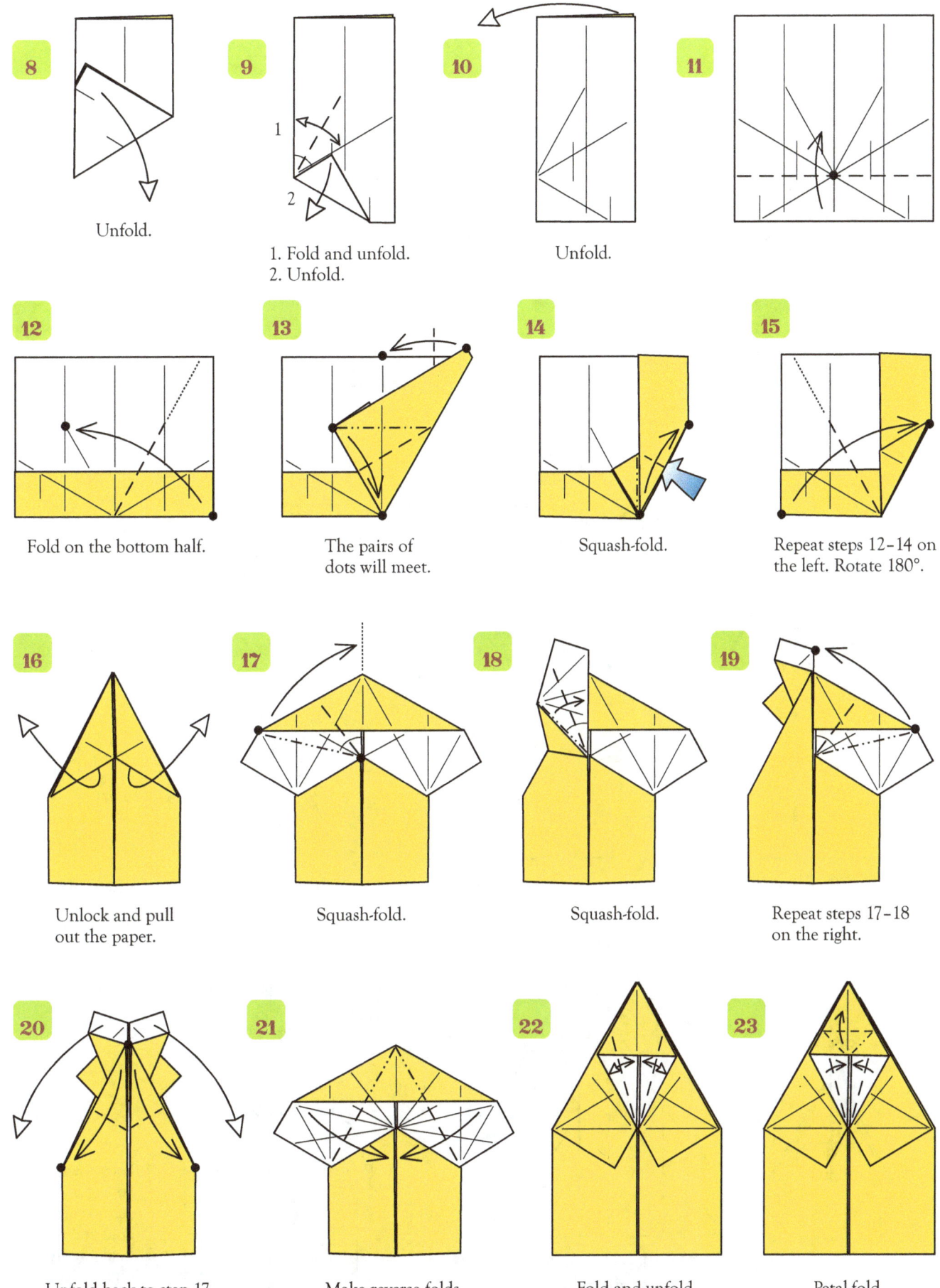

White-tailed Deer 119

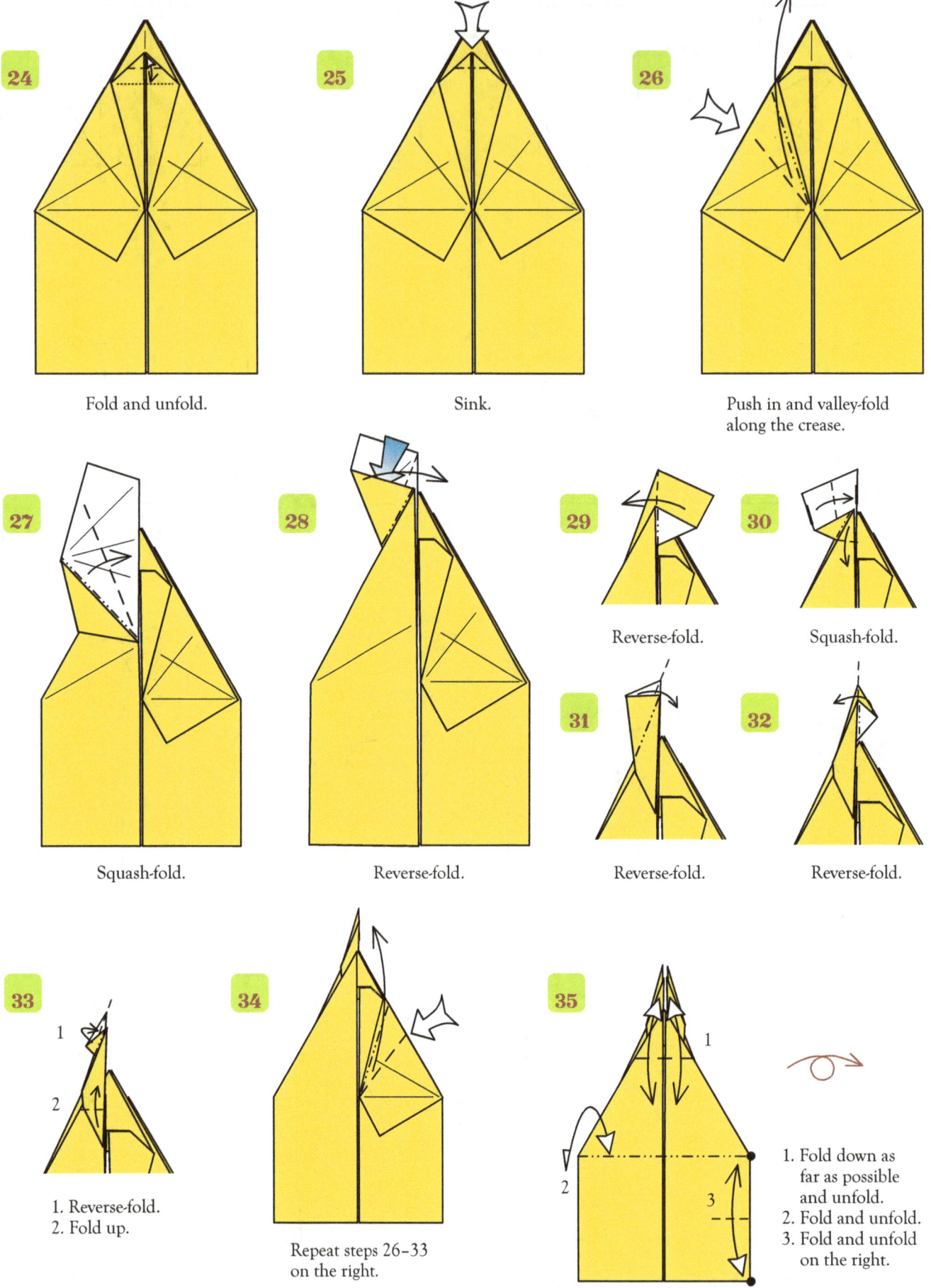

120  Origami Symphony No. 5

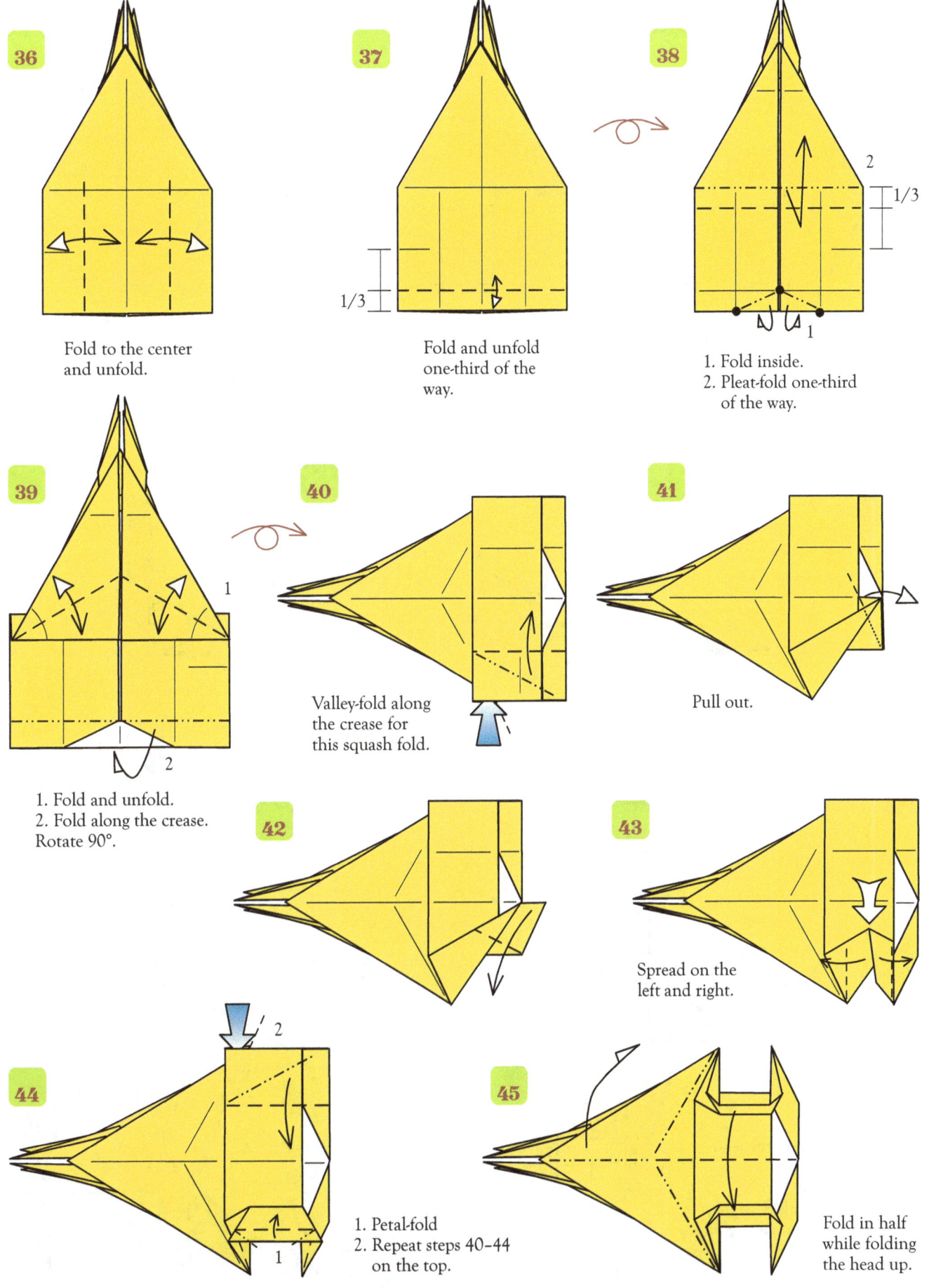

White-tailed Deer 121

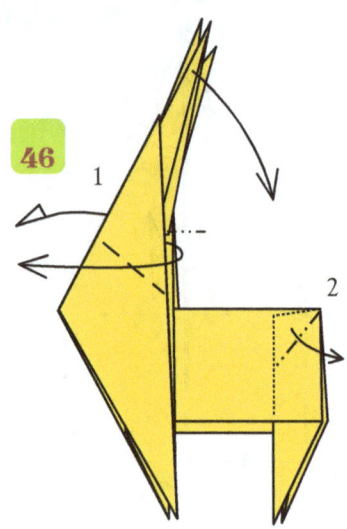

1. Outside-reverse-fold while folding the antlers to the right.
2. Reverse-fold from inside.

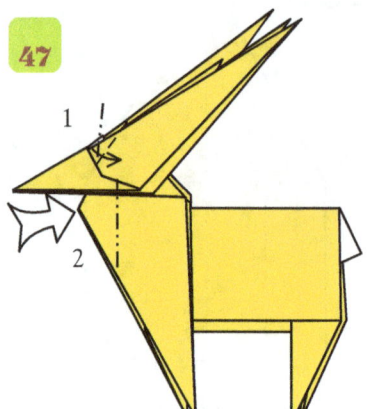

1. Squash-fold, repeat behind.
2. Sink.

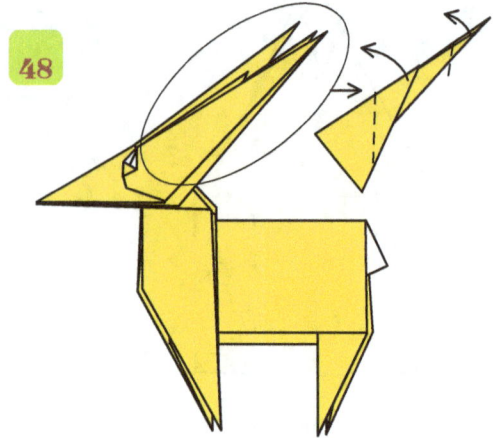

This is an inside view of the antler, which the top parts are covering. Make two spread-squash folds. Repeat on the upper antler.

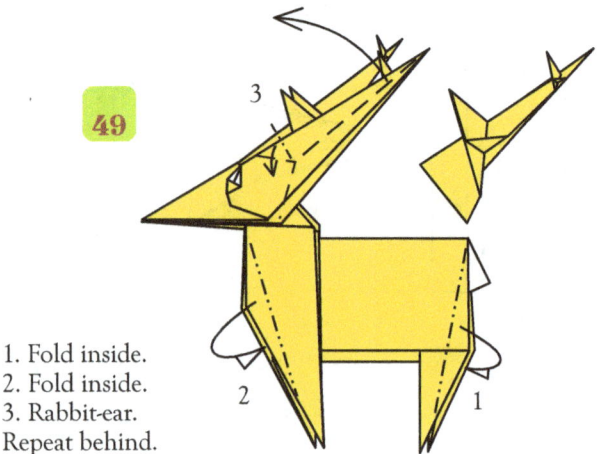

1. Fold inside.
2. Fold inside.
3. Rabbit-ear.
Repeat behind.
An inside view is also shown.

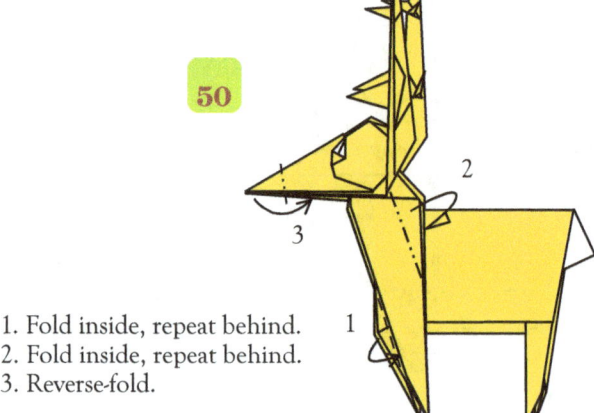

1. Fold inside, repeat behind.
2. Fold inside, repeat behind.
3. Reverse-fold.

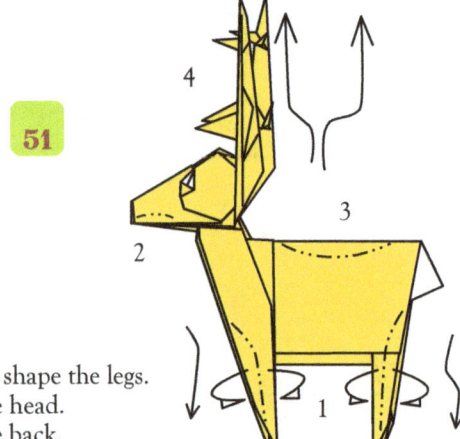

1. Thin and shape the legs.
2. Shape the head.
3. Shape the back.
4. Shape the antlers, so they spread in front and behind.
Repeat behind.

**White-tailed Deer**

122  Origami Symphony No. 5

# Moose

The Moose is the largest member of the deer family. They live in northern regions of the world, where snow can occur. Their hooves are adapted for walking in the snow. Moose eat large amounts of shrubs, woody plants, and aquatic plants. The hump on its back is caused by huge shoulder muscles. Only males have the large antlers which are heavy at 40 pounds. The antlers, called paddles, are shed every winter. New antlers grow in the spring. Moose are excellent swimmers.

1

Fold and unfold.

2

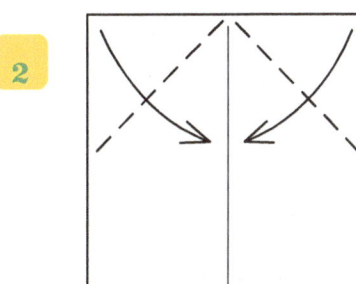

Fold to the center.

3

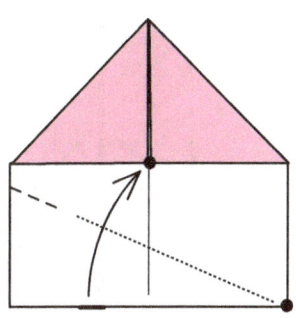

Bring the edge to the center dot. Crease on the left.

4

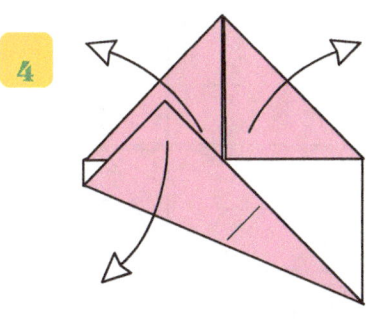

Unfold.

5

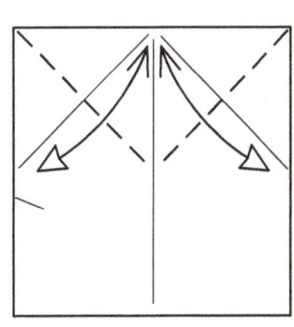

Fold and unfold.

6

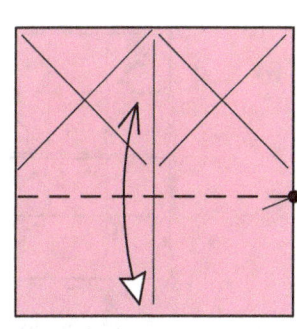

Fold and unfold.

Moose  123

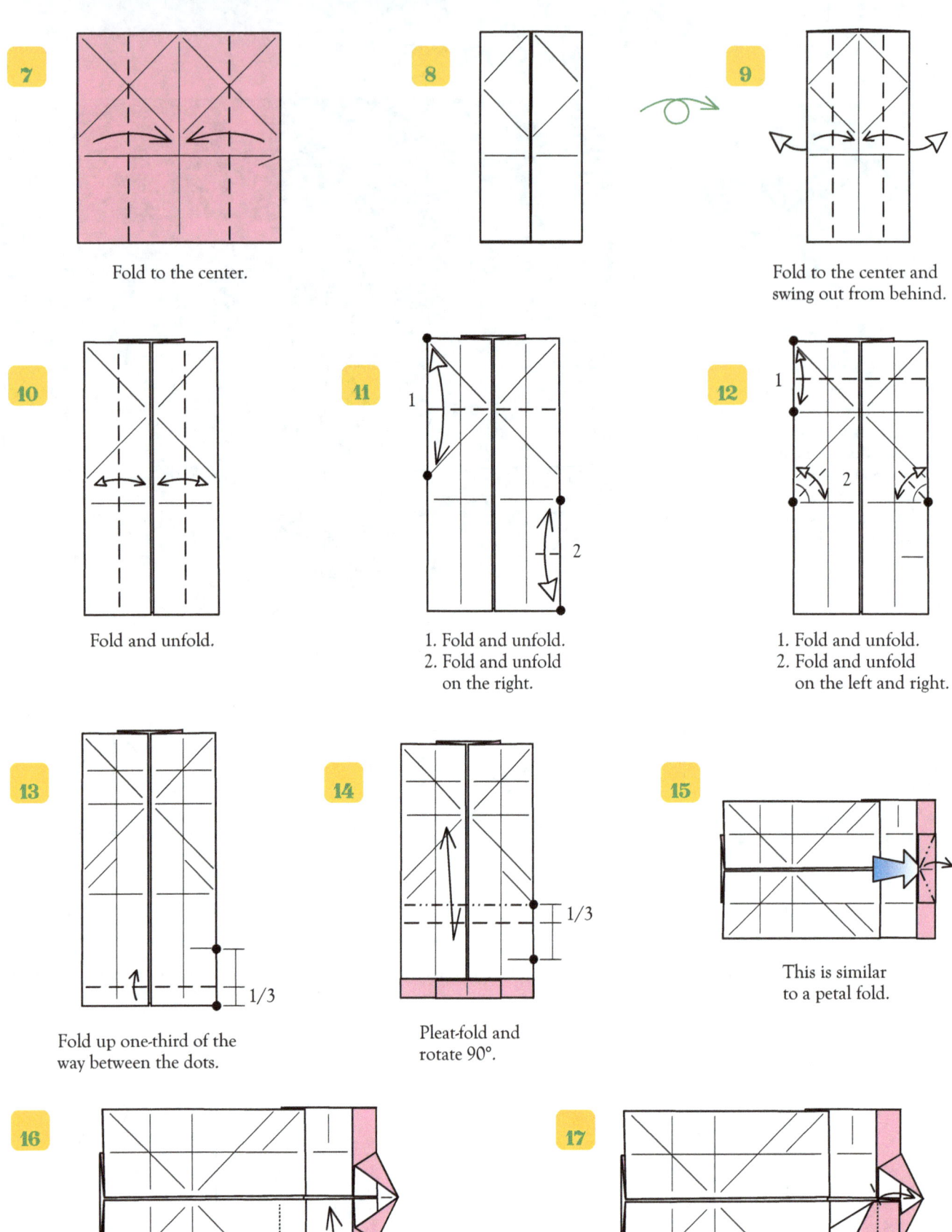

124    Origami Symphony No. 5

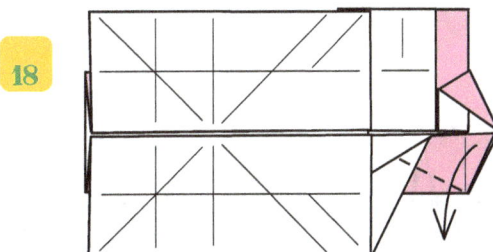

18

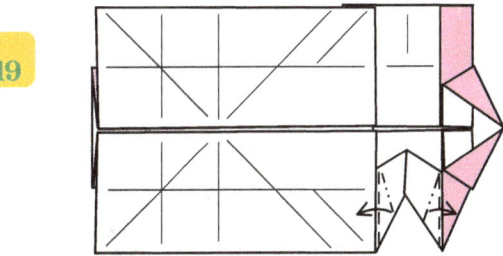

19

Spread and flatten.

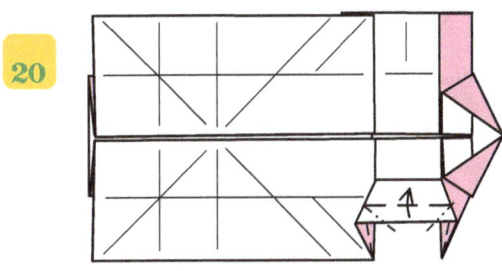

20

Petal-fold.

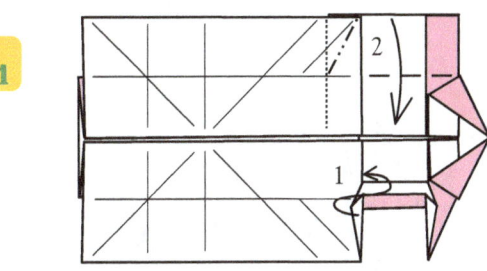

21

1. Tuck inside.
2. Repeat steps 16–21 on the top.

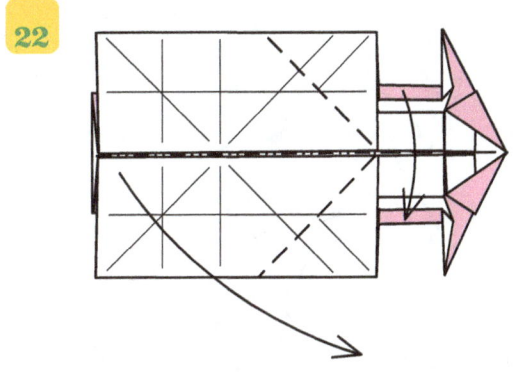

22

Fold the left side in half while folding the body in half.

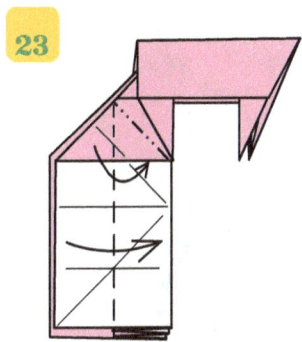

23

Reverse-fold, repeat behind.

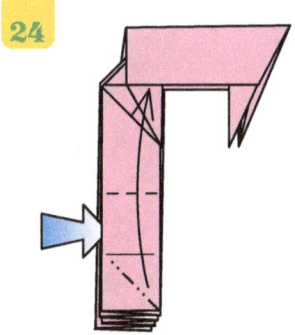

24

Stretch along the creases. Repeat behind.

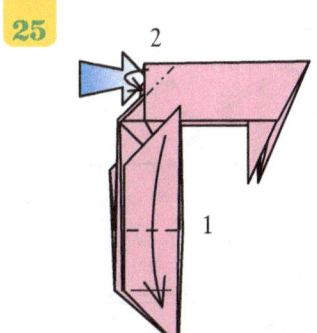

25

1. Fold down, repeat behind.
2. Reverse-fold.

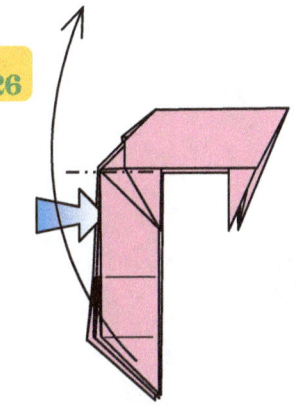

26

Reverse-fold.

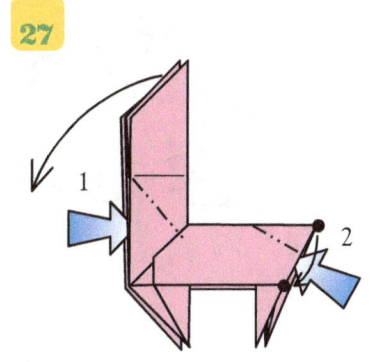

27

1. Reverse-fold.
2. Reverse-fold.

Moose **125**

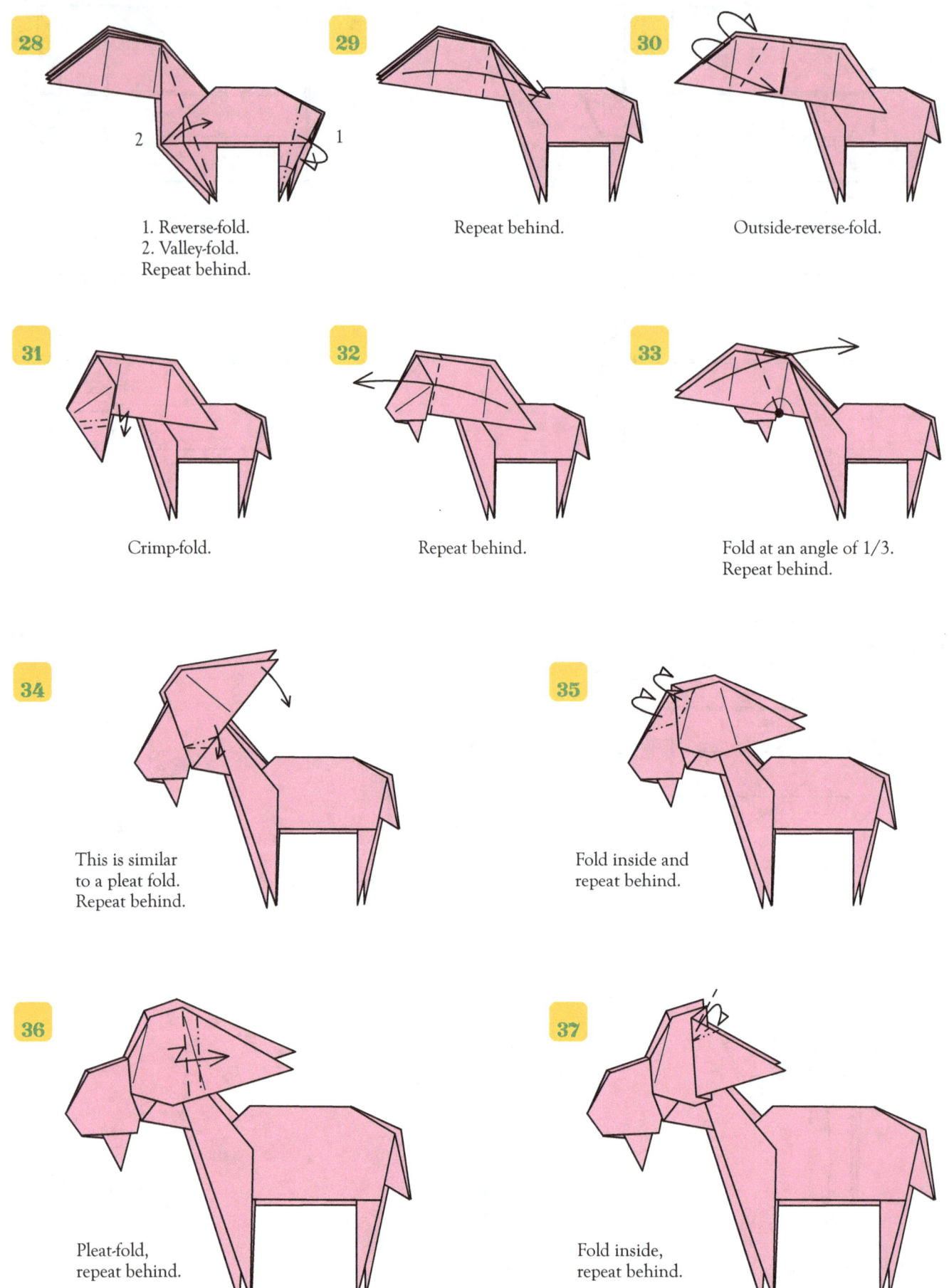

38

Pleat-fold, repeat behind.

39

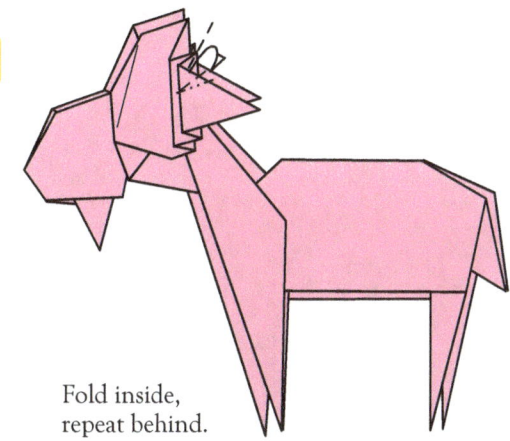

Fold inside, repeat behind.

40

Shape the tip and spread the antlers.

41

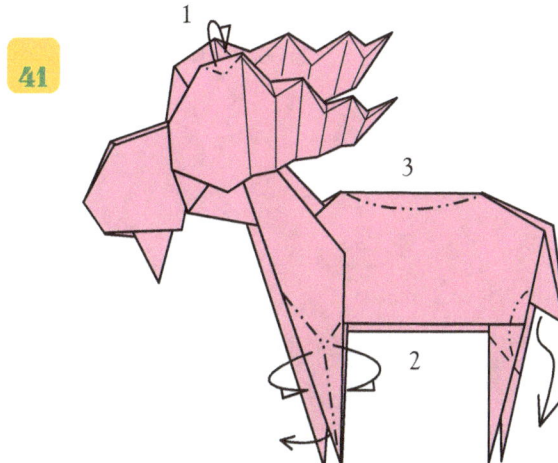

1. Shape the antlers, repeat behind.
2. Shape the legs, repeat behind.
3. Shape the back.

42

Moose

Moose **127**